The Mushroom
at the End of
the World

The Mushroom at the End of the World

On the Possibility of Life in Capitalist Ruins

ANNA LOWENHAUPT TSING

PRINCETON UNIVERSITY PRESS

Princeton and Oxford

Copyright © 2015 by Princeton University Press

Published by Princeton University Press, 41 William Street, Princeton, New Jersey 08540
In the United Kingdom: Princeton University Press, 6 Oxford Street, Woodstock, Oxfordshire OX20 1TW
press.princeton.edu

Jacket art: Homage to Minakata © Naoko Hiromoto

Library of Congress Cataloging-in-Publication Data

Tsing, Anna Lowenhaupt.
The mushroom at the end of the world : on the possibility of life in capitalist ruins / Anna Lowenhaupt Tsing.
pages cm
Includes bibliographical references and index.
ISBN 978-0-691-16275-1 (hardcover : alk. paper) 1. Human ecology. 2. Economic development—Environmental aspects. 3. Environmental degradation. I. Title.
GF21.T76 2015
330.1—dc23
2014037624

British Library Cataloging-in-Publication Data is available

This book has been composed in Sabon Next LT Pro and Syntax

Printed on acid-free paper. ∞

Printed in the United States of America

10 9 8 7 6 5 4 3 2 1

Contents

Enabling Entanglements   vii

PROLOGUE. AUTUMN AROMA   *1*

PART I   What's Left?   *11*

1 | Arts of Noticing   *17*
2 | Contamination as Collaboration   *27*
3 | Some Problems with Scale   *37*

INTERLUDE. SMELLING   *45*

PART II   After Progress: Salvage Accumulation   *55*

4 | Working the Edge   *61*

FREEDOM . . .

5 | Open Ticket, Oregon   *73*
6 | War Stories   *85*
7 | What Happened to the State? Two Kinds of Asian
        Americans   *97*

. . . IN TRANSLATION

8 | Between the Dollar and the Yen   *109*
9 | From Gifts to Commodities—and Back   *121*
10 | Salvage Rhythms: Business in Disturbance   *131*

INTERLUDE. TRACKING   *137*

PART III   Disturbed Beginnings: Unintentional Design   *149*

11 | The Life of the Forest   *155*

COMING UP AMONG PINES . . .

12 | History   *167*
13 | Resurgence   *179*
14 | Serendipity   *193*
15 | Ruin   *205*

. . . IN GAPS AND PATCHES

16 | Science as Translation   *217*
17 | Flying Spores   *227*

INTERLUDE. DANCING   *241*

PART IV   In the Middle of Things   *251*

18 | Matsutake Crusaders: Waiting for Fungal
              Action   *257*
19 | Ordinary Assets   *267*
20 | Anti-ending: Some People I Met along the
              Way   *277*

SPORE TRAIL. THE FURTHER ADVENTURES
OF A MUSHROOM   *285*

Notes   *289*
Index   *323*

Enabling Entanglements

Ever since the Enlightenment, Western philoso-
phers have shown us a Nature that is grand and universal but also passive
and mechanical. Nature was a backdrop and resource for the moral intentionality of Man, which could tame and master Nature. It was left to fabu-
lists, including non-Western and non-civilizational storytellers, to remind
us of the lively activities of all beings, human and not human.

Several things have happened to undermine this division of labor.
First, all that taming and mastering has made such a mess that it is unclear whether life on earth can continue. Second, interspecies entanglements that once seemed the stuff of fables are now materials for serious
discussion among biologists and ecologists, who show how life requires
the interplay of many kinds of beings. Humans cannot survive by
stomping on all the others. Third, women and men from around the
world have clamored to be included in the status once given to Man.
Our riotous presence undermines the moral intentionality of Man's
Christian masculinity, which separated Man from Nature.

The time has come for new ways of telling true stories beyond civiliza-
tional first principles. Without Man and Nature, all creatures can come back
to life, and men and women can express themselves without the strictures
of a parochially imagined rationality. No longer relegated to whispers in the

night, such stories might be simultaneously true and fabulous. How else can we account for the fact that anything is alive in the mess we have made?

Following a mushroom, this book offers such true stories. Unlike most scholarly books, what follows is a riot of short chapters. I wanted them to be like the flushes of mushrooms that come up after a rain: an over-the-top bounty; a temptation to explore; an always too many. The chapters build an open-ended assemblage, not a logical machine; they gesture to the so-much-more out there. They tangle with and interrupt each other—mimicking the patchiness of the world I am trying to describe. Adding another thread, the photographs tell a story alongside the text but do not illustrate it directly. I use images to present the spirit of my argument rather than the scenes I discuss.

Imagine "first nature" to mean ecological relations (including humans) and "second nature" to refer to capitalist transformations of the environment. This usage—not the same as more popular versions—derives from William Cronon's *Nature's Metropolis*.[1] My book then offers "third nature," that is, what manages to live despite capitalism. To even notice third nature, we must evade assumptions that the future is that singular direction ahead. Like virtual particles in a quantum field, multiple futures pop in and out of possibility; third nature emerges within such temporal polyphony. Yet progress stories have blinded us. To know the world without them, this book sketches open-ended assemblages of entangled ways of life, as these coalesce in coordination across many kinds of temporal rhythms. My experiment in form and my argument follow each other.

The book is based on fieldwork conducted during matsutake seasons between 2004 and 2011 in the United States, Japan, Canada, China, and Finland—as well as interviews with scientists, foresters, and matsutake traders there as well as in Denmark, Sweden, and Turkey. Perhaps my own matsutake trail is not yet over: matsutake in places as far afield as Morocco, Korea, and Bhutan beckon. My hope is that readers will experience some of this "mushroom fever" with me in the chapters to come.

Below the forest floor, fungal bodies extend themselves in nets and skeins, binding roots and mineral soils, long before producing mushrooms. All books emerge from similarly hidden collaborations. A list of individuals is inadequate, and so I begin with the collaborative engagements that made this book possible. In contrast to most recent ethnography, the research on which this book is based was pursued in experiments in collaboration. Furthermore, the questions that seemed to me worth pursuing emerged from knots of intense discussion in which I have been only one among many participants.

This book emerged from the work of the Matsutake Worlds Research Group: Timothy Choy, Lieba Faier, Elaine Gan, Michael Hathaway, Miyako Inoue, Shiho Satsuka, and myself. In much of the history of anthropology, ethnography has been a solo performance; our group convened to explore a new anthropology of always-in-process collaboration. The point of ethnography is to learn how to think about a situation together with one's informants; research categories develop *with* the research, not before it. How can one use this method when working with other researchers— each learning from different local knowledge? Rather than knowing the object in advance, as in big science, our group was determined to let our research goals emerge through collaboration. We took up this challenge by trying a variety of forms of research, analysis, and writing.

This book opens a Matsutake Worlds mini-series; Michael Hathaway and Shiho Satsuka will present the next volumes. Consider it an adventure story in which the plot unfolds from one book to the next. Our curiosity about matsutake worlds cannot be contained in one volume or expressed by one voice; stand by to find out what happens next. Furthermore, our books join other genres, including essays and articles.[2] Through the work of the team, plus filmmaker Sara Dosa, Elaine Gan and I designed a web space for stories of pickers, scientists, traders, and forest managers across several continents: www.matsutakeworlds.org. Elaine Gan's art-and-science practice has inspired further collaborations.[3] Sara Dosa's film *The Last Season* adds to these conversations.[4]

Matsutake research takes one not only beyond disciplinary knowledge but also to places where varied languages, histories, ecologies, and cultural traditions shape worlds. Faier, Inoue, and Satsuka are scholars of Japan, and Choy and Hathaway of China. I was to be the group's Southeast Asianist, working with pickers from Laos and Cambodia in the U.S. Pacific Northwest. It turned out, however, that I needed help. Collaboration with Hjorleifur Jonsson and the assistance of Lue Vang and David Pheng were essential to my research with Southeast Asians in the United States.[5] Eric Jones, Kathryn Lynch, and Rebecca McLain of the Institute for Culture and Ecology got me started in the mushroom world and remained amazing colleagues. Meeting Beverly Brown was inspirational. Amy Peterson introduced me to the Japanese-American matsutake community and showed me the ropes. Sue Hilton looked at pines with me. In Yunnan, Luo Wen-hong became a team member. In Kyoto, Noboru Ishikawa was an extraordinary guide and colleague. In Finland, Eira-Maija Savonen arranged everything. Each trip made me aware of the importance of these collaborations.

There are many other kinds of collaborations that go into producing a book. This one draws particularly on two intellectual developments, both local and broad. I had the privilege of learning feminist science studies at the University of California, Santa Cruz, in part from teaching with Donna Haraway. Here I glimpsed how scholarship could cross between natural science and cultural studies not just through critique but also through world-building knowledge. Multispecies storytelling was one of our products. The feminist science studies community in Santa Cruz has continued to make my work possible. Through it, too, I met many later companions. Andrew Mathews kindly reintroduced me to forests. Heather Swanson helped me think through comparison, and Japan. Kirsten Rudestam talked to me about Oregon. I learned from conversations with Jeremy Campbell, Zachary Caple, Roseann Cohen, Rosa Ficek, Colin Hoag, Katy Overstreet, Bettina Stoetzer, and many more.

Meanwhile, the strength of critical feminist studies of capitalism in Santa Cruz and beyond inspired my interest in knowing capitalism beyond its heroic reifications. If I have continued to engage with Marxist categories, despite their sometimes-clunky relation to thick description, it is because of the insights of feminist colleagues, including Lisa Rofel and Sylvia Yanagisako. UC Santa Cruz's Institute for Advanced Feminist Research stimulated my first attempts to describe global supply chains structurally, as translation machines, as did study groups at the University of Toronto (where I was invited by Tania Li) and at the University of Minnesota (where I was invited by Karen Ho). I feel privileged to have had a short moment of encouragement from Julie Graham before her death. The "economic diversity" perspective that she pioneered with Kathryn Gibson helped not just me but many scholars. On questions of power and difference, Santa Cruz conversations with James

Clifford, Rosa Ficek, Susan Harding, Gail Hershatter, Megan Moodie, Bregje van Eekelen, and many more were essential.

A number of grants and institutional arrangements made my work possible. A seed grant from the University of California Pacific Rim Research Program helped sponsor the first stages of my research. A Toyota Foundation award sponsored Matsutake Worlds Research Group joint research in China and Japan. UC Santa Cruz allowed me to take leaves to continue my research. Nils Bubandt and Aarhus University made it possible for me to begin the conceptualization and writing of this book in a calm and stimulating environment. A fellowship from the John Simon Guggenheim Memorial Foundation in 2010–11 made writing possible. The final work on the book overlapped with the beginning of the Aarhus University Research on the Anthropocene project, funded by the Danish National Research Foundation. I am grateful for these opportunities.

Individuals have stepped forward, too, to read drafts, discuss problems, and otherwise make the book possible. Nathalia Brichet, Zachary Caple, Alan Christy, Paulla Ebron, Susan Friedman, Elaine Gan, Scott Gilbert, Donna Haraway, Susan Harding, Frida Hastrup, Michael Hathaway, Gail Hershatter, Kregg Hetherington, Rusten Hogness, Andrew Mathews, James Scott, Heather Swanson, and Susan Wright kindly listened, read, and commented. Miyako Inoue retranslated the poetry. Kathy Chetkovich was an essential writing-and-thinking guide.

This book includes photographs only because of Elaine Gan's generous help in working with them. All emerge from my research, but I have taken the liberty of using several photographs shot by my research assistant, Lue Vang, when we worked together (images preceding chapters 9, 10, 14, and bottom photo of the "Tracking" interlude). I took the others. Elaine Gan made them usable with help from Laura Wright. Elaine Gan also drew the illustrations that mark sections within the chapters. They show fungal spores, rain, mycorrhiza, and mushrooms. I leave it to readers to wander through them.

I owe another enormous set of debts to the many people who agreed to talk and work with me in all my research sites. Pickers interrupted their foraging; scientists interrupted their research; entrepreneurs took time from their businesses. I am grateful. Yet, to protect people's privacy, most individual names in the book are pseudonyms. The exceptions are public figures, including scientists as well as those who offer their views in public spaces. For such spokespersons, it seemed disrespectful to cover up names. A similar intention shapes my use of place names: I name cities but, because this book is not primarily a village study, I avoid local place names when I move to the countryside, where mentioning names might disrupt people's privacy.

Because this book relies on such motley sources, I have included references in notes rather than compile a unified bibliography. For Chinese, Japanese, and Hmong names in the citations, I put the first letter of the family name in bold for the first usage. This allows me to vary surname order, depending on where the author's name happened to enter my research.

A few of the chapters in this book are extended in other forums. Several repeat enough to deserve mention: Chapter 3 is a summary of a longer article I published in *Common Knowledge* 18, no. 3 (2012): 505–524. Chapter 6 is excerpted from "Free in the forest," in *Rhetorics of insecurity*, ed. Zeynep Gambetti and Marcial Godoy-Anativia (New York: New York University Press, 2013), 20–39. Chapter 9 is developed in a longer essay in *Hau* 3, no. 1 (2013): 21–43. Chapter 16 includes material from an article in *Economic Botany* 62, no. 3 (2008): 244–256; although it is only one part of the chapter, this is notable because the journal article was written with Shiho Satsuka. The third interlude exists in a longer version in *Philosophy, Activism, Nature* 10 (2013): 6–14.

The Mushroom
at the End of
the World

Prologue
Autumn Aroma

Takamato ridge, crowded with expanding caps,
filling up, thriving—
the wonder of autumn aroma.

> —*From the eighth-century Japanese poetry collection*
> Man-nyo Shu

WHAT DO YOU DO WHEN YOUR WORLD STARTS TO FALL apart? I go for a walk, and if I'm really lucky, I find mushrooms. Mushrooms pull me back into my senses, not just—like flowers—through their riotous colors and smells but because they pop up unexpectedly, reminding me of the good fortune of just happening to be there. Then I know that there are still pleasures amidst the terrors of indeterminacy.

Terrors, of course, there are, and not just for me. The world's climate is going haywire, and industrial progress has proved much more deadly to life on earth than anyone imagined a century ago. The economy is no longer a source of growth or optimism; any of our jobs could disappear with the next economic crisis. And it's not just that I might fear a spurt of new disasters: I find myself without the handrails of stories that tell where everyone is going and, also, why. Precarity once seemed the fate of the less fortunate. Now it seems that all our lives are precarious—even when, for the moment, our pockets are lined. In contrast to the mid-twentieth century, when poets and philosophers of the global north felt caged by too much stability, now many of us, north and south, confront the condition of trouble without end.

This book tells of my travels with mushrooms to explore indeterminacy and the conditions of precarity, that is, life without the promise of stability. I've read that when the Soviet Union collapsed in 1991, thousands of Siberians, suddenly deprived of state guarantees, ran to the woods to collect mushrooms.[1] These are not the mushrooms I follow, but they make my point: the uncontrolled lives of mushrooms are a gift—and a guide—when the controlled world we thought we had fails.

While I can't offer you mushrooms, I hope you will follow me to savor the "autumn aroma" praised in the poem that begins my prologue. This is the smell of matsutake, a group of aromatic wild mushrooms much valued in Japan. Matsutake is loved as a marker of the autumn season. The smell evokes sadness in the loss of summer's easy riches, but it also calls up the sharp intensity and heightened sensibilities of autumn. Such sensibilities will be needed for the end of global progress's easy summer: the autumn aroma leads me into common life without guarantees. This book is not a critique of the dreams of modernization and progress that offered a vision of stability in the twentieth century; many analysts before me have dissected those dreams. Instead, I address the imaginative challenge of living without those handrails, which once made us think we knew, collectively, where we were going. If we open ourselves to their fungal attractions, matsutake can catapult us into the curiosity that seems to me the first requirement of collaborative survival in precarious times.

Here's how a radical pamphlet put the challenge:

> The spectre that many try not to see is a simple realisation—the world will not be "saved." . . . If we don't believe in a global revolutionary future, we must live (as we in fact always had to) in the present.[2]

When Hiroshima was destroyed by an atomic bomb in 1945, it is said, the first living thing to emerge from the blasted landscape was a matsutake mushroom.[3]

Grasping the atom was the culmination of human dreams of controlling nature. It was also the beginning of those dreams' undoing. The bomb at Hiroshima changed things. Suddenly, we became aware that humans could destroy the livability of the planet—whether intentionally or otherwise. This awareness only increased as we learned about pollution, mass extinction, and climate change. One half of current precarity is the fate of the earth: what kinds of human disturbances can we live with? Despite talk of sustainability, how much chance do we have for passing a habitable environment to our multispecies descendants?

Hiroshima's bomb also opened the door to the other half of today's precarity: the surprising contradictions of postwar development. After the war, the promises of modernization, backed by American bombs, seemed bright. Everyone was to benefit. The direction of the future was well known; but is it now? On the one hand, no place in the world is untouched by that global political economy built from the postwar development apparatus. On the other, even as the promises of development still beckon, we seem to have lost the means. Modernization was supposed to fill the world—both communist and capitalist—with jobs, and not just any jobs but "standard employment" with stable wages and benefits. Such jobs are now quite rare; most people depend on much more irregular livelihoods. The irony of our times, then, is that everyone depends on capitalism but almost no one has what we used to call a "regular job."

To live with precarity requires more than railing at those who put us here (although that seems useful too, and I'm not against it). We might look around to notice this strange new world, and we might stretch our imaginations to grasp its contours. This is where mushrooms help. Matsutake's willingness to emerge in blasted landscapes allows us to explore the ruin that has become our collective home.

Matsutake are wild mushrooms that live in human-disturbed forests. Like rats, raccoons, and cockroaches, they are willing to put up with some of the environmental messes humans have made. Yet they are not pests; they are valuable gourmet treats—at least in Japan, where high prices sometimes make matsutake the most valuable mushroom on earth. Through their ability to nurture trees, matsutake help forests grow in daunting places. To follow matsutake guides us to possibilities of coexistence within environmental disturbance. This is not an excuse for further damage. Still, matsutake show one kind of collaborative survival.

Matsutake also illuminate the cracks in the global political economy. For the past thirty years, matsutake have become a global commodity, foraged in forests across the northern hemisphere and shipped fresh to Japan. Many matsutake foragers are displaced and disenfranchised cultural minorities. In the U.S. Pacific Northwest, for example, most commercial matsutake foragers are refugees from Laos and Cambodia. Because of high prices, matsutake make a substantial contribution to livelihood wherever they are picked, and even encourage cultural revitalizations.

Matsutake commerce, however, hardly leads to twentieth-century development dreams. Most of the mushroom foragers I spoke with have terrible stories to tell of displacement and loss. Commercial foraging is a better than usual way of getting by for those with no other way to make a living. But what kind of economy is this anyway? Mushroom foragers work for themselves; no companies hire them. There are no wages and no benefits; pickers merely sell the mushrooms they find. Some years there are no mushrooms, and pickers are left with their expenses. Commercial wild-mushroom picking is an exemplification of precarious livelihood, without security.

This book takes up the story of precarious livelihoods and precarious environments through tracking matsutake commerce and ecology. In each case, I find myself surrounded by patchiness, that is, a mosaic of open-ended assemblages of entangled ways of life, with each further opening into a mosaic of temporal rhythms and spatial arcs. I argue that only an appreciation of current precarity as an earthwide condition allows us to notice this—the situation of our world. As long as authoritative analysis requires assumptions of growth, experts don't see the heterogeneity of space and time, even where it is obvious to ordinary participants and observers. Yet theories of heterogeneity are still in their infancy. To appreciate the patchy unpredictability associated with our current condition, we need to reopen our imaginations. The point of this book is to help that process along—with mushrooms.

About commerce: Contemporary commerce works within the constraints and possibilities of capitalism. Yet, following in the footsteps of Marx, twentieth-century students of capitalism internalized progress to see only one powerful current at a time, ignoring the rest. This book shows how it is possible to study capitalism without this crippling assumption—by combining close attention to the world, in all its precarity, with questions about how wealth is amassed. How might capitalism look without assuming progress? It might look patchy: *the concentration of wealth is possible because value produced in unplanned patches is appropriated for capital.*

About ecology: For humanists, assumptions of progressive human mastery have encouraged a view of nature as a romantic space of antimodernity.[4] Yet for twentieth-century scientists, progress also unselfconsciously framed the study of landscapes. Assumptions about expansion slipped into the formulation of population biology. New developments in ecology make it possible to think quite differently by introducing cross-species interactions and disturbance histories. In this time of diminished expectations, I look for *disturbance-based ecologies in which many species sometimes live together without either harmony or conquest.*

While I refuse to reduce either economy or ecology to the other, there is one connection between economy and environment that seems important to introduce up front: the history of the human concentration of wealth through making both humans and nonhumans into resources for investment. This history has inspired investors to imbue both people and things with alienation, that is, the ability to stand alone, as if the entanglements of living did not matter.[5] Through alienation, people and things become mobile assets; they can be removed from their life worlds in distance-defying transport to be exchanged with other assets from other life worlds, elsewhere.[6] This is quite different from merely using others as part of a life world—for example, in eating and being eaten. In that case, multispecies living spaces remain in place. Alienation obviates living-space entanglement. The dream of alienation inspires landscape modification in which only one stand-alone asset matters;

everything else becomes weeds or waste. Here, attending to living-space entanglements seems inefficient, and perhaps archaic. When its singular asset can no longer be produced, a place can be abandoned. The timber has been cut; the oil has run out; the plantation soil no longer supports crops. The search for assets resumes elsewhere. Thus, simplification for alienation produces ruins, spaces of abandonment for asset production.

Global landscapes today are strewn with this kind of ruin. Still, these places can be lively despite announcements of their death; abandoned asset fields sometimes yield new multispecies and multicultural life. In a global state of precarity, we don't have choices other than looking for life in this ruin.

Our first step is to bring back curiosity. Unencumbered by the simplifications of progress narratives, the knots and pulses of patchiness are there to explore. Matsutake are a place to begin: However much I learn, they take me by surprise.

This is not a book about Japan, but the reader needs to know something about matsutake in Japan to proceed.[7] Matsutake first appears in Japan's written record in the eighth-century poem that starts this prologue. Already then, the mushroom is praised for its aromatic marking of the autumn season. The mushroom became common around Nara and Kyoto, where people had deforested the mountains for wood to build temples and to fuel iron forges. Indeed, human disturbance allowed *Tricholoma matsutake* to emerge in Japan. This is because its most common host is red pine (*Pinus densiflora*), which germinates in the sunlight and mineral soils left by human deforestation. When forests in Japan are allowed to grow back, without human disturbance, broadleaf trees shade out pines, preventing their further germination.

As red pine spread with deforestation across Japan, matsutake became a valued gift, presented beautifully in a box of ferns. Aristocrats were honored by it. By the Edo period (1603–1868), well-to-do commoners, such as urban merchants, also enjoyed matsutake. The mushroom joined the celebration of the four seasons as a marker of autumn. Outings to pick matsutake in the fall were an equivalent of cherry-blossom viewing parties in the spring. Matsutake became a popular subject for poetry.

> The sound of a temple bell is heard in the cedar forest at dusk,
> The autumn aroma drifts on the roads below.

—AKEMI TACHIBANA (1812–1868)[8]

As in other Japanese nature poetry, seasonal referents helped build a mood. Matsutake joined older signs of the fall season, such as the sound of deer crying or the harvest moon. The coming bareness of winter touched autumn with an incipient loneliness, at the edge of nostalgia, and the poem above offers that mood. Matsutake was an elite pleasure, a sign of the privilege to live within the artful reconstruction of nature for refined tastes.[9] For this reason, when peasants preparing for elite outings sometimes "planted" matsutake (i.e., stuck mushrooms artfully in the ground because naturally occurring matsutake were not available), no one objected. Matsutake had become an element of an ideal seasonality, appreciated not only in poetry but also in all the arts, from tea ceremony to theater.

> The moving cloud fades away, and I smell the aroma of the mushroom.

—KOI NAGATA (1900–1997)[10]

The Edo period was ended by the Meiji Restoration—and Japan's rapid modernization. Deforestation proceeded apace, privileging pine and matsutake. In the Kyoto area, *matsutake* became a generic term for "mushroom." In the early twentieth century, matsutake were particularly common. In the mid-1950s, however, the situation began to change. Peasant woodlands were cut down for timber plantations, paved for suburban development, or abandoned by peasants moving to the city. Fossil fuel replaced firewood and charcoal; farmers no longer used the remaining woodlands, which grew up in dense thickets of broadleaf trees. Hillsides that had once been covered by matsutake were now too shady for pine ecologies. Shade-stressed pines were killed by an invasive nematode. By the mid-1970s, matsutake had become rare across Japan.

This was the time, however, of Japan's rapid economic development, and matsutake were in demand as exquisitely expensive gifts, perks, and bribes. The price of matsutake skyrocketed. The knowledge that matsutake grew in other parts of the world suddenly became relevant. Japanese travelers and residents abroad began to send matsutake to Japan; as importers emerged to funnel the international matsutake trade, non-Japanese pickers rushed in. At first it seemed that there were a plethora of colors and kinds that might appropriately be considered matsutake— because they had the smell. Scientific names proliferated as matsutake in forests across the northern hemisphere suddenly rose from neglect. In the past twenty years, names have been consolidated. All across Eurasia, most matsutake are now *Tricholoma matsutake*.[11] In North America, *T. matsutake* seems to be found only in the east, and in the mountains of Mexico. In western North America, the local matsutake is considered another species, *T. magnivelare*.[12] Some scientists, however, think the generic term "matsutake" is the best way to identify these aromatic mushrooms, since the dynamics of speciation are still unclear.[13] I follow that practice except where I am discussing questions of classification.

Japanese have figured out ways of ranking matsutake from different parts of the world, and ranks are reflected in prices. My eyes were first opened to such rankings when one Japanese importer explained: "Matsutake are like people. American mushrooms are white because the people are white. Chinese mushrooms are black, because the people are black. Japanese people and mushrooms are nicely in between." Not everyone has the same rankings, but this stark example can stand in for the many forms of classification and valuation that structure the global trade.

Meanwhile, people in Japan worry about the loss of the peasant woodlands that have been the source of so much seasonal beauty, from spring blossoms to bright autumn leaves. Starting in the 1970s, volunteer groups mobilized to restore these woodlands. Wanting their work to matter beyond passive aesthetics, the groups looked for ways restored woodlands might benefit human livelihood. The high price of matsutake made it an ideal product of woodland restoration.

And so I return to precarity and living in our messes. But living seems to have gotten more crowded, not only with Japanese aesthetics and ecological histories, but also with international relations and capitalist trading practices. This is the stuff for stories in the book that follows. For the moment, it seems important to appreciate the mushroom.

Oh, matsutake:
The excitement before finding them.

—YAMAGUCHI SODO (1642–1716)[14]

Conjuring time,
Yunnan. Watching
the boss gamble.

Part I
What's Left?

It was a still-bright evening when I realized I was lost and empty-handed in an unknown forest. I was on my first search for matsutake—and matsutake pickers—in Oregon's Cascade Mountains. Earlier that afternoon, I had found the Forest Service's "big camp" for mushroom pickers, but all the pickers were out foraging. I had decided to look for mushrooms myself while I waited for their return.

I couldn't have imagined a more unpromising-looking forest. The ground was dry and rocky, and nothing grew except thin sticks of lodgepole pine. There were hardly any plants growing near the ground, not even grass, and when I touched the soil, sharp pumice shards cut my fingers. As the afternoon wore on, I found one or two "copper tops," dingy mushrooms with a splash of orange and a mealy smell.[1] Nothing else. Worse yet, I was disoriented. Every way I turned, the forest looked the same. I had no idea which direction to go to find my car. Thinking I would be out there just briefly, I had brought nothing, and I knew I would soon be thirsty, hungry—and cold.

I stumbled around and eventually found a dirt road. But which way should I go? The sun was getting lower as I trudged along. I had walked less than a mile when a pickup truck drew up. A bright-faced young man and a wizened old man were inside, and they offered me a ride. The young man introduced himself as Kao. Like his uncle, he said, he was a Mien from the hills of Laos who had come to the United States from a refugee camp in Thailand in the 1980s. They were neighbors in Sacramento, California, and here to pick mushrooms together. They brought me to their camp. The young man went to get water, driving his plastic jugs to a water storage container some ways away. The older man did not know English, but it turned out he knew a little Mandarin Chinese, as did I. As we awkwardly exchanged phrases, he pulled out a smoking bong handcrafted from PVC pipe and lit up his tobacco.

It was dusk when Kao came back with the water. But he beckoned me to go picking with him: There were mushrooms nearby. In the gathering dark, we scrambled up a rocky hillside not far from his camp. I saw nothing but dirt and some scrawny pine trees. But here was Kao with his bucket and stick, poking deep into clearly empty ground and pulling up a fat button. How could this be possible? There had been nothing there—and then there it was.

Kao handed me the mushroom. That's when I first experienced the smell. It's not an easy smell. It's not like a flower or a mouth-watering food. It's disturbing. Many people never learn to love it. It's hard to describe. Some people liken it to rotting things and some to clear beauty—the autumn aroma. At my first whiff, I was just . . . astonished.

My surprise was not just for the smell. What were Mien tribesmen, Japanese gourmet mushrooms, and I doing in a ruined Oregon industrial forest? I had lived in the United States for a long time without ever hearing about any of these things. The Mien camp pulled me back to my earlier fieldwork in Southeast Asia; the mushroom tickled my interest in Japanese aesthetics and cuisine. The broken forest, in contrast, seemed like a science fiction nightmare. To my faulty common sense, we all seemed miraculously out of time and out of place—like something that might jump out of a fairy tale. I was startled and intrigued; I couldn't stop exploring. This book is my attempt to pull you into the maze I found.

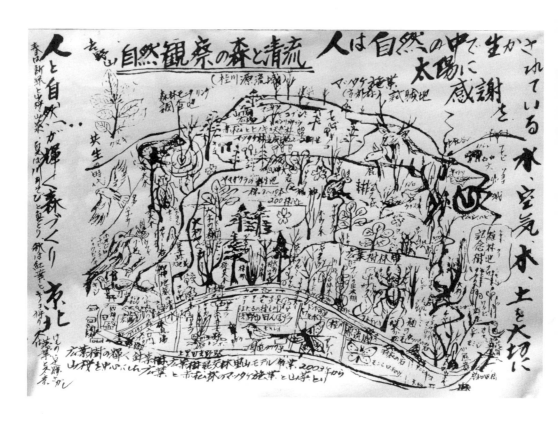

1
Arts of Noticing

I am not proposing a return to the Stone Age. My intent
is not reactionary, nor even conservative, but simply
subversive. It seems that the utopian imagination is
trapped, like capitalism and industrialism and the
human population, in a one-way future consisting only
of growth. All I'm trying to do is figure out how to put a
pig on the tracks.

—*Ursula K. Le Guin*

IN 1908 AND 1909 TWO RAILROAD ENTREPRENEURS
raced each other to build track along Oregon's Deschutes River.[1] The
goal of each was to be the first to create an industrial connection between the towering ponderosas of the eastern Cascades and the stacked
lumberyards of Portland. In 1910, the thrill of competition yielded to an
agreement for joint service. Pine logs poured out of the region, bound
for distant markets. Lumber mills brought new settlers; towns sprung

up as millworkers multiplied. By the 1930s, Oregon had become the nation's largest producer of timber.

This is a story we know. It is the story of pioneers, progress, and the transformation of "empty" spaces into industrial resource fields.

In 1989, a plastic spotted owl was hung in effigy on an Oregon logging truck.[2] Environmentalists had shown that unsustainable logging was destroying Pacific Northwest forests. "The spotted owl was like the canary in the coal mine," explained one advocate. "It was . . . symbolic of an ecosystem on the verge of collapse."[3] When a federal judge blocked old-growth logging to save owl habitat, loggers were furious; but how many loggers were there? Logging jobs had dwindled as timber companies mechanized—and as prime timber disappeared. By 1989, many mills had already closed; logging companies were moving to other regions.[4] The eastern Cascades, once a hub of timber wealth, were now cutover forests and former mill towns overgrown by brush.

This is a story we need to know. Industrial transformation turned out to be a bubble of promise followed by lost livelihoods and damaged landscapes. And yet: such documents are not enough. If we end the story with decay, we abandon all hope—or turn our attention to other sites of promise and ruin, promise and ruin.

What emerges in damaged landscapes, beyond the call of industrial promise and ruin? By 1989, something else had begun in Oregon's cutover forests: the wild mushroom trade. From the first it was linked to worldwide ruination: The 1986 Chernobyl disaster had contaminated Europe's mushrooms, and traders had come to the Pacific Northwest for supplies. When Japan began importing matsutake at high prices— just as jobless Indochinese refugees were settling in California—the trade went wild. Thousands rushed to Pacific Northwest forests for the new "white gold." This was in the middle of a "jobs versus the environment" battle over the forests, yet neither side noticed the mushroomers. Job advocates imagined only wage contracts for healthy white men; the foragers—disabled white veterans, Asian refugees, Native Americans, and undocumented Latinos—were invisible interlopers. Conservationists were fighting to keep human disturbance out of the forests; the entry of thousands of people, had it been noticed, would hardly have been welcome. But the mushroom hunters were mainly not noticed. At most, the Asian presence sparked local fears of invasion: journalists worried about violence.[5]

A few years into the new century, the idea of a trade-off between jobs and the environment seemed less convincing. With or without conservation, there were fewer "jobs" in the twentieth-century sense in the United States; besides, it seemed much more likely that environmental damage would kill all of us off, jobs or no jobs. We are stuck with the problem of living despite economic and ecological ruination. Neither tales of progress nor of ruin tell us how to think about collaborative survival. It is time to pay attention to mushroom picking. Not that this will save us—but it might open our imaginations.

Geologists have begun to call our time the Anthropocene, the epoch in which human disturbance outranks other geological forces. As I write, the term is still new—and still full of promising contradictions. Thus, although some interpreters see the name as implying the triumph of humans, the opposite seems more accurate: without planning or intention, humans have made a mess of our planet.[6] Furthermore, despite the prefix "anthropo-," that is, human, the mess is not a result of our species biology. The most convincing Anthropocene time line begins not with our species but rather with the advent of modern capitalism, which has directed long-distance destruction of landscapes and ecologies. This time line, however, makes the "anthropo-" even more of a problem. Imagining the human since the rise of capitalism entangles us with ideas of progress and with the spread of techniques of alienation that turn both humans and other beings into resources. Such techniques have segregated humans and policed identities, obscuring collaborative survival. The concept of the Anthropocene both evokes this bundle of aspirations, which one might call the modern human conceit, and raises the hope that we might muddle beyond it. Can we live inside this regime of the human and still exceed it?

This is the predicament that makes me pause before offering a description of mushrooms and mushroom pickers. The modern human conceit won't let a description be anything more than a decorative footnote. This "anthropo-" blocks attention to patchy landscapes, multiple temporalities, and shifting assemblages of humans and nonhumans: the very stuff of collaborative survival. In order to make mushroom picking a worthwhile tale, then, I must first chart the work of this "anthropo-" and explore the terrain it refuses to acknowledge.

Consider, indeed, the question of what's left. Given the effectiveness of state and capitalist devastation of natural landscapes, we might ask why anything outside their plans is alive today. To address this, we will need to watch unruly edges. What brings Mien and matsutake together in Oregon? Such seemingly trivial queries might turn everything around to put unpredictable encounters at the center of things.

We hear about precarity in the news every day. People lose their jobs or get angry because they never had them. Gorillas and river porpoises hover at the edge of extinction. Rising seas swamp whole Pacific islands. But most of the time we imagine such precarity to be an exception to how the world works. It's what "drops out" from the system. What if, as I'm suggesting, precarity *is* the condition of our time—or, to put it another way, what if our time is ripe for sensing precarity? What if precarity, indeterminacy, and what we imagine as trivial are the center of the systematicity we seek?

Precarity is the condition of being vulnerable to others. Unpredictable encounters transform us; we are not in control, even of ourselves. Unable to rely on a stable structure of community, we are thrown into shifting assemblages, which remake us as well as our others. We can't rely on the status quo; everything is in flux, including our ability to survive. Thinking through precarity changes social analysis. A precarious world is a world without teleology. Indeterminacy, the unplanned nature of time, is frightening, but thinking through precarity makes it evident that indeterminacy also makes life possible.

The only reason all this sounds odd is that most of us were raised on dreams of modernization and progress. These frames sort out those parts of the present that might lead to the future. The rest are trivial; they "drop out" of history. I imagine you talking back: "Progress? That's an idea from the nineteenth century." The term "progress," referring to a general state, has become rare; even twentieth-century modernization has begun to feel archaic. But their categories and assumptions of improvement are with us everywhere. We imagine their objects every day:

democracy, growth, science, hope. Why would we expect economies to grow and sciences to advance? Even without explicit reference to development, our theories of history are embroiled in these categories. So, too, are our personal dreams. I'll admit it's hard for me to even say this: there might not be a collective happy ending. Then why bother getting up in the morning?

Progress is embedded, too, in widely accepted assumptions about what it means to be human. Even when disguised through other terms, such as "agency," "consciousness," and "intention," we learn over and over that humans are different from the rest of the living world because we look forward—while other species, which live day to day, are thus dependent on us. As long as we imagine that humans are *made* through progress, nonhumans are stuck within this imaginative framework too.

Progress is a forward march, drawing other kinds of time into its rhythms. Without that driving beat, we might notice other temporal patterns. Each living thing remakes the world through seasonal pulses of growth, lifetime reproductive patterns, and geographies of expansion. Within a given species, too, there are multiple time-making projects, as organisms enlist each other and coordinate in making landscapes. (The regrowth of the cutover Cascades and Hiroshima's radioecology each show us multispecies time making.) The curiosity I advocate follows such multiple temporalities, revitalizing description and imagination. This is not a simple empiricism, in which the world invents its own categories. Instead, agnostic about where we are going, we might look for what has been ignored because it never fit the time line of progress.

Consider again the snippets of Oregon history with which I began this chapter. The first, about railroads, tells of progress. It led to the future: railroads reshaped our destiny. The second is already an interruption, a history in which the destruction of forests matters. What it shares with the first, however, is the assumption that the trope of progress is sufficient to know the world, both in success and failure. The story of decline offers no leftovers, no excess, nothing that escapes progress. Progress still controls us even in tales of ruination.

Yet the modern human conceit is not the only plan for making worlds: we are surrounded by many world-making projects, human and not human.[7] World-making projects emerge from practical activities of making lives; in the process these projects alter our planet. To see them, in the shadow of the Anthropocene's "anthropo-," we must reorient our attention. Many preindustrial livelihoods, from foraging to stealing, persist today, and new ones (including commercial mushroom picking) emerge, but we neglect them because they are not a part of progress. These livelihoods make worlds too—and they show us how to look around rather than ahead.

Making worlds is not limited to humans. We know that beavers reshape streams as they make dams, canals, and lodges; in fact, all organisms make ecological living places, altering earth, air, and water. Without the ability to make workable living arrangements, species would die out. In the process, each organism changes everyone's world. Bacteria made our oxygen atmosphere, and plants help maintain it. Plants live on land because fungi made soil by digesting rocks. As these examples suggest, world-making projects can overlap, allowing room for more than one species. Humans, too, have always been involved in multispecies world making. Fire was a tool for early humans not just to cook but also to burn the landscape, encouraging edible bulbs and grasses that attracted animals for hunting. Humans shape multispecies worlds when our living arrangements make room for other species. This is not just a matter of crops, livestock, and pets. Pines, with their associated fungal partners, often flourish in landscapes burned by humans; pines and fungi work together to take advantage of bright open spaces and exposed mineral soils. Humans, pines, and fungi make living arrangements simultaneously for themselves and for others: multispecies worlds.

Twentieth-century scholarship, advancing the modern human conceit, conspired against our ability to notice the divergent, layered, and conjoined projects that make up worlds. Entranced by the expansion of certain ways of life over others, scholars ignored questions of what else was going on. As progress tales lose traction, however, it becomes possible to look differently.

The concept of *assemblage* is helpful. Ecologists turned to assemblages to get around the sometimes fixed and bounded connotations of ecological "community." The question of how the varied species in a species assemblage influence each other—if at all—is never settled: some thwart (or eat) each other; others work together to make life possible; still others just happen to find themselves in the same place. Assemblages are open-ended gatherings. They allow us to ask about communal effects without assuming them. They show us potential histories in the making. For my purposes, however, I need something other than organisms as the elements that gather. I need to see lifeways—and non-living ways of being as well—coming together. Nonhuman ways of being, like human ones, shift historically. For living things, species identities are a place to begin, but they are not enough: ways of being are emergent effects of encounters. Thinking about humans makes this clear. Foraging for mushrooms is a way of life—but not a common characteristic of all humans. The issue is the same for other species. Pines find mushrooms to help them use human-made open spaces. Assemblages don't just gather lifeways; they make them. Thinking through assemblage urges us to ask: How do gatherings sometimes become "happenings," that is, greater than the sum of their parts? If history without progress is indeterminate and multidirectional, might assemblages show us its possibilities?

Patterns of unintentional coordination develop in assemblages. To notice such patterns means watching the interplay of temporal rhythms and scales in the divergent lifeways that gather. Surprisingly, this turns out to be a method that might revitalize political economy as well as environmental studies. Assemblages drag political economy inside them, and not just for humans. Plantation crops have lives different from those of their free-living siblings; cart horses and hunter steeds share species but not lifeways. Assemblages cannot hide from capital and the state; they are sites for watching how political economy works. If capitalism has no teleology, we need to see what comes together—not just by prefabrication, but also by juxtaposition.

Other authors use "assemblage" with other meanings.[8] The qualifier "polyphonic" may help explain my variant. Polyphony is music in which autonomous melodies intertwine. In Western music, the madrigal and the fugue are examples of polyphony. These forms seem archaic and strange to many modern listeners because they were superseded by music in which a unified rhythm and melody holds the composition together. In the classical music that displaced baroque, unity was the goal; this was "progress" in just the meaning I have been discussing: a unified coordination of time. In twentieth-century rock-and-roll, this unity takes the form of a strong beat, suggestive of the listener's heart;

we are used to hearing music with a single perspective. When I first learned polyphony, it was a revelation in listening; I was forced to pick out separate, simultaneous melodies *and* to listen for the moments of harmony and dissonance they created together. This kind of noticing is just what is needed to appreciate the multiple temporal rhythms and trajectories of the assemblage.

For those not musically inclined, it may be useful to imagine the polyphonic assemblage in relation to agriculture. Since the time of the plantation, commercial agriculture has aimed to segregate a single crop and work toward its simultaneous ripening for a coordinated harvest. But other kinds of farming have multiple rhythms. In the shifting cultivation I studied in Indonesian Borneo, many crops grew together in the same field, and they had quite different schedules. Rice, bananas, taro, sweet potatoes, sugarcane, palms, and fruit trees mingled; farmers needed to attend to the varied schedules of maturation of each of these crops. These rhythms were their relation to human harvests; if we add other relations, for example, to pollinators or other plants, rhythms multiply. The polyphonic assemblage is the gathering of these rhythms, as they result from world-making projects, human and not human.

The polyphonic assemblage also moves us into the unexplored territory of the modern political economy. Factory labor is an exemplar of coordinated progress time. Yet the supply chain is infused with polyphonic rhythms. Consider the tiny Chinese garment factory studied by Nellie Chu; like its many competitors, it served multiple supply lines, constantly switching among orders for local boutique brands, knock-off international brands, and generic to-be-branded-later production.[9] Each required different standards, materials, and kinds of labor. The factory's job was to match industrial coordination to the complex rhythms of supply chains. Rhythms further multiply when we move out of factories to watch foraging for an unpredictable wild product. The farther we stray into the peripheries of capitalist production, the more coordination between polyphonic assemblages and industrial processes becomes central to making a profit.

As the last examples suggest, abandoning progress rhythms to watch polyphonic assemblages is not a matter of virtuous desire. Progress felt great; there was always something better ahead. Progress gave us the "progressive" political causes with which I grew up. I hardly know how to think about justice without progress. The problem is that progress stopped making sense. More and more of us looked up one day and realized that the emperor had no clothes. It is in this dilemma that new tools for noticing seem so important.[10] Indeed, life on earth seems at stake. Chapter 2 turns to dilemmas of collaborative survival.

*Conjuring time,
Yunnan. The matsutake
embroidered on this Yi
market goer's vest
performs the promise of
wealth and well-being.
The vest codifies (Yi)
ethnicity and (fungal)
species, making these
units available for a
moment of action within
shifting histories of
encounter.*

2
Contamination as Collaboration

I wanted someone to tell me things were going to be
fine, but no one did.

—*Mai Neng Moua, "Along the Way to the Mekong"*

How does a gathering become a "happening,"
that is, greater than a sum of its parts? One answer is contamination.
We are contaminated by our encounters; they change who we are as we
make way for others. As contamination changes world-making projects, mutual worlds—and new directions—may emerge.[1] Everyone car-
ries a history of contamination; purity is not an option. One value of
keeping precarity in mind is that it makes us remember that changing
with circumstances is the stuff of survival.

But what is survival? In popular American fantasies, survival is all
about saving oneself by fighting off others. The "survival" featured in
U.S. television shows or alien-planet stories is a synonym for conquest
and expansion. I will not use the term that way. Please open yourself to

another usage. This book argues that staying alive—for every species—requires livable collaborations. Collaboration means working across difference, which leads to contamination. Without collaborations, we all die.

Popular fantasies are hardly the whole problem: one-against-all survival has also engaged scholars. Scholars have imagined survival as the advancement of individual interests—whether "individuals" are species, populations, organisms, or genes—human or otherwise. Consider the twin master sciences of the twentieth century, neoclassical economics and population genetics. Each of these disciplines came to power in the early twentieth century with formulations bold enough to redefine modern knowledge. Population genetics stimulated the "modern synthesis" in biology, uniting evolutionary theory and genetics. Neoclassical economics reshaped economic policy, creating the modern economy of its imagination. While practitioners of each have had little to do with each other, the twins set up similar frames. At the heart of each is the self-contained individual actor, out to maximize personal interests, whether for reproduction or wealth. Richard Dawkins's "selfish gene" gets across the idea, useful at many life scales: It is the ability of genes (or organisms, or populations) to look out for their own interests that fuels evolution.[2] Similarly, the life of *Homo economicus*, economic man, is a series of choices to follow his best interests.

The assumption of self-containment made an explosion of new knowledge possible. Thinking through self-containment and thus the self-interest of individuals (at whatever scale) made it possible to ignore contamination, that is, transformation through encounter. Self-contained individuals are not transformed by encounter. Maximizing their interests, they use encounters—but remain unchanged in them. *Noticing* is unnecessary to track these unchanging individuals. A "standard" individual can stand in for all as a unit of analysis. It becomes possible to organize knowledge through logic alone. Without the possibility of transformative encounters, mathematics can replace natural history and ethnography. It was the productiveness of this simplification that made the twins so powerful, and the obvious falsity of the original premise was increasingly forgotten.[3] Economy and ecology thus each became sites for algorithms of progress-as-expansion.

The problem of precarious survival helps us see what is wrong. Precarity is a state of acknowledgment of our vulnerability to others. In order to survive, we need help, and help is always the service of another, with or without intent. When I sprain my ankle, a stout stick may help me walk, and I enlist its assistance. I am now an encounter in motion, a woman-and-stick. It is hard for me to think of any challenge I might face without soliciting the assistance of others, human and not human. It is unselfconscious privilege that allows us to fantasize—counterfactually—that we each survive alone.

If survival always involves others, it is also necessarily subject to the indeterminacy of self-and-other transformations. We change through our collaborations both within and across species. The important stuff for life on earth happens in those transformations, not in the decision trees of self-contained individuals. Rather than seeing only the expansion-and-conquest strategies of relentless individuals, we must look for histories that develop through contamination. Thus, how might a gathering become a "happening"?

Collaboration is work across difference, yet this is not the innocent diversity of self-contained evolutionary tracks. The evolution of our "selves" is already polluted by histories of encounter; we are mixed up with others before we even begin any new collaboration. Worse yet, we are mixed up in the projects that do us the most harm. The diversity that allows us to enter collaborations emerges from histories of extermination, imperialism, and all the rest. Contamination makes diversity.

This changes the work we imagine for names, including ethnicities and species. If categories are unstable, we must watch them emerge within encounters. To use category names should be a commitment to tracing the assemblages in which these categories gain a momentary hold.[4] Only from here can I return to meeting Mien and matsutake in a Cascades forest. What does it mean to be "Mien" or to be "forest"? These identities entered our meeting from histories of transformative ruin, even as new collaborations changed them.

Oregon's national forests are managed by the U.S. Forest Service, which aims to conserve forests as a national resource. Yet the conservation status of the landscape has been hopelessly confused by a hundred-year history of logging and fire suppression. Contamination creates forests, transforming them in the process. Because of this, noticing as well as counting is required to know the landscape.

Oregon's forests played a key role in the U.S. Forest Service's early-twentieth-century formation, during which foresters worked to find kinds of conservation that timber barons would support.[5] Fire suppression was the biggest result: Loggers and foresters could agree on it. Meanwhile, loggers were eager to take out the ponderosa pines that so impressed white pioneers in the eastern Cascades. The great ponderosa stands were logged out by the 1980s. It turned out that they could not reproduce without the periodic fires the Forest Service had stopped. But firs and spindly lodgepole pines were flourishing with fire exclusion—at least if flourishing means spreading in ever denser and more flammable thickets of live, dead, and dying trees.[6] For several decades, Forest Service management has meant, on the one hand, trying to make the ponderosas come back, and, on the other, trying to thin, cut, or otherwise control flammable fir and lodgepole thickets. Ponderosa, fir, and lodgepole, each finding life through human disturbance, are now creatures of contaminated diversity.

Surprisingly, in this ruined industrial landscape, new value emerged: matsutake. Matsutake fruit especially well under mature lodgepole, and mature lodgepole exists in prodigious numbers in the eastern Cascades because of fire exclusion. With the logging of ponderosa pines and fire exclusion, lodgepoles have spread, and despite their flammability, fire exclusion allows them a long maturity. Oregon matsutake fruit only after forty to fifty years of lodgepole growth, made possible by excluding fire.[7] The abundance of matsutake is a recent historical creation: contaminated diversity.

And what are Southeast Asian hill people doing in Oregon? Once I realized that almost everyone in the forest was there for explicitly "ethnic" reasons, finding out what these ethnicities implied became urgent. I needed to know what created communal agendas that included mushroom hunting; thus I followed the ethnicities they named for me. The pickers, like the forests, must be appreciated in becoming, not just counted. Yet almost all U.S. scholarship on Southeast Asian refugees ignores ethnic formation in Southeast Asia. To counteract this omission, allow me an extended story. Despite their specificity, Mien stand in here for all the pickers—and the rest of us too. Transformation through collaboration, ugly and otherwise, is the human condition.

The distant ancestors of Kao's Mien community are imagined as emerging already in contradiction and on the run. Moving through the hills of southern China to hide from imperial power, they also treasured imperial documents exempting them from taxation and corvée. A little more than a hundred years ago, some moved farther out of the way—into the northern hills of what are now Laos, Thailand, and Vietnam. They brought a distinctive script, based on Chinese characters and used for writing to spirits.[8] As both refusal and acceptance of Chinese authority, the script is a neat expression of contaminated diversity: Mien are Chinese, and not Chinese. Later they would learn to be Lao/Thai, but not Lao/Thai, and then American, and not American.

Mien are not known for their respect for national boundaries; communities have repeatedly crossed back and forth, especially when armies threaten. (Kao's uncle learned Chinese and Lao from cross-border movement.) Yet, despite this mobility, Mien are hardly an autonomous tribe, free from the control of the state. Hjorleifur Jonsson has shown how Mien lifeways have repeatedly changed in relation to state agendas. In the first half of the twentieth century, for example, Mien in Thailand organized their communities around the opium trade. Only large, polygynous households controlled by powerful senior men could keep hold of the opium contracts. Some households had one hundred members. The Thai state did not mandate this family organization; it arose from the Mien encounter with opium. In a similarly unplanned process in the late twentieth century, Mien in Thailand came to identify as an "ethnic group" with distinctive customs; Thai policy toward minorities made this identity possible. Meanwhile, along the Laos/Thailand border, Mien slipped back and forth, evading state policy on both sides even while being shaped by it.[9]

Those cross-boundary Asian hills have known many peoples, and Mien sensibilities have developed in engagement with these shifting groups as all have negotiated imperial governance and rebellion, licit and illicit trade, and millennial mobilization. To understand how Mien came to be matsutake pickers requires considering their relationship with another group now in the Oregon forests, Hmong. Hmong are like Mien in many ways. They also ran south from China; they also crossed borders and occupied the high altitudes suited to commercial opium farming; they also value their distinctive dialects and traditions. A mid-twentieth-century millennial movement started by an illiterate farmer produced a completely original Hmong script. This was the time of the U.S.-Indochina War, and Hmong were in the thick of it. As linguist William Smalley points out, discarded military ordnance in the area would have exposed this inspired farmer to English, Russian, and Chinese writing, and he might also have seen Lao and Thai.[10] Emerging from the trash of war, this distinctive and multiply derivative Hmong script, like that of the Mien, is a wonderful icon for contaminated diversity.

Hmong are proud of their patrilineal clan organization, and, according to ethnographer William Geddes, clans have been key to forming long-distance ties among men.[11] Clan relations allowed military leaders to recruit outside their face-to-face networks. This proved relevant when the United States took over imperial oversight after the French defeat by Vietnamese nationalists in 1954, thus inheriting the loyalty of French-trained Hmong soldiers. One of those soldiers became General Vang Pao, who mobilized Hmong in Laos to fight in behalf of the United States, becoming what 1970s CIA director William Colby called "the biggest hero of the Vietnam War."[12] Vang Pao recruited not just individuals but villages and clans into the war. Although his claims to represent Hmong disguised the fact that Hmong also fought for the communist Pathet Lao, Vang Pao made his cause simultaneously a Hmong cause and a U.S. anticommunist cause. Through his control over opium transport, bombing targets, and CIA rice drops, as well as his charisma, Vang Pao generated enormous ethnic loyalty, consolidating one kind of "Hmong."[13] It is hard to think of a better example of contaminated diversity.

Some Mien fought in Vang Pao's army. Some followed Hmong to the Ban Vinai refugee camp Vang Pao helped to have established in Thailand after he fled Laos following the U.S. withdrawal in 1975. But the war did not give Mien the sense of ethnic-political unity it gave Hmong. Some Mien fought for other political leaders, including Chao La, a Mien general. Some left Laos for Thailand long before the communist victory in Laos. Jonsson's oral histories of Mien in the United States suggest that what are often imagined as innocent "regional" groupings of Laotian Mien—northern Mien, southern Mien—refer to divergent histories of forced resettlement by Vang Pao and Chao La, respectively.[14] War, he argues, creates ethnic identities.[15] War forces people to move but also cements ties to reimagined ancestral cultures. Hmong helped to stimulate the mix, and Mien came to participate.

In the 1980s, Mien who had crossed from Laos to Thailand joined U.S. programs to bring anticommunists from Southeast Asia to the United States and allow them, through refugee status, to become citizens. The refugees arrived in the United States just as welfare was being cut; they were offered few resources for livelihood or assimilation. Most of those from Laos and Cambodia had neither money nor Western education; they moved into off-the-grid jobs such as matsutake picking. In the Oregon woods, they use skills honed in Indochinese wars. Those experienced in jungle fighting rarely get lost, since they know how to find their way in unfamiliar forests. Yet the forest has not stimulated a generic Indochinese—or American—identity. Mimicking the structure of Thai refugee camps, Mien, Hmong, Lao, and Khmer keep their places separate. Yet white Oregonians sometimes call them all "Cambodians," or, with even more confusion, "Hong Kongs." Negotiating multiple forms of prejudice and dispossession, contaminated diversity proliferates.

I hope that at this point you are saying, "This is hardly news! I can think of plenty of similar examples from the landscape and people around me." I agree; contaminated diversity is everywhere. If such stories are so widespread and so well known, the question becomes: Why don't we use these stories in how we know the world? One reason is that contaminated diversity is complicated, often ugly, and humbling. Contaminated diversity implicates survivors in histories of greed, violence, and environmental destruction. The tangled landscape grown up from corporate logging reminds us of the irreplaceable graceful giants that came before. The survivors of war remind us of the bodies they climbed over—or shot—to get to us. We don't know whether to love or hate these survivors. Simple moral judgments don't come to hand.

Worse yet, contaminated diversity is recalcitrant to the kind of "summing up" that has become the hallmark of modern knowledge. Contaminated diversity is not only particular and historical, ever changing, but also relational. It has no self-contained units; its units are encounter-based collaborations. Without self-contained units, it is impossible to compute costs and benefits, or functionality, to any "one" involved. No self-contained individuals or groups assure their self-interests oblivious to the encounter. Without algorithms based on self-containment, scholars and policymakers might have to learn something about the cultural and natural histories at stake. That takes time, and too much time, perhaps, for those who dream of grasping the whole in an equation. But who put them in charge? If a rush of troubled stories is the best way to tell about contaminated diversity, then it's time to make that rush part of our knowledge practices. Perhaps, like the war survivors themselves, we need to tell and tell until all our stories of death and near-death and gratuitous life are standing with us to face the challenges of the present. It is in listening to that cacophony of troubled stories that we might encounter our best hopes for precarious survival.

This book tells a few such stories, which take me not only to the Cascades but also to Tokyo auctions, Finnish Lapland, and a scientist's lunchroom, where I am so excited I spill my tea. Following all these stories at once is as challenging—or, once one gets the hang of it, as simple—as singing a madrigal in which each singer's melody courses in and out of the others. Such interwoven rhythms perform a still lively temporal alternative to the unified progress-time we still long to obey.

3
Some Problems with Scale

No, no, you are not thinking; you are just being logical.

—*Physicist Niels Bohr defending "spooky action at a
distance"*

TO LISTEN TO AND TELL A RUSH OF STORIES IS A
method. And why not make the strong claim and call it a science, an addition to knowledge? Its research object is contaminated diversity; its unit of analysis is the indeterminate encounter. To learn anything we must revitalize arts of noticing and include ethnography and natural history. But we have a problem with scale. A rush of stories cannot be neatly summed up. Its scales do not nest neatly; they draw attention to interrupting geographies and tempos. These interruptions elicit more stories. This is the rush of stories' power as a science. Yet it is just these interruptions that step out of the bounds of most modern science, which demands the possibility for infinite expansion without changing the research framework. Arts of noticing are considered archaic because

they are unable to "scale up" in this way. The ability to make one's research framework apply to greater scales, without changing the research questions, has become a hallmark of modern knowledge. To have any hope of thinking with mushrooms, we must get outside this expectation. In this spirit, I lead a foray into mushroom forests as "anti-plantations."

The expectation of scaling up is not limited to science. Progress itself has often been defined by its ability to make projects expand without changing their framing assumptions. This quality is "scalability." The term is a bit confusing, because it could be interpreted to mean "able to be discussed in terms of scale." Both scalable and nonscalable projects, however, can be discussed in relation to scale. When Fernand Braudel explained history's "long durée" or Niels Bohr showed us the quantum atom, these were not projects of scalability, although they each revolutionized thinking about scale. Scalability, in contrast, is the ability of a project to change scales smoothly without any change in project frames. A scalable business, for example, does not change its organization as it expands. This is possible only if business relations are not transformative, changing the business as new relations are added. Similarly, a scalable research project admits only data that already fit the research frame. Scalability requires that project elements be oblivious to the indeterminacies of encounter; that's how they allow smooth expansion. Thus, too, scalability banishes meaningful diversity, that is, diversity that might change things.

Scalability is not an ordinary feature of nature. Making projects scalable takes a lot of work. Even after that work, there will still be interactions between scalable and nonscalable project elements. Yet, despite the contributions of thinkers such as Braudel and Bohr, the connection between scaling up and the advancement of humanity has been so strong that scalable elements receive the lion's share of attention. The nonscalable becomes an impediment. It is time to turn attention to the nonscalable, not only as objects for description but also as incitements to theory.

A theory of nonscalability might begin in the work it takes to create scalability—and the messes it makes. One vantage point might be that early and influential icon for this work: the European colonial plantation. In their sixteenth- and seventeenth-century sugarcane plantations in Brazil, for example, Portuguese planters stumbled on a formula for smooth expansion. They crafted self-contained, interchangeable project elements, as follows: exterminate local people and plants; prepare now-empty, unclaimed land; and bring in exotic and isolated labor and crops for production. This landscape model of scalability became an inspiration for later industrialization and modernization. The sharp contrast between this model and the matsutake forests that form the subject of this book is a useful platform from which to build a critical distance from scalability.[1]

Consider the elements of the Portuguese sugarcane plantation in colonial Brazil. First, the cane, as Portuguese knew it: Sugarcane was planted by sticking a cane in the ground and waiting for it to sprout. All the plants were clones, and Europeans had no knowledge of how to breed this New Guinea cultigen. The interchangeability of planting stock, undisturbed by reproduction, was a characteristic of European cane. Carried to the New World, it had few interspecies relations. As plants go, it was comparatively self-contained, oblivious to encounter.

Second, cane labor: Portuguese cane-growing came together with their newly gained power to extract enslaved people from Africa. As cane workers in the New World, enslaved Africans had great advantages from growers' perspectives: they had no local social relations and thus no established routes for escape. Like the cane itself, which had no history of either companion species or disease relations in the New World, they were isolated. They were on their way to becoming self-contained, and thus standardizable as abstract labor. Plantations were organized to further alienation for better control. Once central milling operations were started, all operations had to run on the time frame of the mill. Workers had to cut cane as fast as they could, and with full attention, just to avoid injury. Under these conditions, workers did, indeed, become self-contained and interchangeable units. Already considered commodities, they were given jobs made interchangeable by the regularity and coordinated timing engineered into the cane.

Interchangeability in relation to the project frame, for both human work and plant commodities, emerged in these historical experiments. It was a success: Great profits were made in Europe, and most Europeans were too far away to see the effects. The project was, for the first time, scalable—or, more accurately, seemingly scalable.[2] Sugarcane plantations expanded and spread across the warm regions of the world. Their contingent components—cloned planting stock, coerced labor, conquered and thus open land—showed how alienation, interchangeability, and expansion could lead to unprecedented profits. This formula shaped the dreams we have come to call progress and modernity. As Sidney Mintz has argued, sugarcane plantations were the model for factories during industrialization; factories built plantation-style alienation into their plans.[3] The success of expansion through scalability shaped capitalist modernization. By envisioning more and more of the world through the lens of the plantation, investors devised all kinds of new commodities. Eventually, they posited that everything on earth—and beyond—might be scalable, and thus exchangeable at market values. This was utilitarianism, which eventually congealed as modern economics and contributed to forging more scalability—or at least its appearance.

Contrast the matsutake forest: unlike sugarcane clones, matsutake make it evident that they cannot live without transformative relations with other species. Matsutake mushrooms are the fruiting bodies of an underground fungus associated with certain forest trees. The fungus gets its carbohydrates from mutualistic relations with the roots of its host trees, for whom it also forages. Matsutake make it possible for host trees to live in poor soils, without fertile humus. In turn, they are nourished by the trees. This transformative mutualism has made it impossible for humans to cultivate matsutake. Japanese research institutions have thrown millions of yen into making matsutake cultivation possible, but so far without success. Matsutake resist the conditions of the plantation. They require the dynamic multispecies diversity of the forest—with its contaminating relationality.[4]

Furthermore, matsutake foragers are far from the disciplined, interchangeable laborers of the cane fields. Without disciplined alienation, no scalable corporations form in the forest. In the U.S. Pacific Northwest, foragers flock to the forest following "mushroom fever." They are independent, finding their way without formal employment.

Yet it would be a mistake to see matsutake commerce as a primitive survival; this is the misapprehension of progress blinders. Matsutake commerce does not occur in some imagined time before scalability. It is dependent on scalability—in ruins. Many pickers in Oregon are displaced from industrial economies, and the forest itself is the remains of scalability work. Both matsutake commerce and ecology depend on interactions between scalability and its undoing.

The U.S. Pacific Northwest was the crucible of U.S. timber policy and practice in the twentieth century. This region attracted the timber industry after it had already destroyed midwestern forests—and just as scientific forestry became a power in U.S. national governance. Private and public (and, later, environmentalist) interests battled it out in the Pacific Northwest; the scientific-industrial forestry on which they tenuously agreed was a creature of many compromises. Still, here is a place to see forests treated as much like scalable plantations as they might ever be. During the heyday of joint public-private industrial forestry in the 1960s and 1970s, this meant monocrop even-aged timber stands.[5] Such management took a huge amount of work. Unwanted tree species, and indeed all other species, were sprayed with poison. Fires were absolutely excluded. Alienated work crews planted "superior" trees. Thinning was brutal, regular, and essential. Proper spacing allowed maximum rates of growth as well as mechanical harvesting. Timber trees were a new kind of sugarcane: managed for uniform growth, without multispecies interference, and thinned and harvested by machines and anonymous workers.

Despite its technological prowess, the project of turning forests into plantations worked out unevenly at best. Earlier, timber companies had made a killing by just harvesting the most expensive trees; when national forests were opened for logging after World War II, they continued "high grading," a practice dignified under standards that said mature trees were better replaced by fast-growing youngsters. Clear-cutting, or "even-aged management," was introduced to move beyond the inefficiencies of such pick-and-choose harvesting. But the regrowing trees of scientific-industrial management were not so inviting, profit-wise. Where the great timber species had earlier been maintained by Native American burning, it was difficult to reproduce the "right" species. Firs and lodgepole pines grew up where great ponderosas had once held dominance. Then the price of Pacific Northwest timber plummeted. Without easy pickings, timber companies began to search elsewhere for cheaper trees. Without the political clout and funds of big timber, the region's Forest Service districts lost funding, and maintaining plantation-like forests became cost-prohibitive. Environmentalists started going to the courts, asking for stricter conservation protections. They were blamed for the crashing timber economy, but the timber companies—and most of the big trees—had already left.[6]

By the time I wandered into the eastern Cascades, in 2004, fir and lodgepole had made great advances across what once had been almost pure stands of ponderosa pine. Although signs along the highways still said "Industrial Timber," it was hard to imagine industry. The landscape was covered with thickets of lodgepole and fir: too small for most timber users; not scenic enough for recreation. But something else had emerged in the regional economy—matsutake. Forest Service researchers in the 1990s found that the annual commercial value of the mushrooms was as least as much as the value of the timber.[7] Matsutake had stimulated a nonscalable forest economy in the ruins of scalable industrial forestry.

The challenge for thinking with precarity is to understand the ways projects for making scalability have transformed landscape and society, while also seeing where scalability fails—and where nonscalable ecological and economic relations erupt. It is key to take note of the careers of both scalability and nonscalability. But it would be a huge mistake to assume that scalability is bad and nonscalability is good. Nonscalable projects can be as terrible in their effects as scalable ones. Unregulated loggers destroy forests more rapidly than scientific foresters. The main distinguishing feature between scalable and nonscalable projects is not ethical conduct but rather that the latter are more diverse because they are not geared up for expansion. Nonscalable projects can be terrible or benign; they run the range.

New eruptions of nonscalability do not mean that scalability has disappeared. In an era of neoliberal restructuring, scalability is increasingly reduced to a technical problem rather than a popular mobilization in which citizens, governments, and corporations should work together. As chapter 4 explores, the articulation between scalable accounting and nonscalable workplace relations is increasingly accepted as a model for capitalist accumulation. Production does not have to be scalable as long as elites are able to regularize their account books. Can we keep sight of the continuing hegemony of scalability projects while immersing ourselves in the forms and tactics of precarity?

Part 2 of this book traces the interplay between scalable and nonscalable in forms of capitalism in which scalable accounting allows nonscalable labor and natural resource management. In this "salvage" capitalism, supply chains organize the translation process in which wildly diverse forms of work and nature are made commensurate—for capital. Part 3 returns to matsutake forests as anti-plantations in which transformative encounters create the possibilities of life. The contaminated diversity of ecological relations takes center stage.

But first, a foray into indeterminacy: the central feature of the assemblages I follow. So far, I've defined assemblages in relation to their negative features: their elements are contaminated and thus unstable; they refuse to scale up smoothly. Yet assemblages are defined by the strength of what they gather as much as their always-possible dissipation. They make history. This combination of ineffability and presence is evident in smell: another gift of the mushroom.

Interlude
Smelling

"What leaf? What mushroom?"

—*John Cage's translation of a classic poem by Basho*

WHAT IS THE STORY OF A SMELL? NOT AN ETHNOGRAPHY of smelling, but the story of the smell itself, wafting into the nostrils of people and animals, and even impressing the roots of plants and the membranes of soil bacteria? Smell draws us into the entangled threads of memory and possibility.

Matsutake guides not just me but many others. Moved by the smell, people and animals across the northern hemisphere brave wild terrain searching for it. Deer select matsutake over other mushroom choices. Bears turn over logs and excavate ditches searching for it. And several Oregon mushroom hunters told me of elk with bloody muzzles from uprooting matsutake from the sharp pumice soil. The smell, they said, draws elk from one patch straight to another. And what is smell but a particular form of chemical sensitivity? In this interpretation, trees too are touched by the smell of matsutake, allowing it into their roots. As with truffles, flying insects have been seen circling underground caches. In contrast, slugs, other fungi, and many kinds of soil bacteria are repulsed by the smell, moving out of its range.

Smell is elusive. Its effects surprise us. We don't know how to put much about smell into words, even when our reactions are strong and certain. Humans breathe and smell in the same intake of air, and describing smell seems almost as difficult as describing air. But smell, unlike air, is a sign of the presence of another, to which we are already responding. Response always takes us somewhere new; we are not quite ourselves any more—or at least the selves we were, but rather ourselves in encounter with another. Encounters are, by their nature, indeterminate; we are unpredictably transformed. Might smell, in its confusing mix of elusiveness and certainty, be a useful guide to the indeterminacy of encounter?

Indeterminacy has a rich legacy in human appreciation of mushrooms. American composer John Cage wrote a set of short performance pieces called *Indeterminacy*, many of which celebrate encounters with mushrooms.[1] Hunting wild mushrooms, for Cage, required a particular kind of attention: attention to the here and now of encounter, in all its contingencies and surprises. Cage's music was all about this "always different" here and now, which he contrasted to the enduring "sameness" of classical composition; he composed to get the audience to listen as much to ambient sounds as composed music. In one famous composition, *4'33"*, no music is played at all, and the audience is forced to just listen. Cage's attention to listening as things occurred brought him to appreciate indeterminacy. The Cage quotation with which I began this chapter is his translation of seventeenth-century Japanese poet Matsuo Basho's haiku, "matsutake ya shiranu ki no ha no hebari tsuku," which I have seen translated as "Matsutake; And on it stuck / The leaf of some unknown tree."[2] Cage decided that the indeterminacy of encounter was not clear enough in such translations. First he settled on "That that's unknown brings mushroom and leaf together," which nicely expresses the indeterminacy of encounter. But, he thought, it is too ponderous. "What leaf? What mushroom?" can also take us into that open-endedness that Cage so valued in learning from mushrooms.[3]

Indeterminacy has been equally important in what scientists learn from mushrooms. Mycologist Alan Rayner finds the indeterminacy of fungal growth one of the most exciting things about fungi.[4] Human bodies achieve a determinate form early in our lives. Barring injury, we'll never be all that different in shape than we were as adolescents. We can't grow extra limbs, and we're stuck with the one brain we've each got. In contrast, fungi keep growing and changing form all their lives. Fungi are famous for changing shape in relation to their encounters and environments. Many are "potentially immortal," meaning they die from disease, injury, or lack of resources, but not from old age. Even this little fact can alert us to how much our thoughts about knowledge and existence just assume determinate life form and old age. We rarely imagine life without such limits—and when we do we stray into magic. Rayner challenges us to think with mushrooms, otherwise. Some aspects of our lives are more comparable to fungal indeterminacy, he points out. Our daily habits are repetitive, but they are also open-ended, responding to opportunity and encounter. What if our indeterminate life form was not the shape of our bodies but rather the shape of our motions over time? Such indeterminacy expands our concept of human life, showing us how we are transformed by encounter. Humans and fungi share such here-and-now transformations through encounter. Sometimes they encounter each other. As another seventeenth-century haiku put it: "Matsutake / Taken by someone else / Right in front of my nose."[5] What person? What mushroom?

The smell of matsutake transformed me in a physical way. The first time I cooked them, they ruined an otherwise lovely stir-fry. The smell was overwhelming. I couldn't eat it; I couldn't even pick out the other vegetables without encountering the smell. I threw the whole pan away and ate my rice plain. After that I was cautious, collecting but not eating. Finally, one day, I brought the whole load to a Japanese colleague, who was head over heels in delight. She had never seen so much matsutake in her life. Of course she prepared some for dinner. First, she showed me how she tore apart each mushroom, not touching it with a knife. The metal of the knife changes the flavor, she said, and, besides, her mother told her that the spirit of the mushroom doesn't like it. Then she grilled the matsutake on a hot pan without oil. Oil changes the smell, she explained. Worse yet, butter, with its strong smell. Matsutake must be dry grilled or put into a soup; oil or butter ruins it. She served the grilled matsutake with a bit of lime juice. It was marvelous! The smell had begun to delight me.

Over the next few weeks, my senses changed. It was an amazing year for matsutake, and they were everywhere. Now, when I caught a whiff, I felt happy. I lived for several years in Borneo, where I had had a similar experience with durian, that marvelously stinky tropical fruit. The first time I was served durian I thought I would vomit. But it was a good year for durian, and the smell was everywhere. Before long I found myself thrilled by the smell; I couldn't remember what had sickened me. Similarly, matsutake: I could no longer remember what I had found so disturbing. Now it smelled like joy.

I'm not the only one who has that reaction. Koji Ueda runs a beautifully trim vegetable shop in Kyoto's traditional market. During the matsutake season, he explained, most people who come into the store don't want to buy (his matsutake are expensive); they want to smell. Just coming into the store makes people happy, he said. That's why he sells matsutake, he said: for the sheer pleasure it gives people.

Perhaps the happiness factor in smelling matsutake is what pressed Japanese odor engineers to manufacture an artificial matsutake smell. Now you can buy matsutake-flavored potato chips and matsutake-flavored instant miso soup. I've tried them, and I can sense a distant memory of matsutake at the edge of my tongue, but it's nothing like encountering a mushroom. Still, many Japanese have only known matsutake in this form, or as the frozen mushrooms used in matsutake rice or matsutake pizza. They wonder what the fuss is all about and feel indulgently critical toward those who go on and on about matsutake. Nothing can smell all that good.

Matsutake lovers in Japan know this scorn and cultivate a defensive exuberance about the mushroom. The smell of matsutake, they say, recalls times past that these young people never knew, much to their detriment. Matsutake, they say, smells like village life and a childhood visiting grandparents and chasing dragonflies. It recalls open pinewoods, now crowded out and dying. Many small memories come together in the smell. It brings to mind the paper dividers on village interior doors, one woman explained; her grandmother would change the papers every New Year and use them to wrap the next year's mushrooms. It was an easier time, before nature became degraded and poisonous.

Nostalgia can be put to good uses. Or so explained Makoto Ogawa, the elder statesman of matsutake science in Kyoto. When I met him, he had just retired. Worse yet, he had cleaned out his office and thrown away books and scientific articles. But he was a walking library of matsutake science and history. Retirement had made it easier for him to talk about his passions. His matsutake science, he explained, had always involved advocacy for both people and nature. He had dreamed that showing people how to nurture matsutake forests might revitalize connections between city and countryside—as urban people became interested in rural life, and villagers had a valuable product to sell. Meanwhile, even as matsutake research could be funded by economic excitement, it had many benefits for basic science, especially in understanding relations among living things in changing ecologies. If nostalgia was a part of this project, so much the better. This was his nostalgia too. He took my research team to see what once was a thriving matsutake forest behind an old temple. Now the hill was alternately dark with planted conifers and choked with evergreen broadleaf trees, with only a few dying pines. We found no matsutake. Once, he recalled, that hillside was teeming with mushrooms. Like Proust's madeleines, matsutake are redolent with *temps perdu*.

Dr. Ogawa savors nostalgia with considerable irony and laughter. As we stood in the rain beside the matsutake-less temple forest, he explained the Korean origin of Japanese regard for matsutake. Before you hear the story, consider that there is no love lost between Japanese nationalists and Koreans. For Dr. Ogawa to remind us that Korean aristocrats started Japanese civilization works against the grain of Japanese desire. Besides, civilization, in his tale, is not all for the good. Long before they came to central Japan, Dr. Ogawa related, Koreans had cut down their forests to build temples and fuel iron forging. They had developed in their homeland the human-disturbed open pine forests in which matsutake grow long before such forests emerged in Japan. When Koreans expanded to Japan in the eighth century, they cut down forests. Pine forests sprung up from such deforestation, and with them matsutake. Koreans smelled the matsutake—and they thought of home. The first nostalgia: the first love of matsutake. It was in longing for Korea that Japan's new aristocracy first glorified the now famous autumn aroma, Dr. Ogawa told us. No wonder, too, that Japanese abroad are so obsessed with matsutake, he added. He ended with a funny story about a Japanese American matsutake hunter he met in Oregon who, in a badly garbled mixture of Japanese and English, saluted Dr. Ogawa's research, saying, "We Japanese are matsutake crazy!"

Dr. Ogawa's stories tickled me because they situated nostalgia, but they also drove home another point: matsutake grows only in deeply disturbed forests. Matsutake and red pine are partners in central Japan, and both grow only where people have caused significant deforestation. All over the world, indeed, matsutake are associated with the most disturbed kinds of forests: places where glaciers, volcanoes, sand dunes—or human actions—have done away with other trees and even organic soil. The pumice flats I walked in central Oregon are in some ways typical of the kind of land matsutake knows how to inhabit: land on which most plants and other fungi can find no hold. On such impoverished landscapes, the indeterminacies of encounter loom. What pioneer has found its way here, and how can it live? Even the hardiest of seedlings is unlikely to make it unless it finds a partner in an equally hardy fungus to draw nutrients from the rocky ground. (What leaf? What mushroom?) The indeterminacy of fungal growth matters too. Might it encounter the roots of a receptive tree? A change in substrate or potential nutrition? Through its indeterminate growth, the fungus learns the landscape.

There are humans to encounter as well. Will they inadvertently nurture the fungus while cutting firewood and gathering green manure? Or will they introduce hostile plantings, import exotic diseases, or pave the area for suburban development? Humans matter on these landscapes. And humans (like fungi and trees) bring histories with them to meet the challenges of the encounter. These histories, both human and not human, are never robotic programs but rather condensations in the indeterminate here and now; the past we grasp, as philosopher Walter Benjamin puts it, is a memory "that flashes in a moment of danger."[6] We enact history, Benjamin writes, as "a tiger's leap into that which has gone before."[7] Science studies scholar Helen Verran offers another image: Among Australia's Yolngu people, she relates, the recollection of the ancestors' dreaming is condensed for present challenges in a rite at the climax of which a spear is thrown into the center of the storytellers' circle. The toss of the spear merges the past in the here and now.[8] Through smell, all of us know that spear's throw, that tiger's leap. The past we bring to encounters is condensed in smell. To smell childhood visits with one's grandparents condenses a great chunk of Japanese history, not just the vitality of village life in the mid-twentieth century, but the nineteenth-century deforestation that came before, denuding the landscape, and the urbanization and abandonment of the forests that later followed.

While some Japanese may smell nostalgia in the forests made by their disturbances, this is not, of course, the only feeling that people bring to such wild places. Consider the smell of matsutake again. It is time to tell you that most people of European origin can't stand the smell. A Norwegian gave the Eurasian species its first scientific name, *Tricholoma nauseosum*, the nauseating Trich. (In recent years, taxonomists made an exception to usual rules of precedence to rename the mushroom, acknowledging Japanese tastes, as *Tricholoma matsutake*.) Americans of European descent tend to be equally unimpressed by the smell of the Pacific Northwest's *Tricholoma magnivelare*. "Mold," "turpentine," "mud," white pickers said, when I asked them to characterize the smell. More than one moved our conversation to the foul smell of rotting fungi. Some were familiar with California mycologist David Arora's characterization of the smell as "a provocative compromise between 'red hots' and dirty socks."[9] Not exactly something you would want to eat. When Oregon's white pickers prepare the mushroom as food, they pickle it or smoke it. The processing masks the smell, making the mushroom anonymous.

It is not surprising, perhaps, that U.S. scientists have studied the smell of matsutake to see what it repels (slugs), but Japanese scientists have studied the smell to consider what it attracts (some flying insects).[10] Is it the "same" smell if people bring such different sensibilities to the encounter? Does that problem stretch to slugs and gnats as well as people? What if noses—as in my experience—change? What if the mushroom too can change through its encounters?

Matsutake in Oregon associate with many host trees. Oregon pickers can distinguish the host tree with which a particular matsutake has grown—partly from the size and shape, but partly from the smell. The subject came up one day when I examined some truly bad-smelling matsutake being offered for sale. The picker explained that he found these mushrooms under white fir, an unusual host tree for matsutake. Loggers, he said, call white fir "piss fir" because of the bad smell the wood emits when you cut it. The mushrooms smelled as bad as a wounded fir.

To me, they did not smell like matsutake at all. But wasn't this smell some piss fir–matsutake combination, made in the encounter?

There is an intriguing nature-culture knot in such indeterminacies. Different ways of smelling and different qualities of smell are wrapped up together. It seems impossible to describe the smell of matsutake without telling all the cultural-and-natural histories condensed together in it. Any attempt at definitive untangling—perhaps like artificial matsutake scent—is likely to lose the point: the indeterminate experience of encounter, with its tiger's leap into history. What else is smell?

The smell of matsutake wraps and tangles memory and history—and not just for humans. It assembles many ways of being in an affect-laden knot that packs its own punch. Emerging from encounter, it shows us history-in-the-making. Smell it.

Capitalist edge effects, Oregon. A buyer sets up by the side of the highway. Commerce connects undisciplined labor and resources with central locations for inventory, where capitalist value is amassed in translation.

Part II
After Progress: Salvage Accumulation

I FIRST HEARD OF MATSUTAKE FROM MYCOLOGIST David Arora, who studied matsutake camps in Oregon between 1993 and 1998. I was looking for a culturally colorful global commodity, and Arora's stories of matsutake intrigued me. He told me of the buyers set up tents by the side of the highway to buy mushrooms at night. "They have nothing to do all day, so they'll have plenty of time to talk to you," he ventured.

And there the buyers were—but so much more! In the big camp, I seemed to have stepped into rural Southeast Asia. Mien wearing sarongs boiled water in kerosene cans over stone tripods and hung strips of game and fish over the stove to dry. Hmong all the way from North Carolina brought home-canned bamboo shoots for sale. Lao noodle tents sold not only *pho* but also the most authentic *laap* I had eaten in the United States, all raw blood, chilies, and intestines. Lao karaoke blared from battery-powered speakers. I even met a Cham picker, although he did not speak Cham, which I thought perhaps I could manage from its closeness to Malay. Mocking my linguistic limitations, a Khmer teenager wearing grunge boasted that he spoke four languages: Khmer, Lao, English, and Ebonics. Local Native Americans sometimes came to sell their mushrooms. There were also both whites and Latinos, although most avoided the official camp, staying in the woods alone or in small groups. And visitors: A Sacramento Filipino followed Mien friends up here one year, although he said he never got the point. A Portland Korean thought maybe he might join.

Yet there was something not at all cosmopolitan about the scene as well: A rift separated these pickers and buyers from shops and consumers in Japan. Everyone knew that the mushrooms (except for a small percentage bought for Japanese American markets) were going to Japan. Every buyer and bulker longed to sell directly to Japan—but none had any idea how. Misconceptions about the matsutake trade both in Japan and in other supply sites proliferated. White pickers swore that the value of the mushrooms in Japan was as an aphrodisiac. (While matsutake in Japan do have phallic connotations, no one eats them as a drug.) Some complained about the Chinese Red Army, which, they said, drafted people to pick, which depressed global prices. (Pickers in China are independent, just as in Oregon.) When someone discovered extremely high prices in Tokyo on the Internet, no one realized that these prices referred to *Japanese* matsutake. One exceptional bulker, of Chinese origin and fluent in Japanese, whispered to me about these misunderstandings—but he was an outsider. Except for this man, Oregon pickers, buyers, and bulkers were completely in the dark about the Japanese side of the trade. They made up fantasy landscapes of Japan, and they did not know how to assess them. They had their own matsutake world: a patch of practices and meanings that brought them together as matsutake suppliers—but did not inform the mushrooms' further passage.

This rift between U.S. and Japanese segments of the commodity chain guided my search. Different processes for making and accessing value characterized each segment. Given this diversity, what makes this part of that global economy we call capitalism?

4
Working the Edge

It may seem odd to want to tackle capitalism with a theory that stresses ephemeral assemblages and multidirectional histories. After all, the global economy has been the centerpiece of progress, and even radical critics have described its forward-looking motion as filling up the world. Like a giant bulldozer, capitalism appears to flatten the earth to its specifications. But all this only raises the stakes for asking what else is going on—not in some protected enclave, but rather everywhere, both inside and out.

Impressed by the rise of factories in the nineteenth century, Marx showed us forms of capitalism that required the rationalization of wage labor and raw materials. Most analysts have followed this precedent, imagining a factory-driven system with a coherent governance structure, built in cooperation with nation-states. Yet today—as then—much of the economy takes place in radically different scenes. Supply chains snake back and forth not only across continents but also across standards; it would be hard to identify a single rationality across the chain. Yet assets are still amassed for further investment. How does this work?

A supply chain is a particular kind of commodity chain: one in which lead firms direct commodity traffic.[1] Throughout this part, I explore the supply chain linking matsutake pickers in the forests of Oregon with those who eat the mushrooms in Japan. The chain is surprising and full of cultural variety. The factory work through which we know capitalism is mainly missing. But the chain illuminates something important about capitalism today: Amassing wealth is possible without rationalizing labor and raw materials. Instead, it requires acts of translation across varied social and political spaces, which, borrowing from ecologists' usage, I call "patches." Translation, in Shiho Satsuka's sense, is the drawing of one world-making project into another.[2] While the term draws attention to language, it can also refer to other forms of partial attunement. Translations across sites of difference *are* capitalism: they make it possible for investors to accumulate wealth.

How do mushrooms foraged as trophies of freedom become capitalist assets—and later, exemplary Japanese gifts? Answering this question requires attention to the unexpected assemblages of the chain's component links, as well as the translation processes that draw the links together into a transnational circuit.

Capitalism is a system for concentrating wealth, which makes possible new investments, which further concentrate wealth. This process is accumulation. Classic models take us to the factory: factory owners concentrate wealth by paying workers less than the value of the goods that the workers produce each day. Owners "accumulate" investment assets from this extra value.

Even in factories, however, there are other elements of accumulation. In the nineteenth century, when capitalism first became an object of inquiry, raw materials were imagined as an infinite bequest from Nature to Man. Raw materials can no longer be taken for granted. In our food procurement system, for example, capitalists exploit ecologies not only by reshaping them but also by taking advantage of their capacities. Even in industrial farms, farmers depend on life processes outside their control, such as photosynthesis and animal digestion. In capitalist farms, living things made within ecological processes are coopted for the concentration of wealth. This is what I call "salvage," that is, taking advantage of value produced without capitalist control. Many capitalist raw materials (consider coal and oil) came into existence long before capitalism. Capitalists also cannot produce human life, the prerequisite of *labor*. "Salvage accumulation" is the process through which lead firms amass capital without controlling the conditions under which commodities are produced. Salvage is not an ornament on ordinary capitalist processes; it is a feature of how capitalism works.[3]

Sites for salvage are simultaneously inside and outside capitalism; I call them "pericapitalist."[4] All kinds of goods and services produced by pericapitalist activities, human and nonhuman, are salvaged for capitalist accumulation. If a peasant family produces a crop that enters capitalist food chains, capital accumulation is possible through salvaging the value created in peasant farming. Now that global supply chains have come to characterize world capitalism, we see this process everywhere. "Supply chains" are commodity chains that translate value to the benefit of dominant firms; translation between noncapitalist and capitalist value systems is what they do.

Salvage accumulation through global supply chains is not new, and some well-known earlier examples can clarify how it works. Consider the nineteenth-century ivory supply chain connecting central Africa and Europe as told in Joseph Conrad's novel *Heart of Darkness*.[5] The story turns around the narrator's discovery that the European trader he much admired has turned to savagery to procure his ivory. The savagery is a surprise because everyone expects the European presence in Africa to be a force for civilization and progress. Instead, civilization and progress turn out to be cover-ups and translation mechanisms for getting access to value procured through violence: classic salvage.

For a brighter view of supply-chain translation, consider Herman Melville's account of the nineteenth-century procurement of whale oil for Yankee investors.[6] *Moby-Dick* tells of a ship of whalers whose rowdy cosmopolitanism contrasts sharply with our stereotypes of factory discipline; yet the oil they obtain from killing whales around the world enters a U.S.-based capitalist supply chain. Strangely, all the harpooners on the *Pequod* are unassimilated indigenous people from Asia, Africa, America, and the Pacific. The ship is unable to kill a single whale without the expertise of people who are completely untrained in U.S.

industrial discipline. But the products of this work must eventually be translated into capitalist value forms; the ship sails only because of capitalist financing. The conversion of indigenous knowledge into capitalist returns is salvage accumulation. So too is the conversion of whale life into investments.

Before you conclude that salvage accumulation is archaic, let me turn to a contemporary example. Technological advances in managing inventory have energized today's global supply chains; inventory management allows lead firms to source their products from all kinds of economic arrangements, capitalist and otherwise. One firm that helped put such innovations in place is the retail giant Wal-Mart. Wal-Mart pioneered the required use of universal product codes (UPCs), the black-and-white bars that allow computers to know these products as inventory.[7] The legibility of inventory, in turn, means that Wal-Mart is able to ignore the labor and environmental conditions through which its products are made: pericapitalist methods, including theft and violence, may be part of the production process. With a nod to Woody Guthrie, we might think about the contrast between production and accounting through the two sides of the UPC tag.[8] One side of the tag, the side with the black-and-white bars, allows the product to be minutely tracked and assessed. The other side of the tag is blank, indexing Wal-Mart's total lack of concern with how the product is made, since value can be translated through accounting. Wal-Mart has become famous for forcing its suppliers to make products ever more cheaply, thus encouraging savage labor and destructive environmental practices.[9] Savage and salvage are often twins: Salvage translates violence and pollution into profit.

As inventory moves increasingly under control, the requirement to control labor and raw materials recedes; supply chains make value from translating values produced in quite varied circumstances into capitalist inventory. One way of thinking about this is through scalability, the technical feat of creating expansion without the distortion of changing relations. The legibility of inventory allows scalable retail expansion for Wal-Mart without requiring that production be scalable. Production is left to the riotous diversity of nonscalability, with its relationally particular dreams and schemes. We know this best in "the race to the bottom": the role of global supply chains in promoting coerced labor, dangerous sweatshops, poisonous substitute ingredients, and irresponsible environmental gouging and dumping. Where lead firms pressure suppliers to provide cheaper and cheaper products, such production conditions are predictable outcomes. As in *Heart of Darkness*, unregulated production is translated in the commodity chain, and even reimagined as progress. This is frightening. At the same time, as J. K. Gibson-Graham argue in their optimistic reach toward a "postcapitalist politics," economic diversity can be hopeful.[10] Pericapitalist economic forms can be sites for rethinking the unquestioned authority of capitalism in our lives. At the very least, diversity offers a chance for multiple ways forward—not just one.

In her insightful comparison between the supply chains for French green beans (*haricots verts*) that link West Africa with France and East Africa with Great Britain, respectively, geographer Susanne Freidberg offers a sense of how supply chains, drawing variously on colonial and national histories, may encourage quite different economic forms.[11] French neocolonial schemes mobilize peasant cooperatives; British supermarket standards encourage expatriate scam operations.[12] Within and across differences such as these, there is room for building a politics to confront and navigate salvage accumulation. But following Gibson-Graham to call this politics "postcapitalist" seems to me premature. Through salvage accumulation, lives and products move back and forth between noncapitalist and capitalist forms; these forms shape each other and interpenetrate. The term "pericapitalist" acknowledges that those of us caught in such translations are never fully shielded from capitalism; pericapitalist spaces are unlikely platforms for a safe defense and recuperation.

At the same time, the more prominent critical alternative—shutting one's eyes to economic diversity—seems even more ridiculous in these times. Most critics of capitalism insist on the unity and homogeneity of the capitalist system; many, like Michael Hardt and Antonio Negri, argue that there is no longer a space outside of capitalism's empire.[13] Everything is ruled by a singular capitalist logic. As for Gibson-Graham, this claim is an attempt to build a critical political position: the possibility of transcending capitalism. Critics who stress the uniformity of capitalism's hold on the world want to overcome it through a singular solidarity. But what blinders this hope requires! Why not instead admit to economic diversity?

My goal in bringing up Gibson-Graham and Hardt and Negri is not to dismiss them; indeed, I think they are perhaps the early twenty-first century's most trenchant anticapitalist critics. Furthermore, by setting out strongly contrasting goal posts between which we might think and play, they jointly do us an important service. Is capitalism a single, over-arching system that conquers all, or one segregated economic form among many?[14] Between these two positions, we might see how capitalist and noncapitalist forms interact in pericapitalist spaces. Gibson-Graham advise us, quite correctly I think, that what they call "noncapitalist" forms can be found everywhere in the midst of capitalist worlds—rather than just in archaic backwaters. But they see such forms as alternatives to capitalism. Instead, I would look for the noncapitalist elements on which capitalism depends. Thus, for example, when Jane Collins reports that workers in Mexican garment assembly factories are expected to know how to sew before they begin their jobs, *because they are women*, we are offered a glimpse of noncapitalist and capitalist economic forms working together.[15] Women learn to sew growing up at home; salvage accumulation is the process that brings this skill into the factory to the benefit of owners. To understand capitalism (and not just its alternatives), then, we can't stay inside the logics of capitalists; we need an ethnographic eye to see the economic diversity through which accumulation is possible.

It takes concrete histories to make any concept come to life. And isn't mushroom collecting a place to look, after progress? The rifts and bridges of the Oregon-to-Japan matsutake commodity chain show capitalism achieved through economic diversity. Matsutake foraged and sold in pericapitalist performances become capitalist inventory as they are sent to Japan a day later. Such translation is the central problem of many global supply chains. Let me begin by describing the first part of the chain.[16]

Americans don't like middlemen, who, they say, just rip off value. But middlemen are consummate translators; their presence directs us to salvage accumulation. Consider the North American side of the commodity chain that brings matsutake from Oregon to Japan. (The Japanese side—with its many middlemen—will be considered later.) Independent foragers pick the mushrooms in national forests. They sell to independent buyers, who sell, in turn, to bulkers' field agents, who sell to other bulkers or to exporters, who sell and ship, at last, to importers in Japan. Why so many middlemen? The best answer may be a history.

Japanese traders began importing matsutake in the 1980s, when the scarcity of matsutake in Japan first became clear. Japan was bursting with investment capital, and matsutake were prime luxuries, equally suitable as perks, gifts, or bribes. American matsutake were still an expensive novelty in Tokyo, and restaurants competed to get some. Emerging matsutake traders in Japan were like other Japanese traders of that time, ready to use their capital to organize supply chains.

The mushrooms were expensive, so the incentives for suppliers were good. North American traders remember the 1990s as a time of extraordinary prices—and high-risk gambling. If a supplier was able to hit the Japanese markets correctly, the payoff was huge. But with an inconsistent and easy-to-spoil forest product and rapidly changing demand, the possibilities for total wipeout were also great. Everyone spoke of those days in casino metaphors. One Japanese trader compared the importers then to the Mafia in international ports after World War I: It was not just that the importers were gambling but that they were also catalyzing gambling—and keeping the gambling going.

Japanese importers needed local know-how, and they began through alliances with exporters. In the Pacific Northwest, the first exporters were Asian Canadians in Vancouver—and because of their precedent, most U.S. matsutake continue to be exported by their firms. These exporters were not interested only in matsutake. They shipped seafood, or cherries, or log homes to Japan; matsutake were added to those activities. Some—especially the Japanese immigrants—told me they added matsutake to sweeten long-term relations with importers. They were willing to ship matsutake at a loss, they said, to keep their relations intact.

Alliances between exporters and importers formed a basis for the transpacific trade. But the exporters—experts in fish, or fruit, or timber—knew nothing about how to get the mushrooms. In Japan, matsutake come to the market via an agricultural cooperative, or from individual farmers. In North America, matsutake are scattered across enormous national (U.S.) or commonwealth (Canadian) forests. This is where the small companies that I call "bulkers" come in; bulkers gather mushrooms to sell to exporters. Bulkers' field agents buy mushrooms from "buyers" who buy from pickers. Field agents, like buyers, must know the terrain and the people likely to search it.

In the earliest days of the U.S. Pacific Northwest matsutake trade, most field agents, buyers, and pickers were white men who found solace in the mountains, such as Vietnam veterans, displaced loggers, and rural "traditionalists" who rejected liberal urban society. After 1989, an increasing number of refugees from Laos and Cambodia came to pick, and field agents had to stretch their abilities to work with Southeast Asians. Southeast Asians eventually became buyers, and a few became field agents. Working around each other, the whites and Southeast Asians found a common vocabulary in "freedom," which could mean many things dear to each group, even if they were not the same. Native Americans found resonance, but Latino pickers did not share the rhetoric of freedom. Despite this variation, the overlapping concerns of self-exiled whites and Southeast Asian refugees became the heartbeat of the trade; freedom brought out the matsutake.

Through shared concerns with freedom, the U.S. Pacific Northwest became one of the world's great matsutake exporting areas. Yet this way of life was segregated from the rest of the commodity chain. Bulkers and buyers longed to export matsutake directly to Japan but did not succeed. Neither buyers nor bulkers could get beyond the already diffi-cult exchange with Canadian exporters of Asian origin, for whom En-glish was not often a first language. They complained about unfair prac-tices, but in fact they were useless at the cultural translation necessary for the making of inventory. For it is not just language that separates pickers, buyers, and bulkers in Oregon from Japanese traders; it is the conditions of production. Oregon mushrooms are contaminated with the cultural practices of "freedom."

The story of an exception makes the point. "Wei" first went to Japan from his native China to study music; when he found he could not make a living, he entered the Japanese vegetable import trade. He be-came fluent in Japanese, although still prickly about some features of life in Japan. When his company wanted someone to go to North Amer-ica, he volunteered. This is how he became an idiosyncratic combina-tion of field agent, bulker, and exporter. He goes to the matsutake area to watch the buying, just like other field agents, but he has a direct line to Japan. Unlike the other field agents, he is constantly on the phone with Japanese traders, gauging opportunities and prices. He also talks to Japanese Canadian exporters, although he does not sell his mushrooms through them; because he can talk to them in Japanese, they constantly ask him to explain conditions in the field, including the behavior of the field agents whose mushrooms they buy. Meanwhile, the other field agents refuse to include him in their company and conspire against his buyers. He is not welcomed into their discussions, and, indeed, is shunned by the freedom-loving mountain men.

Unlike the other field agents, Wei pays his buyers a salary, rather than a commission. He demands the loyalty and discipline of employees, refusing them the freewheeling independence of the other buyers. He buys matsutake for particular shipments, with particular characteristics, rather than buying for the pleasure and prowess of free competition, as the others do. He is already making inventory in the buying tents. His difference highlights the distinctiveness of the freedom assemblage as a patch.

As international matsutake commerce entered the twenty-first century, regularization was afoot in Japan. Prices there stabilized as supply chains in many countries developed, as rankings of foreign matsutake congealed, and as perk-money in Japan diminished and the demand for matsutake became more specialized. The prices of Oregon matsutake in Japan became relatively stable—considering, of course, that matsutake is still a wild product with an irregular supply. However, this stability was not reflected in Oregon, where prices continued to roller-coaster, even if never returning to 1990s' highs. When I talked to Japanese importers about this discrepancy, they explained it as a matter of American "psychology." An importer who specialized in Oregon matsutake was thrilled to show me photographs from his visits and reminisce about his Wild West experiences in Oregon. White and Southeast Asian pickers and buyers, he explained, would not produce mushrooms without the excitement of what he called an "auction," and the more the price fluctuated, the better the buying. (In contrast, he said, Mexican pickers in Oregon were willing to accept a constant price, but the others dominated the trade.) His job was to facilitate American peculiarities; his company had a parallel specialist in Chinese matsutake, whose job was to accommodate Chinese quirks. By facilitating varied cultural economies, his company could build its business through mushrooms from around the world.

It was this man's expectation of the necessity of cultural translation that first alerted me to the problem of salvage accumulation. In the 1970s, Americans expected the globalization of capital to mean the spread of U.S. business standards all over the world. In contrast, Japanese traders had become specialists in building international supply chains and using them as mechanisms of translation to bring goods into Japan without Japanese production facilities or employment standards. As long as these goods could be made into legible inventory in their transit to Japan, Japanese traders could use them to accumulate capital. By the end of the century, Japanese economic power had slipped, and twentieth-century Japanese business innovations were eclipsed by neoliberal reforms. But no one cares to reform the matsutake commodity chain; it is too small and too "Japanese." Here is a place, then, to look for the Japanese trading strategies that rocked the world. At their center is translation between diverse economies. Traders as translators become masters of salvage accumulation.

Before taking on translation, however, I need to visit the freedom assemblage.

Freedom . . .

5
Open Ticket, Oregon

In the middle of nowhere

—Official slogan of an aspiring matsutake town in Finland

ONE COLD OCTOBER NIGHT IN THE LATE 1990S, THREE
Hmong American matsutake pickers huddled in their tent. Shivering,
they brought their gas cooking stove inside to provide a little warmth.
They went to sleep with the stove on. It went out. The next morning, all
three were dead, asphyxiated by the fumes. Their deaths left the campground vulnerable, haunted by their ghosts. Ghosts can paralyze you,
taking away your ability to move or speak. The Hmong pickers moved
away, and the others soon moved too.

The U.S. Forest Service did not know about the ghosts. They wanted
to rationalize the pickers' camping area, to make it accessible to police
and emergency services, and easier for campground hosts to enforce
rules and fees. In the early 1990s, Southeast Asian pickers had camped
where they pleased, like everyone else who visits the national forests. But
whites complained that Southeast Asians left too much litter. The Forest

Service responded by shunting the pickers to a lonely access road. At the time of the deaths, the pickers were camped all along the road. But soon afterward, the Forest Service built a great grid, with numbered camping spaces, scattered portable toilets, and, after many complaints, a large tank of water at the (rather distant) campground entrance.

The campsites had no amenities, but the pickers—escaping from the ghosts—quickly made them their own. Mimicking the structure of the refugee camps in Thailand where many had spent more than a decade, they segregated themselves into ethnic groups: on one end, Mien and then those Hmong willing to stay; half a mile away, Lao and then Khmer; in an isolated hollow, way back, a few whites. The Southeast Asians built structures of slim pine poles and tarps and put their tents inside, sometimes with the addition of wood stoves. As in rural Southeast Asia, possessions were hung from the rafters, and an enclosure gave privacy for dip baths. In the center of the camp, a big tent sold hot bowls of *pho*. Eating the food, listening to the music, and observing the material culture, I thought I was in the hills of Southeast Asia, not the forests of Oregon.

The Forest Service's idea about emergency access did not work out as it imagined. A few years later, someone called emergency services in behalf of a critically wounded picker. Regulations aimed only at the mushroom camp required the ambulance to wait for police escort before entering. The ambulance waited for hours. When the police finally showed up, the man was dead. Emergency access had not been limited by terrain but by discrimination.

This man, too, left a dangerous ghost, and no one slept near his campsite except Oscar, a white man and one of the few local residents to seek out Southeast Asians, who did it once, drunk, on a dare. Oscar's success in getting through the night led him to try picking mushrooms on a nearby mountain, sacred to local Native Americans and the home of their ghosts. But the Southeast Asians I knew stayed away from that mountain. They knew about ghosts.

Oregon's center of matsutake commerce in the first decade of the twenty-first century was a place not marked on any map, "in the middle of nowhere." Everyone in the trade knew where it was, but it wasn't a town or a recreation site; it was officially invisible. Buyers had established a cluster of tents along the highway, and every evening pickers, buyers, and field agents gathered there, turning it into a theater of lively suspense and action. Because the place is self-consciously off the map, I decided to make up a name to protect people's privacy, and to add some characters from the up-and-coming matsutake trading spot down the road. My composite field site is "Open Ticket, Oregon."

"Open ticket" is actually the name of a mushroom-buying practice. In the evening after returning from the woods, pickers sell their mushrooms for the buyer's price per pound, adjusted in relation to the mushroom's size and maturity, its "grade." Most wild mushrooms carry a stable price. But the price of matsutake shoots up and down. Within the night, the price may easily shift by $10 per pound or more. Within the season, price shifts are much greater. Between 2004 and 2008, prices shifted between $2 and $60 per pound for the best mushrooms—and this range is nothing compared with earlier years. "Open ticket" means that a picker may return to the buyer for the difference between the original price paid and a higher price offered on the same night. Buyers—who earn a commission based on the poundage they buy—offer open ticket to entice pickers to sell early in the evening, rather than waiting to see if prices will rise. Open ticket is testimony to the unspoken power of pickers to negotiate buying conditions. It also illustrates the strategies of buyers, who continually try to put each other out of business. Open ticket is a practice of making and affirming freedom for both pickers and buyers. It seems an apt name for a site of freedom's performance.

For what is exchanged every evening is not just mushrooms and money. Pickers, buyers, and field agents are engaged in dramatic enactments of freedom, as they separately understand it, and they exchange these, encouraging each other, along with their trophies: money and mushrooms. Sometimes, indeed, it seemed to me that the really important exchange was the freedom, with the mushroom-and-money trophies as extensions—proofs, as it were—of the performance. After all, it was the feeling of freedom, galvanizing "mushroom fever," that energized buyers to put on their best shows and pressed pickers to get up the next dawn to search for mushrooms again.

But what is this freedom about which pickers spoke? The more I asked about it, the more unfamiliar it became to me. This is not the freedom imagined by economists, who use that term to talk about the regularities of individual rational choice. Nor is it political liberalism. This mushroomers' freedom is irregular and outside rationalization; it is performative, communally varied, and effervescent. It has something to do with the rowdy cosmopolitanism of the place; freedom emerges from open-ended cultural interplay, full of potential conflict and misunderstanding. I think it exists only in relation to ghosts. Freedom is the negotiation of ghosts on a haunted landscape; it does not exorcise the haunting but works to survive and negotiate it with flair.

Open Ticket is haunted by many ghosts: not only the "green" ghosts of pickers who died untimely deaths; not only the Native American communities removed by U.S. laws and armies; not only the stumps of great trees cut down by reckless loggers, never to be replaced; not only the haunting memories of war that will not seem to go away; but also the ghostly appearance of forms of power—held in abeyance—that enter the everyday work of picking and buying. Some kinds of power are there, but not there; this haunting is a place from which to begin to understand this multiply culturally layered enactment of freedom. Consider these absences that make Open Ticket what it is:

Open Ticket is far from the concentration of power; it is the opposite of a city. It is missing social order. As Seng, a Lao picker, put it, "Buddha is not here." Pickers are selfish and greedy, he said; he was impatient to return to the temple where things were properly arranged. But, meanwhile, Dara, a Khmer teenager, explained that this is the only place she can grow up away from the violence of gangs. Yet Thong is a (former?) Lao gang member; I think he is getting away from warrants for his arrest. Open Ticket is a hodgepodge of flights from the city. White Vietnam vets told me they wanted to be away from crowds, which sparked flashbacks from the war and uncontrollable panic attacks. Hmong and Mien told me they were disappointed in America, which had promised them freedom but instead crowded them into tiny urban apartments; only in the mountains could they find the freedom they remembered from Southeast Asia. Mien in particular hoped to reconstitute a remembered village life in the matsutake forest. Matsutake picking was a time to see dispersed friends and to be away from the constraints of crowded families. Nai Tong, a Mien grandmother, explained that her daughter called her every day to beg her to come home to take care of the grandchildren. But she calmly repeated that she had at least to make up the money for her picking permit; she could not go back yet. The important bits were left unsaid in those calls: Escaping from apartment life, she had the freedom of the hills. The money was less important than the freedom.

Matsutake picking is not the city, although haunted by it. Picking is also not labor—or even "work." Sai, a Lao picker, explained that "work" means obeying your boss, doing what he tells you to. In contrast, matsutake picking is "searching." It is looking for your fortune, not doing your job. When a white campground owner, sympathetic to the pickers, talked to me about how the pickers deserved more because they work so hard, getting up at dawn and staying through sun and snow, something nagged at me about her view. I had never heard a picker talk like that. No pickers I met imagined the money they gained from matsutake as a return on their labor. Even Nai Tong's time babysitting was more akin to work than mushroom picking.

Tom, a white field agent who had spent years as a picker, was particularly clear about rejecting labor. He had been an employee of a big timber company, but one day he put his equipment in his locker, walked out the door, and never looked back. He moved his family into the woods and earned from what the land would give him. He has gathered cones for seed companies and trapped beaver for skins. He has picked all kinds of mushrooms—not to eat but to sell, and he has taken his skills into the buying scene. Tom tells me how liberals have ruined American society; men no longer know how to be men. The best answer is to reject what liberals think of as "standard employment."

Tom goes to great lengths to explain to me that the buyers he works with are not employees but independent businessmen. Even though he gives them large amounts of cash every day to buy mushrooms, they can sell to any field agent—and I know they do. It's an all cash business, too, without contracts, so if a buyer decides to abscond with his cash, he says, there is nothing he can do about it. (Amazingly, buyers who abscond often come back to deal with another field agent.) But the scales he lends buyers for weighing mushrooms, he points out, are his; he could call the police about the scales. He tells the story of a recent buyer who absconded with several thousand dollars—but made the mistake of taking the scale. Tom drove down the road in the direction he believed the buyer took, and, sure enough, there was the scale abandoned by the side of the road. The cash was gone of course; but that was the risk of independent business.

Pickers bring many kinds of cultural heritage to their rejection of labor. Mad Jim celebrates his Native American ancestors in matsutake picking. After many jobs, he said, he was working as a bartender on the coast. A Native woman walked in with a $100 bill; shocked, he asked where she got it. "Picking mushrooms," she told him. Jim went out the next day. It wasn't easy to learn: he crawled through the brush; he followed animals. Now he knows how to stalk the dunes for the matsutake buried deep in the sand. He knows where to look under tangled rhododendron roots in the mountains. He has never gone back to wage work.

Lao-Su works in a Wal-Mart warehouse in California when he is not picking matsutake, making $11.50 an hour. To get that pay rate, however, he had to agree to work without medical benefits. When he hurt his back on the job and was unable to lift merchandise, he was given a long leave to recover. While he hopes the company will take him back, he says he gets more money from matsutake picking than from Wal-Mart anyway, despite the fact that the mushroom season is only two months long. Besides, he and his wife look forward to joining the vibrant Mien community in Open Ticket every year. They consider it a vacation; on weekends, their children and grandchildren sometimes come up to join them in picking.

Matsutake picking is not "labor," but it is haunted by labor. So, too, property: Matsutake pickers act as if the forest was an extensive commons. The land is not officially a commons. It is mainly national forest, with some adjacent private land, all fully protected by the state. But the pickers do their best to ignore questions of property. White pickers are particularly aggravated by federal property and do their best to thwart restrictions on using it. Southeast Asian pickers are generally warmer to government, expressing wishes that it would do more. Unlike white pickers, many of whom are proud of picking without a permit, most Southeast Asians register with the Forest Service for permission to pick. However, the fact that law enforcement tends to single out Asians for infractions even without evidence—as one Khmer buyer put it, "driving while being Asian"—makes it seem less worth the effort to stay within the law. Not many do.

Vast lands without boundary markers makes staying in approved picking zones quite difficult, as I found from my own experience. Once, a sheriff staked out my car to catch me without a permit when I returned with mushrooms. Even as an avid reader of maps, I had been unable to tell whether this place was on or off limits.[1] I was lucky; I was just at the border. But it wasn't marked. Once, too, after I had pleaded with a Lao family for days to take me picking, they agreed, if I would drive. We chugged through forest on unmarked dirt roads for what seemed hours before they told me we had arrived at the place they wanted to pick. When I pulled over, they asked me why I wasn't trying to hide the car. Only then did I realize that we were surely trespassing.

The fines are steep. During my fieldwork, the fine for picking in a national park was $2,000 on the first offense. But law enforcement is thin on the ground, and the roads and trails are many. The national forest is crisscrossed with abandoned logging roads; these make it possible for pickers to travel across extensive forestland. Young men, too, are willing to hike many miles, looking for the most isolated mushroom patches—perhaps on forbidden lands, perhaps not. When the mushrooms get to the buyers, no one asks.[2]

But what is "public property" if not an oxymoron? Certainly, the Forest Service has trouble with it in these times. Legislation requires that public forests be thinned for fire protection for a square mile around private inholdings; this requires a lot of public funds to save a few private assets.[3] Meanwhile, private timber companies do that thinning, making further profits from public forests. And, while logging is allowed within Late Successional Reserves, pickers are forbidden—because no one has found funds for an environmental impact assessment. If pickers have trouble sorting out which kinds of lands are off-limits, they are not alone in their confusion. The difference between the two kinds of confusion is also instructive. The Forest Service is asked to uphold *property*, even if it means neglecting the *public*. The pickers do their best to hold property in abeyance as they pursue a commons haunted by the possibility of their own exclusion.

Freedom/haunting: two sides of the same experience. Conjuring a future full of pasts, a ghost-ridden freedom is both a way to move on and a way to remember. In its fever, picking escapes the separation of persons and things so dear to industrial production. The mushrooms are not yet alienated commodities; they are effects of the pickers' free-dom. Yet this scene only exists because the two-sided experience has purchase in a strange sort of commerce. Buyers translate freedom tro-phies into trade through dramatic performances of "free market com-petition." Thus market freedom enters freedom's jumble, making the holding in abeyance of concentrated power, labor, property, and alien-ation seem strong and effective.

It's time to get back to the buying in Open Ticket. It's late afternoon, and some of the white field agents are sitting around joking. They accuse each other of lying and call each other "vultures" and "Wile E. Coyote." They are right. They agree to open at the price of $10 a pound for num-ber one mushrooms, but almost no one does. The minute the tents open, the competition is on. The field agents call their buyers to offer opening prices—perhaps $12 or even $15 if they agreed on $10. It is up to the buyers to report back about what is happening in the buying tents. Pickers come in and ask about the prices. But the price is a secret—unless you are a regular seller, or, alternatively, you are already showing your mush-rooms. Other buyers send their friends, disguised as pickers, to find the price, so it is not something to tell just anyone. Then, when a buyer wants to raise prices, to beat the competition, he or she is supposed to call the field agent. If not, the buyer will have to pay the price difference from his or her commission—but this is a tactic many are willing to try. Soon enough, calls ricochet between pickers, buyers, and field agents. The prices are shifting. "It's dangerous!" one field agent would tell me as he stalked around the buying area, watching the scene. He could not talk to me during the buying; it demanded his full attention. Barking commands into his cell phone, each tried to stay ahead—and to trip up the others. Meanwhile, field agents are on the phone to their bulking companies and exporters, learning how high they can go. It's exciting and exacting work to put the others out of business as well as one can.

"Imagine the time before cell phones!" one field agent reminisced. Everyone lined up at the two public phone booths, trying to get through as the prices changed. Even now, every field agent surveys the buying field like a general on an old-fashioned battlefield, his phone, like a field radio, constantly at his ear. He sends out spies. He must react quickly. If he raises the price at the right time, his buyers will get the best mushrooms. Better yet, he might push a competitor to raise the price too high, forcing him to buy too many mushrooms, and, if all goes really right, to close down for a few days. There are all kinds of tricks. If the price spikes, a buyer can get pickers to take his mushrooms to sell to other buyers: Better the money than the mushrooms. There will be rude laughter for days, fuel for another round of calling the others liars—and yet, no one goes out of business despite all these efforts.[4] This is a performance of competition—not a necessity of business. The *point* is the drama.

Let's say it's dark now, and pickers are lined up to sell at a buying tent. They have picked this buyer not only because of his prices, but because they know he is a skilled sorter. Sorting is just as important as basic prices, because a buyer assigns a grade to each mushroom, and the price depends on the grade. And what an art sorting is! Sorting is an eye-catching, rapid-fire dance of the arms with the legs held still. White men make it look like juggling; Lao women—the other champion buyers—make it look like Royal Lao dancing. A good sorter knows a lot about the mushrooms just from touching them. Matsutake with insect larvae will spoil the batch before it arrives in Japan; it is essential that the buyer refuse them. But only an inexperienced buyer cuts into the mushroom to look for larvae. Good buyers know from the feel. They can also smell the provenance of the mushroom: its host tree; the region it comes from; other plants, such as rhododendron, which affect the size and shape. Everyone enjoys watching a good buyer sort. It is a public performance full of prowess. Sometimes pickers photograph the sorting. Sometimes they also photograph their best mushrooms, or the money, especially when it is hundred dollar bills. These are trophies of the chase.

Buyers try to assemble "crews," that is, loyal pickers, but pickers do not feel the obligation to continue selling to any buyer. So buyers court pickers, using ties of kinship, language, and ethnicity, or special bonuses. Buyers offer pickers food and coffee—or, sometimes, stronger beverages, such as alcoholic tonics laced with herbs and scorpions. Pickers sit around eating and drinking outside buyers' tents; where they share common war experiences with the buyers, the camaraderie may last until late at night. But such groups are evanescent; all it takes is a rumor of a high price or a special deal, and pickers are off to another tent, another circle. Yet the prices are not so different. Might performance be part of the point? Competition and independence mean freedom for all.

Sometimes pickers have been known to wait, sitting in their pickup trucks with their mushrooms, because they are dissatisfied with everyone's prices. But they must sell before the evening is over; they cannot keep the mushrooms. Waiting too is part of the performance of freedom: freedom to search wherever one pleases—holding propriety, labor, and property at arm's length; freedom to bring one's mushrooms to any buyer, and for the buyers, to any field agent; freedom to put the other buyers out of business; freedom to make a killing or lose it all.

Once I told an economist about this buying scene, and he was excited, telling me this was the true and basic form of capitalism, without the pollution of powerful interests and inequalities. This was real capitalism, he said, where the playing field was level, as it should be. But is Open Ticket's picking and buying capitalism? The problem is that there isn't any capital. There is a lot of money changing hands, but it slips away, never forming an investment. The only accumulation is happening downstream, in Vancouver, Tokyo, and Kobe, where exporters and importers use the matsutake trade to build their firms. Open Ticket's mushrooms join streams of capital there, but they are not procured in what seems to me a capitalist formation.

But there are clearly "market mechanisms": or are there? The whole point of competitive markets, according to economists, is to lower prices, forcing suppliers to procure goods in more efficient ways. But Open Ticket's buying competition has the explicit goal of *raising* prices. Everyone says so: pickers, buyers, bulkers. The purpose of playing with prices is to see if the price can be increased, so that everyone at Open Ticket benefits. Many seem to think that there is an ever-flowing spring of money in Japan, and the goal of competitive theater is to force open the pipes so that the money will flow to Open Ticket. Old timers all remember 1993, when the price of matsutake in Open Ticket rose briefly to $600 a pound in the hands of pickers. All you had to do was find one fat button, and you had $300![5] Even after that high, they say, in the 1990s a single picker could make several thousand dollars in one day. How might access to that flow of money be opened again? Open Ticket buyers and bulkers stake their bets on competition to raise prices.

It seems to me that there are two framing circumstances that allow this set of beliefs and practices to flourish. First, American businessmen have naturalized the expectation that the U.S. government will apply muscle in their behalf: As long as they perform "competition," the government will twist the arms of foreign business partners to make sure American companies get the prices and market share they want.[6] Open Ticket matsutake trading is much too small and inconspicuous to get that kind of government attention. Still, it is within this national expectation that buyers and bulkers engage in competitive performances to get the Japanese to offer them the best prices. As long as they show themselves properly "American," they expect to succeed.

Second, Japanese traders are willing to put up with such displays as signs of what the importer I mentioned called "American psychology." Japanese traders expect to work in and around strange performances; if this is what brings in the goods, it should be encouraged. Later, exporters and importers can translate the exotic products of American freedom into Japanese inventory—and, through inventory, accumulation.

What is this "American psychology" then? There are too many people and histories in Open Ticket to plunge directly into the coherence through which we usually imagine "culture." The concept of assemblage—an open-ended entanglement of ways of being—is more useful. In an assemblage, varied trajectories gain a hold on each other, but indeterminacy matters. To learn about an assemblage, one unravels its knots. Open Ticket's performances of freedom require following histories that stretch far beyond Oregon but show how Open Ticket's entanglements might have come into being.[7]

6
War Stories

In France they have two kinds, freedom and communist.
In the U.S. they just have one kind: freedom.

—*Open Ticket Lao buyer, explaining why he came to the*
United States, not France

THE FREEDOM ABOUT WHICH SO MANY PICKERS AND
buyers speak has far-flung referents as well as local ones. In Open Ticket,
most explain their commitments to freedom as stemming from terrifying and tragic experiences in the U.S.-Indochina War and the civil wars
that followed. When pickers talk about what shaped their lives, including their mushroom picking, most talk about surviving war. They are
willing to brave the considerable dangers of the matsutake forest because it extends their living survival of war, a form of haunted freedom
that goes everywhere with them.

Yet engagements with war are culturally, nationally, and racially
specific. The landscapes pickers construct vary with their legacies of

engagement with war. Some pickers wrap themselves in war stories without ever having lived through war. One wry Lao elder explained why even young Lao pickers wear camouflage: "These people weren't soldiers; they're just pretending to be soldiers." When I asked about the dangers of being invisible to white deer hunters, a Hmong picker evoked a different imaginary: "We wear camouflage so we can hide if we see the hunters first." If they saw him, hunters might hunt him, he implied. Pickers navigate the freedom of the forest through a maze of differences. Freedom as they described it is both an axis of commonality and a point from which communally specific agendas divide. Despite further differences within such agendas, a few portraits can suggest the varied ways the matsutake hunt is energized by freedom. This chapter extends my exploration of what pickers and buyers meant by freedom by turning to the stories they told about war.

Frontier romanticism runs high in the mountains and forests of the Pacific Northwest. It is common for whites to glorify Native Americans *and* identify with the settlers who tried to wipe them out. Self-sufficiency, rugged individualism, and the aesthetic force of white masculinity are points of pride. Many white mushroom pickers are advocates of U.S. conquest abroad, limited government, and white supremacy. Yet the rural northwest has also gathered hippies and iconoclasts. White veterans of the U.S.-Indochina War bring their war experiences into this rough and independent mix, adding a distinctive mixture of resentment and patriotism, trauma and threat. War memories are simultaneously disturbing and productive in forming this niche. War is damaging, they tell us, but it also makes men. Freedom can be found in war as well as against war.

Two white veterans suggest the range of how freedom is expressed. Alan felt lucky when an aggravated childhood injury caused him to be sent home from Indochina. For the next six months he served as a driver on an American base. One day he received orders to return to Vietnam. He drove his jeep back to the depot and walked out of the base, AWOL. He spent the next four years hiding in the Oregon mountains, where he gained a new goal: to live in the woods and never pay rent. Later, when the matsutake rush came, it suited him perfectly. Alan imagines himself as a gentle hippie who works against the combat culture of other vets. Once he went to Las Vegas and had a terrible flashback when surrounded by Asians at the casino. Life in the forest is his way of keeping clear of psychological danger.

Not all war experience is so benign. When I first met Geoff I was overjoyed to find someone with so much knowledge about the forest. Telling me of the pleasures of his childhood in eastern Washington, he described the countryside with a passionate eye for detail. My enthusiasm to work with Geoff was transformed, however, when I talked with Tim, who explained that Geoff had served a long and difficult tour in Vietnam. Once, his group had jumped from a helicopter into an ambush. Many of the men were killed, and Geoff was shot through the neck but, miraculously, survived. When Geoff came home, he screamed so much at night that he could not stay home, and so he returned to the woods. But his war years were not over. Tim described a time when he and Geoff had surprised a group of Cambodian pickers on a mushroom patch Geoff thought of as one of his special places. Geoff had opened fire, and the Cambodians scrambled into the bushes to get away. Once Tim and Geoff shared a cabin, but Geoff spent the night brooding and sharpening his knife. "Do you know how many men I killed in Vietnam?" he asked Tim. "One more wouldn't make a bit of difference."

White pickers imagine themselves not only as violent vets but also as self-sufficient mountain men: loners, tough, and resourceful. One point of connection with those who did not fight is hunting. One white buyer, too old for Vietnam but a strong supporter of U.S. wars, explained that hunting, like war, builds character. We spoke of then Vice President Cheney, who had shot a friend while bird hunting; it was through the ordinariness of accidents such as this that hunting makes men, he said. Through hunting, even noncombatants can experience the forest landscape as a site for making freedom.

Cambodian refugees cannot easily join established Pacific Northwest legacies; they have had to make up their own histories of freedom in the United States. Such histories are guided not only by U.S. bombardment and the subsequent terrors of the Khmer Rouge regime and civil war, but also by their moment of entry into the United States: the shutting down of the U.S. welfare state in the 1980s. No one offered Cambodians stable jobs with benefits. Like other Southeast Asian refugees, they had to make something from what they had—including their war experiences. The matsutake boom made forest foraging, with its opportunities for making a living through sheer intrepidness, an appealing option.

What then is freedom? One white field agent, exalting the pleasures of war, suggested I speak with Ven, a Cambodian who, the field agent said, would show me that even Asians love U.S. imperial war. Given that Ven spoke to me with this introduction, I was not surprised by his endorsement of American freedom as a military quest. Yet our conversation took turns that I don't imagine the field agent would have expected, and yet it echoed other Cambodians in the forest. First, in the confusions of the Cambodian civil war, it was never quite clear on which side one was fighting. Where white vets imagined freedom on a starkly divided racial landscape, Cambodians told stories in which war bounced one from one side to the other without one's knowledge. Second, where white vets sometimes took to the hills to live out war's traumatic freedom, Cambodians offered a more optimistic vision of recovery in the forests of American freedom.

At the age of thirteen, Ven left his village to join an armed struggle. His goal was to repel Vietnamese invaders. He says he did not know the national affiliations of his group; he later found it to be a Khmer Rouge affiliate. Because of his youth, the commander befriended him and he was kept safe, close to the leaders. Later, however, the commander fell out of favor, and Ven became a political detainee. His group of detainees was sent to the jungle to fend for themselves. By chance, this turned out to be an area Ven knew from his fighting days. Where others saw empty jungle, he knew the concealed paths and forest resources. At this point in the story, I expected him to say that he escaped, especially since he was beaming with pride about his jungle knowledge. But no: He showed the group a hidden spring, without which they would not have had fresh water. Perhaps there was something empowering about this forest detention, even in its coercions. Returning to the forest draws from this spark—but only, he explained, in the safety of American imperial freedom.

Other Cambodians spoke about mushroom foraging as healing from war. One woman described how weak she was when she first came to the United States; her legs were so frail that she could hardly walk. Mushroom foraging has brought back her health. Her freedom, she explained, is freedom of motion.

Heng told me about his experiences in a Cambodian militia. He was the leader of thirty men. But while patrolling one day he stepped on a land mine, which blew off his leg. He begged his comrades to shoot him, since the life of a one-legged man in Cambodia was beyond what he imagined as human. Through luck, however, he was picked up by a UN mission and transported to Thailand. In the United States he gets along well on his artificial leg. Still, when he told his relatives that he would pick mushrooms in the forest, they scoffed. They refused to take him with them, since, they said, he would never be able to keep up. Finally, an aunt dropped him off at the base of a mountain, telling him to find his own way. He found mushrooms! Ever since, the matsutake harvest has been an affirmation of his mobility. Another of his buddies is missing the other leg, and he jokes that together in the mountains, they are "complete."

The Oregon mountains are both a cure for and a connection to old habits and dreams. I was startled into seeing this one day when I asked Heng about deer hunters. I had been picking by myself that afternoon when suddenly shots rang out nearby. I was terrified; I didn't know which way to run. I asked Heng about it later. "Don't run!" he said. "To run shows that you are afraid. I would never run. That's why I am a leader of men." The woods are still full of war, and hunting is its reminder. The fact that almost all the hunters are white, and that they tend to be contemptuous of Asians, makes the parallels to war yet more apparent. This theme was even more consequential for Hmong pickers, who, unlike most Cambodians, identify as hunters as well as hunted.

During the U.S.-Indochina War, the Hmong became the front line of the U.S. invasion of Laos. Recruited by General Vang Pao, whole villages gave up agriculture to subsist on CIA airdrops of food. The men called in U.S. bombers, putting their bodies on the line so that Americans could destroy the country from the skies.[1] It is not surprising that this policy exacerbated tensions between the Lao targets of the bombing and the Hmong. Hmong refugees have done relatively well in the United States, but war memories run strong. The landscapes of wartime Laos are very much alive for Hmong refugees, and this shapes both the politics of freedom and freedom's everyday activities.

Consider the case of Hmong hunter and U.S. Army sharpshooter Chai Soua Vang. In November 2004, he climbed into a deer blind in a Wisconsin forest just as the white landowners were touring the property. The landowners confronted him, telling him to leave. It seems they shouted racial epithets, and someone shot at him. In response, he shot eight of them with his semiautomatic rifle, killing six.

The story was news, and the main tenor in which it was told was outrage. CBS News quoted local Deputy Tim Zeigle, who said Vang was "chasing after [the landowners] and killing them. He hunted them down."[2] Hmong community spokesmen immediately took their distance from Vang and focused on saving the reputation of the Hmong people. Although younger Hmong spoke up against racism in the trial that followed Vang's arrest, no one publicly suggested why Vang might have assumed a sharpshooter's stance to eliminate his adversaries.

The Hmong I spoke with in Oregon all seemed to know, and to empathize. What Vang did appeared utterly familiar; he could have been a brother or a father. Although Vang was too young to have participated in the U.S.-Indochina War, his actions showed how well he was socialized in the landscapes of that war. There every man who was not a comrade was an enemy, and war meant to kill or be killed. The elder men of the Hmong community still live very much in the world of these battles; at Hmong gatherings, the logistics of particular battles—the topography, timing, and surprises—are the subject of men's conversations. One Hmong elder whom I had asked about his life used the opportunity to tell me about how to throw back grenades and what to do if you are shot. The logistics of wartime survival *were* the substance of his life.

Hunting recalls the familiarity of Laos for Hmong in the United States. The Hmong elder explained his coming of age in Laos: as a boy, he had learned to hunt, and he used his hunting skills in jungle fighting. Now in the United States, he teaches his sons how to hunt. Hunting brings Hmong men into a world of tracking, survival, and manhood.

Hmong mushroom pickers are comfortable in the forest because of hunting. Hmong rarely get lost; they use the forest-navigation skills they know from hunting. The forest landscape reminds older men of Laos: Much is different, but there are wild hills and the necessity of keeping your wits about you. Such familiarity brings the older generation back to pick each year; like hunting, this is a chance to remember forest landscapes. Without the sounds and smells of the forest, the elder told me, a man dwindles. Mushroom picking layers together Laos and Oregon, war and hunting. The landscapes of war-torn Laos suffuse present experience. What seemed to me nonsequiturs shocked me into awareness of such layers: I asked about mushrooms, and Hmong pickers answered by telling me of Laos, of hunting, or of war.

Tou and his son Ger kindly took my assistant Lue and me for many a matsutake hunt. Ger was an exuberant teacher, but Tou was a quiet elder. As a result, I valued the things he said all the more. One afternoon after a long and pleasurable forage, Tou collapsed into the front seat of the car with a sigh. Lue translated from Hmong. "It's just like Laos," Tou said, telling us of his home. His next comment made no sense to me: "But it's important to have insurance." It took me the next half hour to figure out what he meant. He offered a story: A relative of his had gone back to Laos for a visit, and the hills had so drawn him that he left one of his souls behind when he returned to the United States. He soon died as a result. Nostalgia can cause death, and then it's important to have life insurance, because that allows the family to buy the oxen for a proper funeral. Tou was experiencing the nostalgia of a landscape made familiar by hiking and foraging. This is also the landscape of hunting—and of war.

As Buddhists, ethnic Lao tend to object to hunting. Instead, Lao are the businessmen of the mushroom camps. Most Southeast Asian mushroom buyers are Lao. In the campgrounds, Lao have opened noodle tents, gambling, karaoke, and barbeque shops. Many of the Lao pickers I met originated from or were displaced to Laotian cities. They are often lost in the woods. But they enjoy the risks of mushroom picking and explain it as an entrepreneurial sport.

I first started thinking about cultural engagements with war when I was hanging out with Lao pickers. Camouflage is popular among Lao men. Most are further covered by protective tattoos—some gained in the army, some in gangs, and some in martial arts. Lao rowdiness is the justification for Forest Service rules that disallow gunfire in the camp-grounds. Compared with other picker groups, the Lao I met seemed less wounded by the actual moment of war—and yet more involved in its simulation in the forest. But what is a wound? U.S. bombing in Laos displaced 25 percent of the rural population, forcing fleeing refugees into cities—and, when possible, abroad.[3] If Lao refugees in the United States have some characteristics of camp followers, is this not also a wound?

Some Lao pickers grew up in army families. Sam's father served in the Royal Lao Army; he was set to follow in his father's footsteps by en-listing in the U.S. Army. The fall before his recruitment he joined some friends for a last hurrah—picking mushrooms. He made so much money that he called off his army plans. He even brought his parents to pick. He also discovered the pleasures of illegal picking one season when he made $3,000 in one day by trespassing on national park lands.

Like white pickers, the Lao I knew looked for out-of-bounds and hidden matsutake patches. (In contrast, Cambodian, Hmong, and Mien pickers more often used careful observation in well-known common spots.) Lao pickers also—again like whites—took pleasure in boasting of their forays outside the law and their ability to get out of scrapes. (Other pickers went outside the law more quietly.) As entrepreneurs, Lao were mediators, with all the pleasures and dangers of mediation. In my own inexperience, I found the entrepreneurial grasp of combat readiness a confusing set of juxtapositions. Yet I could tell it somehow worked as advocacy for high-risk enterprise.

Thong, a strong and handsome man in his mid-thirties, seemed to me a man of contradictions: a fighter, a fine dancer, a reflective thinker, a judgmental critic. Because of his strength, Thong picks in high, inac-cessible places. He told of his encounter with a policeman who stopped him for speeding one night more than forty miles from the mushroom camp. He told the policeman to go ahead and impound his car; he would walk through the frozen night. The policeman gave in, he said, and let him go. When Thong said that mushroom pickers are in the forest to escape warrants, I thought he might be speaking for himself. So, too, until quite recently he was married. In the process of getting a divorce, he quit a well-paying job to pick mushrooms. At the least, I believe he aimed to escape the obligations of child support. The contradictions multiply. He went out of his way to express contempt for pickers who abandon their children for the forest. He is not in touch with his children.

Meta thinks a lot about Buddhism. Meta spent two years in a monastery; returned to the world, he works to renounce material things. Mushroom picking is a way to do this work of renunciation. Most of his belongings are in his car. Money comes to him easily but disappears just as easily. He does not mire himself in possession. This does not mean he is ascetic in a Western sense. When he is drunk, he sings a tender tenor karaoke.

Only among Lao pickers did I meet children of mushroom pickers who, as adults, became mushroom pickers themselves. Paula first came picking with her parents, who later moved to Alaska. But she maintains her parents' social networks in the Oregon forests, thus earning the room for maneuver claimed by much more seasoned pickers. Paula is daring. She and her husband arrived ready to pick ten days before the U.S. Forest Service opened the season. When the police caught them with mushrooms in their truck, her husband pretended that he couldn't speak English, while Paula berated the officials. Paula is cute and looks like a child; she can get away with more sass than others. Still, I was surprised at the chutzpah she claimed. She said she dared the police to interfere with her activities. They asked her where she found the mushrooms. "Under green trees." Where were these green trees? "All trees are green trees," she insisted. Then she pulled out her cell phone and started calling her supporters.

What is freedom? U.S. immigration policy differentiates "political refugees" from "economic refugees," granting asylum only to the former. This requires immigrants to endorse "freedom" as a condition of their entry. Southeast Asian Americans had the opportunity to learn such endorsements in refugee camps in Thailand, where many spent years preparing themselves for U.S. immigration. As the Lao buyer quoted at the beginning of this chapter quipped in explaining why he picked the United States rather than France: "In France they have two kinds, freedom and communist. In the U.S. they just have one kind: freedom." He went on to say that he prefers mushroom picking to a steady job with a good income—he has been a welder—because of the freedom.

Lao strategies for enacting freedom contrast sharply with those of the other picker group that vies for the title "most harassed by the law": Latinos. Latino pickers tend to be undocumented migrants who fit mushroom foraging into a year-round schedule of outdoor work. During mushroom season many live hidden in the forest instead of in the legally required industrial camps and motels where identification and picking permits might be checked. Those I knew had multiple names, addresses, and papers. Mushroom arrests could lead not just to fines but also to loss of vehicles (for faulty papers) and deportation. Instead of sassing the law, Latino pickers tried to stay out of the way, and, if caught, juggle papers and sources of legitimation and support. In contrast, most Lao pickers, as refugees, are citizens and, embracing freedom, hustle for more room.

Contrasts such as these motivated my search to understand the cultural engagements with war that shape the practices of freedom of white veterans and Cambodian, Hmong, and Lao refugees. Veterans and refugees negotiate American citizenship through endorsing and enacting freedom. In this practice, militarism is internalized; it infuses the landscape; it inspires strategies of foraging and entrepreneurship.

Among commercial matsutake pickers in Oregon, freedom is a "boundary object," that is, a shared concern that yet takes on many meanings and leads in varied directions.[4] Pickers arrive every year to search out matsutake for Japanese-sponsored supply chains because of their overlapping yet diverging commitments to the freedom of the forest. Pickers' war experiences motivate them to come back year after year to extend their living survival. White vets enact trauma; Khmer heal war wounds; Hmong remember fighting landscapes; Lao push the envelope. Each of these historical currents mobilizes the practice of picking mushrooms as the practice of freedom. Thus, without any corporate recruitment, training, or discipline, mountains of mushrooms are gathered and shipped to Japan.

7
What Happened to the State?
Two Kinds of Asian Americans

Lightly dressed *shigin* friends went up to the mountain,
A shady wilderness crowded with pines.
We parked our cars and went into the mountains to look
   for mushrooms.
Suddenly, a whistle broke the desolation of the forest.
All rushing there, we shouted for joy.
In the autumn light, being beside ourselves, we felt like
   children again.

—*Sanou Uriuda, "Matsutake Hunting at Mt. Rainier"*[1]

EVERYTHING ABOUT OPEN TICKET SURPRISED ME,
but especially the feel of Southeast Asian village life in the middle of the
Oregon forest. My disorientation was only amplified when I found a different group of matsutake pickers: Japanese Americans. Despite many differences from my Chinese American background, Japanese Americans
felt familiar to me, like family. Yet this ease struck me sharply, a splash of

cold water. I realized that something huge and perplexing had happened to U.S. citizenship between early- and late-twentieth-century immigrations. A wild new cosmopolitanism has inflected what it means to be an American: a jostling of unassimilated fragments of cultural agendas and political causes from around the world. My surprise, then, was not the ordinary shock of cultural difference. American precarity—living in ruins—is in this unstructured multiplicity, this uncongealed confusion. No longer a melting pot, we live with unrecognizable others. And if I tell this story within Asian American worlds, do not think it stops there. This cacophony is the feel of precarious living for both white and colored Americans—with repercussions around the world. It is most clearly seen, however, in relation to its alternatives, such as assimilation.

The first people to go "matsutake crazy" in Oregon were Japanese who came to the region in that short window of opportunity between the banishment of the Chinese in 1882 and the "Gentlemen's Agreement" stopping Japanese immigration in 1907.[2] Some of the first Japanese immigrants worked as loggers and found matsutake in the forest. When they settled into farming, they returned to the forest every season: for *warabi* ferns in the spring, *fuki* shoots in the summer, and matsutake in the fall. By the early twentieth century, matsutake outings—picnic lunches with matsutake foraging—were a popular leisure activity, as celebrated in the poem that opens this chapter.

Uriuda's poem is a useful signpost of both pleasures and dilemmas. The matsutake hunters drive cars into the mountains; they are enthusiastic Americans even as they retain Japanese sensibilities. Like others who ventured out of Meiji Japan, the immigrants were serious translators, learning other cultures. Beside themselves, they became children—in both American and Japanese ways. Then something changed: World War II.

Since arriving in the United States, Japanese had struggled over bans against citizenship and land ownership. Despite this, they had succeeded at farming—especially with labor-intensive fruits and vegetables, such as cauliflower, which needed to be shaded from light, and berries, which needed hand picking. World War II broke that trajectory, removing them from their farms. Oregon's Japanese Americans were interned in "War Relocation Camps." Their citizenship dilemmas were turned inside out.

I first heard Uriuda's poem sung in Japanese in a classical style during a gathering of Japanese Americans celebrating their matsutake heritage in 2006. The elderly man who sang it had first learned classical singing when he was interned in the camps. Indeed, many "Japanese" hobbies flourished there. But even as it was possible to pursue Japanese hobbies, the camps changed what it meant to be Japanese in the United States. When they came back after the war, most had lost access to their possessions and their farms. (Juliana Hu Pegues notes that the same year Japanese American farmers were sent away to camps, the United States opened the Bracero program to bring in Mexican farm laborers.)[3] They were treated with suspicion. In response, they did their best to become model Americans.

As one man recalled, "We stayed away from everything Japanese-y. If you had a pair of [Japanese] slippers, you left them at the door when you went out." Japanese daily habits were not for public display. Young people stopped learning Japanese. Total immersion into American culture was expected, without bicultural extensions, and children led the way. Japanese Americans became "200 percent American."[4] At the same time, Japanese arts had flourished in the camps. Traditional poetry and music, in decline before the war, were revived. Camp activities became the basis for postwar clubs. These would be private leisure activities. Japanese culture, matsutake picking included, became increasingly popular, but it formed a segregated addition to the performance of American selves. "Japanese-ness" flourished only as an American-style hobby.

Perhaps you can catch a glimmer of my disconcertment. Japanese American matsutake pickers are quite different from Southeast Asian refugees—and I can't explain the difference away by "culture" or by "time" spent in the United States, the usual sociological stories of differences among immigrants. Second-generation Southeast Asian Americans are nothing like Japanese American *Nisei* in their performance of citizenship. The difference has to do with historical events—indeterminate encounters, if you will—in which relations between immigrant groups and the demands of citizenship are formed. Japanese Americans were subject to coercive assimilation. The camps taught them that to be an American required serious work in transforming oneself from inside out. Coercive assimilation showed me its contrast: Southeast Asian refugees have become citizens in a moment of neoliberal multiculturalism. A love for freedom may be enough to join the American crowd.

The contrast hit me in a personal way. My mother came to study in the United States from China just after World War II, when the two countries were allies; after the triumph of communism in China, the U.S. government did not let her go home. Through the 1950s and early 1960s, our family, like other Chinese Americans, was under FBI surveillance as possible enemy aliens. Thus my mother, too, learned a coercive assimilation. She learned to cook hamburgers, meatloaf, and pizza, and when she had children, she refused to allow us to learn Chinese, even though she was still struggling with English. She believed that if we spoke Chinese, our English might show the trace of an accent, revealing us as not quite American. It was unsafe to be bilingual, to carry one's body in the wrong way, or to eat the wrong foods.

When I was a child, my family used the term "American" to mean white, and we watched Americans carefully as sources of both emulation and cautionary tales. In the 1970s, I joined Asian American student groups whose participants were of Chinese, Japanese, and Filipino origin; even our most radical politics took for granted the coerced assimilation each of these groups had experienced. My background thus prepared me for an easy empathy with the Japanese American matsutake pickers I met in Oregon: I felt comfortable with their way of being Asian American. The elders were second-generation immigrants who spoke hardly a word of Japanese, and who were as likely to go out for cheap Chinese food as to prepare traditional Japanese dishes. They were proud of their Japanese heritage—as witnessed in their devotion to matsutake. But that pride was expressed in self-consciously American ways. Even the matsutake dishes we cooked together were cosmopolitan hybrids that violated every Japanese culinary principle.

In contrast, I had been utterly unprepared to discover the Asian American cultures of Open Ticket's matsutake camps. Mien camps struck me with particular force because they reminded me not of the Asian America I knew but of some combination of my mother's remembered China and the villages in Borneo where I had done fieldwork. Mien come to the Cascades in multigenerational groups of kin and neighbors with the explicit aim of recuperating village life. They remain committed to differences that mattered in Laos; because Lao sit on the floor, Mien sit on the low stools my mother still longs for as a reminder of China. They refuse raw vegetables—that's for Lao—but prepare soups and sautés with chopsticks, as do Chinese. No meatloaf or hamburgers are cooked in Mien mushroom camps. Because so many Southeast Asians are gathered together, deliveries of Asian vegetables from California family garden plots arrive all the time. Every evening, cooked dishes are exchanged with neighbors, and visitors talk over smoking bongs into the night. When I saw one of my Mien hosts squatting in a sarong and shelling overripe yard-long beans or sharpening her machete, I felt transported to the upland villages in Indonesia where I first learned about Southeast Asia. This wasn't the United States that I knew.

The other Southeast Asian groups in Open Ticket are less dedicated to recreating village life; some are from cities, not villages. Still, they have one thing in common with these Mien: a lack of interest in—even an unfamiliarity with—the kind of American assimilation with which I grew up. I wondered, How did they get away with this? At first, I was awed, and perhaps a little jealous. Later, I recognized that they had been asked to assimilate too, in a different mode. This is where freedom and precarity come back into the story: freedom coordinates wildly diverse expressions of American citizenship, and it provides the only official rudder for precarious living. But this means that between the arrival of Japanese Americans and the coming of Lao and Cambodian Americans something important has changed in the relationship of the state and its citizens.

The pervasive quality of Japanese American assimilation was shaped by the cultural politics of the U.S. welfare state from the New Deal through the late twentieth century. The state was empowered to order people's lives with attractions as well as coercion. Immigrants were exhorted to join the "melting pot," to become full Americans by erasing their pasts. Public schools were a venue for making Americans. The affirmative action policies of the 1960s and 1970s not only opened schools but also made it possible for minorities educated in public schools to find professional placements despite their racial exclusion from networks of influence. Japanese Americans were cajoled as well as prodded into the American fold.

It is the erosion of this apparatus of state welfare that most simply helps to explain why the Southeast Asian Americans of Open Ticket have developed such a different relationship to American citizenship. Since the mid-1980s, when they arrived as refugees, all kinds of state programs have been dismantled. Affirmative action has been criminalized, funds cut for public schools, unions chased out, and standard employment has become a vanishing ideal for anyone, much less entry-level workers. Even if they had managed to become perfect copies of white Americans, there would be few rewards. And the immediate challenges of making a living loom.

In the 1980s, the refugees had few resources and needed public assistance. Yet welfare in the strict sense was being radically downsized. In California, the destination of many Open Ticket Southeast Asians, eighteen months became the limit for state assistance. Many of the Lao and Cambodian Americans in Open Ticket received some language education and job training, but rarely of a sort that actually helped them get a job. They were left to find their own way in American society.[5] For those few who had Western-style educations, English, or money, there were options. The rest were in the difficult position of finding traction for the resources and skills they had, such as, for example, surviving a war. The freedom they had endorsed to enter the United States had to be translated into livelihood strategies.

Histories of survival shaped what they could use as livelihood skills. It is a tribute to their resourcefulness that they used them. But this also created differences among the refugees. Consider some of these differences. A Lao buyer from a family of businesswomen in the capital city, Vientiane, explained that she decided to leave because communism was bad for profits. Vientiane is on the Mekong River, across from Thailand, and leaving meant finding a night to swim the river. She could have been shot; she had a young daughter to carry. Still, despite the danger, the experience showed her that she must seize opportunities. The freedom that pushed her toward the United States was the freedom of the market.

In contrast, Hmong pickers were adamant about freedom as anti-communism combined with ethnic autonomy. Older Hmong in Open Ticket had fought for General Vang Pao's CIA army in Laos. The middle-aged had spent years after the communist victory going back and forth between refugee camps in Thailand and rebel camps in Laos. Both these life trajectories combined jungle survival and ethnopolitical loyalty. These were skills that could be used in the United States for kin-based investments, for which Hmong Americans have become known. Sometimes such commitments need to be revived—by life in the wild.

Everyone I talked to dreamed about livelihood strategies self-consciously tied to their ethnic and political stories. No one in Open Ticket thought immigration meant erasing one's past to become an American. An ethnic Lao from northeastern Cambodia would like to run trucks between Cambodia and Laos. An ethnic Khmer from Vietnam, whose family crossed the border to defend Cambodia, thought his family's patriotism made him a good candidate for a military career. While many of these dreams would remain unfulfilled, they told me something about dreaming: these were not the new start we still call "the American dream."

The more you stare at it, the more the idea that you *should* start over to become an American seems strange. What was this American dream then? Clearly, it was more than an effect of economic policy. Might it have been a version of Christian conversion, American-style, in which the sinner opens up to God and resolves to banish his former sinful life? The American dream requires relinquishing one's old self, and perhaps this is one form of conversion.

Protestant revivalism has been key to composing the "we" of the American polity since the American Revolution.[6] Furthermore, Protestantism guided the twentieth-century project of American secularization—designed to reject illiberal Christianity while promoting unmarked liberal forms. Susan Harding has shown how U.S. public education in the mid-twentieth century was shaped by projects of secularization, in which some versions of Christianity were promoted as examples of "tolerance," while other versions were parochialized as exotic remnants of earlier times.[7] In its secular forms, then, this cosmological politics exceeds Christianity; to be an American, you must convert, not to Christianity, but to American democracy.

In the mid-twentieth century, assimilation was a project of this American Protestant secularism. Immigrants were expected to "convert" by taking on the full array of white American bodily practices and speech habits. Speech was particularly important—the speaking of the "we." That's why my mother wouldn't let me learn Chinese. It would be a sign of the devil, so to speak, peeking out of my American habitus. This is the conversion wave that hit Japanese Americans after World War II.

It did not necessarily mean becoming a Christian. The Japanese Americans I worked with are mainly Buddhists. Indeed, Buddhist "churches" (as some participants call them) help tie the community together. The one I visited is a curious hybrid. The hall for weekly worship has a colorful Buddhist altar in front. But the rest of the room is an exact model of an American Protestant church. There are rows of wooden pews, complete with holders on the seatbacks for hymnals and announcements. The basement has space for Sunday School classes and for fundraising dinners and bake sales. The core congregation is Japanese American, but they are proud to have a white pastor, whose Buddhism augments their American identity. The congregation's "American" conversion sponsors religious legibility.

Contrast Open Ticket's Southeast Asian refugees. Thinking through cosmological politics, they were also "converted" to American democracy. They each had a conversion ritual in a Thai refugee camp—the interview that allowed them to enter the United States. At this interview, they were required to endorse "freedom" and to show their anticommunist credentials. Else they would be enemy aliens: outside the fold. To enter the country, a rigorous assertion of freedom was necessary. The refugees might not know much English, but they needed one word: freedom.

In addition, some of Open Ticket's Hmong and Mien Americans have converted to Christianity. Yet—as Thomas Pearson has shown for Vietnamese Montagnard-Dega refugees in North Carolina—they have, from a U.S. Protestant point of view, a strange kind of Christian practice.[8] The point of conversion for an American Protestant is to be able to say, "I once was lost, but now I have accepted God." Instead, the refugees say, "Communist soldiers pointed at me, but God made me invisible." "War scattered my family in the jungle, but God brought us back together." God operates like indigenous spirits, warding off danger. Instead of needing interior transformation, the converts I met came under protection through endorsing *freedom*.

Again the contrast: A centripetal (in-spinning) logic of conversion drew my family and my Japanese American friends into an inclusive, expansive United States of assimilative Americanization. A centrifugal (out-spinning) logic of conversion, held together by a single boundary object, freedom, shaped Open Ticket's Southeast Asian refugees. These two kinds of conversion can coexist. Yet each was carried on a distinct historical wave of citizenship politics.

It seems quite predictable, then, these two kinds of matsutake pickers do not mix. Japanese Americans picked commercially at the beginning of Japan's import boom; but by the late 1980s, they were overtaken by white and Southeast Asian pickers. Now they pick for their friends and family rather than to sell. Matsutake is a treasured gift and a food that confirms one's Japanese cultural roots. And matsutake picking is fun—a chance for elders to show off their knowledge, for kids to play in the woods, and for everyone to share delicious *bento* lunches.

This kind of leisure is possible because the Japanese Americans I accompanied had entered a class niche of urban employment. When they returned from the camps after World War II, as I explained, they had lost their access to farms. Still, many resettled as close to the places they knew as they could. Some became factory workers and were able to join newly integrated unions. Others opened small restaurants or worked in hotels. It was a time of growing wealth for Americans. Their children went to public schools and became dentists, pharmacists, and store managers. Some married white Americans. Yet people keep track of each other; the community is close. Matsutake help maintain the community even though no one depends on them to defray living expenses.

One of the best-loved matsutake forests of this community is a pine-studded, moss-covered valley, as smooth and clean as the grounds of a Japanese temple. Japanese Americans are proud of how carefully they maintain the area for both people and plants. Even the foraging areas of the deceased are remembered and respected. In the mid-1990s, a bold, white bulker-buyer from Open Ticket brought a load of commercial pickers to this area. The commercial pickers were not used to careful harvesting; they needed to cover a lot of ground to make the day's pick. They tore up the moss and left the place a mess. A confrontation ensued. Japanese Americans brought in the Forest Service, who advised the buyer that commerce inside national forests is prohibited. The buyer accused the agency of racial discrimination. "Why should Japanese have special rights?" he reminisced to me, still sore. Finally, the Forest Service closed the area to commercial picking. The buyer went back to Open Ticket. But without enforcement, commercial pickers still sneak in, and hostilities between Japanese and Southeast Asian Americans still smolder. Clearly, they are different kinds of Asian Americans. As one Japanese American picker unself-consciously quipped, "The forests were great until the Asians came." Who?

Let me return to Southeast Asian pickers' freedom. Certainly, it includes sneaking into forbidden places when one can get away with it. But freedom is more than personal daring; it is an engagement with an emerging political formation. I am sure I am not the only product of integration who was taken by surprise by the strength of twenty-first-century resentment of this program, particularly by rural whites, who feel left out and left behind. Some white pickers and buyers call their position "traditionalism." They oppose integration; they want to savor their own values, without contamination from others. They also call this "freedom." This is not a multicultural plan. And yet, ironically, it has helped bring to life the most cosmopolitan cultural formation the United States has ever known. The new traditionalists reject racial mixing and the muscular legacy of the welfare state that made mixing possible—through coercive assimilation. As they dismantle assimilation, new formations emerge. Without central planning, immigrants and refugees hold on to their best chances to make a living: their war experiences, languages, and cultures. They join American democracy through that single word, "freedom." They are free, indeed, to continue transnational politics and trade; they may plot to overthrow foreign regimes and stake their fortunes on international fashions. In contrast to earlier immigrants, they need not study to become American from inside out. In the wake of the welfare state, this concurrence of freedom agendas—in all its unruly diversity—has seized the time.

And what better participants in global supply chains! Here are nodes of ready and willing entrepreneurs, with and without capital, able to mobilize their ethnic and religious fellows to fill almost any kind of economic niche. Wages and benefits are not needed. Whole communities can be mobilized—and for communal reasons. Universal standards of welfare hardly seem relevant. These are projects of freedom. Capitalists looking for salvage accumulation, take note.

. . . in Translation

*Translating value, Tokyo.
Matsutake, calculator,
telephone: still life
at an intermediate
wholesaler's booth.*

8
Between the Dollar and the Yen

I HAVE BEEN ARGUING THAT COMMERCIAL MUSHROOM picking exemplifies the general condition of precarity—and in particular of livelihood without "regular jobs." But how did we get into a situation in which so few jobs with wages and benefits are available, even in the world's richest country? Worse yet, how did we lose the expectation and taste for such jobs? This is a recent situation; many white pickers knew such jobs, or at least such expectations, from their earlier lives. Something changed. This chapter makes the bold assertion that the view from a neglected commodity chain can illuminate this surprisingly abrupt— and global—change.

But isn't matsutake economically negligible? Shouldn't it offer only the view from a frog in a well? On the contrary: the modest success of the Oregon-to-Japan matsutake commodity chain is the tip of an iceberg, and following the iceberg to its underwater girth brings up forgotten stories that still grip the planet. Things that seem small often turn out to be big. It is the very negligible quality of the matsutake commodity chain that hid it from the view of twenty-first-century reformers, thus preserving a late-twentieth-century history that shook the world.

This is the history of encounters between Japan and the United States that shaped the global economy. Shifting relations between U.S. and Japanese capital, I argue, led to global supply chains—and to the end of expectations of progress aimed toward collective advancement.

Global supply chains ended expectations of progress because they allowed lead corporations to let go of their commitment to controlling labor. Standardizing labor required education and regularized jobs, thus connecting profits and progress. In supply chains, in contrast, goods gathered from many arrangements can lead to profits for the lead firm; commitments to jobs, education, and well-being are no longer even rhetorically necessary. Supply chains require a particular kind of salvage accumulation, involving translation across patches. The modern history of U.S.-Japanese relations is a counterpoint of call-and-response that spread this practice around the world.

Two bookends frame the tale. In the mid-nineteenth century, U.S. ships threatened Edo Bay in order to "open" the Japanese economy for American businessmen; this sparked a Japanese revolution that overturned the national political economy and pushed Japan into international commerce. Japanese refer to the indirect upending of Japan through the icon of the "Black Ships" that carried the U.S. threat. This icon is useful in considering what happened—in reverse—150 years later, at the end of the twentieth century, when the threat of Japan's commercial power indirectly upended the U.S. economy. Scared by the success of Japanese investments, American business leaders destroyed the corporation as a social institution and propelled the U.S. economy into the world of Japanese-style supply chains. One might call this "Reverse Black Ships." In the great wave of mergers and acquisitions of the 1990s, with their corporate reshufflings, the expectation that U.S. corporate leaders ought to provide employment disappeared. Instead, labor would be outsourced elsewhere—into more and more precarious situations. The matsutake commodity chain linking Oregon and Japan is just one of many global outsourcing arrangements inspired by the success of Japanese capital between the 1960s and the 1980s.

This history was quickly covered up. In the 1990s, American businessmen reclaimed preeminence in the world economy, while the Japanese economy fell drastically. By the twenty-first century, Japan's economic power had been forgotten, and progress, fueled by American ingenuity, appeared to account for the global shift to outsourcing. This is where a humble commodity chain comes in to help us cut through obfuscations. What economic models allowed its organizational forms to emerge? The only way to answer this question is to follow twentieth-century Japanese economic innovations. These were not created in isolation: they formed from tensions and dialogues across the Pacific. The matsutake commodity chain places us firmly in U.S.-Japanese economic interactions, and from here we can notice this chunk of forgotten history. In what follows, I let the thread of the story unroll quite far from matsutake. Yet at each step I need the chain's reminders to resist the lull of current erasures. This is not just a story, then, but also a method: big histories are always best told through insistent, if humble, details.

Money can open the tale. Both the U.S. dollar and the yen came into being in a world dominated by Spanish pesos, minted since the sixteenth century from the exploitation of Latin American silver. Neither the United States nor Japan were early players, as the United States only came into existence in the eighteenth century, and Japan was ruled by inward-looking lords, who strictly regulated foreign trade, from the seventeenth to the nineteenth centuries. The grand futures of neither the dollar nor the yen were evident at their births. By the mid-nineteenth century, however, the dollar had gained the clout of imperial gunboats deployed in its name.

U.S. businessmen resented the tight control over foreign trade exerted by the Tokugawa shogunate.[1] In 1853, Matthew Perry, commodore of the U.S. Navy, took up their cause by leading a fleet of armed ships to Edo Bay. Intimidated by this show of force, the shogunate signed the Convention of Kanagawa in 1854, which opened ports for U.S. trade.[2] Japanese elites were aware of the subjugation of China in the wake of that country's opposition to British "free trade" opium. To avoid war, they signed away their rights. But domestic crisis followed, resulting in the toppling of the shogunate. A new era opened with the brief civil war known as the Meiji Restoration. The winning group looked to Western modernity for their inspiration. In 1871, the Meiji government established the yen as the Japanese national currency, intending it to move within European and American circuits. Thus the dollar, indirectly, helped give birth to the yen.

Meiji-era elites were not satisfied, however, to let foreigners control trade. They quickly worked to learn Western conventions and to establish their own firms as domestic equivalents to foreign ones. The government brought in foreign experts and sent young men abroad to study Western languages, laws, and trading practices. The young men came home and established professions, industries, banks, and trading companies, which flourished in Japan's push for "the modern." The new money was embedded in new contract laws, political forms, and debates about value.

Meiji Japan was full of entrepreneurial energies, and international trade quickly emerged as an important sector of the economy.[3] Japan lacked natural resources for industrialization, and the importation of raw materials was seen as an essential service for the building of the nation. Trading was among the most successful Meiji enterprises, and it became associated with rising new industries such as the production of cotton thread and textiles. Meiji-era traders saw their job as mediating between Japan and foreign economic worlds. Traders were trained through experience in foreign countries, gaining the doubled cultural agility that allowed them to negotiate across radical difference. Their work exemplifies Satsuka's concept of "translation," in which learning another culture both bridges and maintains difference.[4] The new traders learned how commodities were traded in other places, and they used that knowledge to make advantageous contracts for Japan. In the terms economists use, they were specialists in "imperfect markets," that is, markets in which information is not freely available to all buyers and sellers. Meiji-era traders coordinated markets across national borders; they also worked across incommensurable value systems. As Japanese have continued to imagine a "Japan" that exists in dynamic difference with something called "the West," this understanding of international trading as translation has persisted, informing contemporary business practices. Trading *creates* capitalist value through its work of translation.

Meiji-era traders associated themselves with industrial enterprises. Industry needed raw materials gained through trade; trade and industry flourished together. In the early twentieth century, the boom economy associated with World War I allowed large conglomerates to form, encompassing banking, mining, industry, and foreign trade.[5] In contrast to twentieth-century U.S. corporate giants, these conglomerates, the *zaibatsu*, were coordinated by finance capital, not production: Banking and trading were central to their mission. From the first they were involved with government business (Mitsui, for example, had provided the money to overthrow the shogunate);[6] in the run-up to World War II, pressed by Japanese nationalists, the zaibatsu became increasingly entangled with imperial expansion. When Japan lost the war, the zaibatsu were the first targets of the U.S. occupation.[7] The yen lost its value; the Japanese economy was in shambles.

In the first days of the occupation, it seemed that the United States was favoring smaller firms, and even the advancement of labor. Soon enough, however, the American occupiers arranged for the rehabilitation of once-disgraced nationalists and rebuilt the Japanese economy as a bulwark against communism. It was in this climate that associations of banks, industrial enterprises, and specialists in trade formed again, although less formally, as *keiretsu* "enterprise groups."[8] At the heart of most enterprise groups was a general trading company in partnership with a bank.[9] The bank transferred money to the trading company, which, in turn, made smaller loans to its associated enterprises. The bank did not have to monitor these small loans, which the trading company used to facilitate the formation of supply chains. This model is well made to stretch across national borders. Trading companies advanced loans—or equipment, technical advice, or special marketing agreements—to their supply chain partners overseas. The trading company's job was to translate goods procured in varied cultural and economic arrangements into inventory. It is hard not to see in this arrangement the roots of the current hegemony of global supply chains, with their associated form of salvage accumulation.[10]

I first learned about supply chains in studying logging in Indonesia, and this is a place to see how the Japanese supply-chain model works.[11] During Japan's building boom in the 1970s and 1980s, Japanese imported Indonesian trees to make plywood construction molds. But no Japanese cut down Indonesian trees. Japanese general trading companies offered loans, technical assistance, and trade agreements to firms from other countries, which cut logs to Japanese specifications. This arrangement had many advantages for Japanese traders. First, it avoided political risk. Japanese businessmen were aware of the political difficulties of Chinese Indonesians who, resented for their wealth and willingness to cooperate with the more ruthless policies of the Indonesian government, were targets in periodic riots. Japanese businessmen evaded

such difficulties for themselves by advancing money to Chinese Indonesians, who made the deals with Indonesian generals and took the risks.
Second, the arrangement facilitated transnational mobility. Japanese traders had already deforested the Philippines and much of Malaysian Borneo by the time they got to Indonesia. Rather than adapting to a new
country, the traders could merely bring in agents willing to work with
them in each location. Indeed, Filipino and Malaysian loggers, financed
by Japanese traders, were ready and able to go to work in cutting down
Indonesian trees. Third, supply-chain arrangements facilitated Japanese
trade standards while ignoring environmental consequences. Environmentalists looking for targets could find only a grab bag of varied companies,
many Indonesian; no Japanese were in the forests. Fourth, supply-chain
arrangements accommodated illegal logging as a layer of subcontracting, which harvested trees protected by environmental regulations. Illegal loggers sold their logs to the larger contractors, who passed them on
to Japan. No one need be responsible. And—even after Indonesia started
its own plywood businesses, in a supply-chain hierarchy modeled on
Japanese trade—the wood was so cheap! The cost could be calculated
without regard to the lives and livelihoods of loggers, trees, or forest
residents.

Japanese trading companies made the logging of Southeast Asia possible. They were equally busy with other commodities and in other
parts of the world.[12] Let me return to the early post–World War II period
when these arrangements were emerging to see how this system developed. Some of the first postwar supply chains from Japan made use of
ties with Japan's former colony, Korea. At this time, the United States
was the world's richest country and the best destination for every country's wares, but it had imposed a strict quota on goods imported from
Japan. Historian Robert Castley tells the story of how Japan helped
build South Korea's economy to avoid U.S. quotas.[13] By transferring
light industry to South Korea, Japanese traders could export more products freely to the United States. Yet Japanese direct investment was resented in Korea. Thus Japan adopted what Castley calls a "putting out"
approach. "It involved merchants (or firms) supplying subcontractors
with loans, credit, machinery and equipment to produce or finish
goods, which would be sold in distant markets by the merchant."[14] Castley notes the power of traders and bankers in this strategy: "the Japanese

offered long-term contracts with overseas suppliers and frequently loans for the development of resources."[15] This form of expansion, he says, was a form of political as well as economic security in Japan.

The putting-out system transferred less profitable manufacturing sectors and older technologies to South Korea, clearing the way for Japanese businesses to upgrade. According to this model, which Japanese proponents later graced with the image of "flying geese," Korean businesses would always be one cycle of innovation behind Japan.[16] But all would be flying forward, in part because Koreans could then transfer their own outdated manufacturing sectors to the poorer countries of Southeast Asia, allowing Koreans to inherit new rounds of Japanese innovation. South Korean elites were happy to benefit from Japanese capital—some of it transferred as war reparations. The resulting business networks formed models for the transnational expansion of capital in Japan, including the work of the Japanese-controlled Asian Development Bank.

By the 1970s, many kinds of supply chains snaked in and out of Japan. General trading companies organized cross-continental supply chains for raw materials, becoming some of the richest companies in the world. Banks sponsored enterprises across Asia with links to Japan. Meanwhile, producers had organized their own supply chains, sometimes called "vertical keiretsu" in the English-language literature. Car companies, for example, subcontracted the development and manufacture of parts, saving costs. Mom-and-Pop suppliers made industrial components at home. Salvage accumulation and supply-chain subcontracting had grown together.

The combined result was so successful that U.S. businesses, and their government supporters, could feel the heat. The success of Japanese cars was particularly painful to American pundits who had become used to thinking of the U.S. economy in relation to its cars. The appearance of Japanese cars in the United States, and the related decline of Detroit's car companies, sparked public awareness of Japan's rising economic fortunes. Some business leaders jumped to learn from Japanese success, showing interest in "quality control" and "corporate culture."[17] Other business leaders sought U.S. reprisals against Japan. A wave of public fear emerged. One index was the 1982 murder of Chinese American Vincent Chin, mistaken for a Japanese by unemployed white autoworkers in Detroit.[18]

The threat posed by Japan unleashed a U.S. revolution. Reverse Black Ships overturned the U.S. order of things, but through U.S. efforts. Empowered by public fears of U.S. decline, a small group of activist stockholders and business school professors, who might otherwise have never gained a hearing, were allowed to dismantle American corporations.[19] The activists of the 1980s "shareholders' revolution" reacted to what they saw as the erosion of U.S. power. To regain it, they aimed to take back corporations for their owners, the stockholders, rather than leaving them in the hands of professional managers. They began to buy up corporations to strip them of assets and resell them. By the 1990s, the movement had won; the radical chic of "leveraged buyouts" became the mainstream investment strategy of "mergers and acquisitions." As corporations rid themselves of all but their most profitable sectors, most of what had once been inside those corporations was contracted to distant suppliers. Supply chains, and thus commitment to their distinctive form of salvage accumulation, took off as the dominant form of capitalism in the United States. This worked so well for investors that by the turn of the century, U.S. business leaders had forgotten that this shift was part of a struggle for position and had recast it as the leading edge of an evolutionary process. They were busy cramming the world into this process, and had, indeed, made headway in enforcing an American version in Japan.[20]

To understand how Japan's threat had faded requires going back a bit—and allowing money to emerge as a protagonist of the story. In the 1980s and 1990s, lots of things shifted because of confrontations between the dollar and the yen.

In 1949, the yen was pegged to the U.S. dollar as part of the Bretton Woods agreements. As the Japanese economy flourished, in part through nonreciprocated exports to the United States, the U.S. balance of payments with Japan suffered.[21] From the U.S. perspective, the yen was "undervalued," making Japanese goods cheap in the United States and U.S. exports to Japan too dear there. U.S. anxieties about the yen were one small part of the situation in 1971 that led to the U.S. abandonment of the gold standard. In 1973, the yen was allowed to float. Then in 1979, the U.S. raised interest rates, attracting investment in the dollar and keeping its value high. Because the Japanese economy continued to export to the United States, the Japanese government bought and sold

U.S. dollars to keep the price of the yen low. In the first half of the 1980s, capital flowed out of Japan, keeping the yen weak in relation to the dollar. By 1985, U.S. business leaders had panicked about this situation. In response, the U.S. engineered an international agreement, the Plaza Accord. The value of the dollar was lowered, and the yen rose. By 1988, the yen had doubled its value in relation to the dollar. Japanese consumers could buy almost everything abroad—including matsutake. National pride rose; this was the moment of *The Japan That Can Say No*.[22] However, the situation made it difficult for Japanese companies to export their goods, which now were priced too high.

Japanese companies responded by sending more production abroad. So did their suppliers in South Korea, Taiwan, and Southeast Asia, also reeling from the change in currency values. Supply chains traveled everywhere. Here's how two American sociologists describe the situation:

> Faced with the sudden increase of the dollar value of their factor inputs, and eager to keep their prices low and thus maintain their contracts with American retailers, Asian businesses quickly began to diversify. Most of Taiwan's light industries . . . moved to . . . mainland China, but also to Southeast Asia. . . . Large segments of Japanese export-oriented industries moved to Southeast Asia. In addition some firms, such as Toyota, Honda, and Sony, established portions of their business in North America. South Korean businesses also moved labor-intensive operations to Southeast Asia, as well as to other developing countries in Latin America and central Europe. In each place that they established their new businesses, low-price supplier networks began to form.[23]

The Japanese national economy went into shock—first with the "bubble economy" of inflated real estate and stock prices in the late 1980s, then the "lost decade" of recession in the 1990s, then the further financial crisis of 1997.[24] But supply chains took off as never before: not just Japanese-sponsored chains but chains from all Japan's supplier sites, which now had their own chains. Supply-chain capitalism became a presence around the world. But Japan was no longer in charge.

One company's history sharply etches the change between Japanese and U.S. leadership of global supply chains: Nike, the trendsetting brand of athletic shoes. Nike began as a U.S. outpost of a Japanese distribution chain for athletic shoes. (Distribution is an element of many

Japanese supply chains.) Subject to the disciplines of the Japanese trading regime, Nike learned the supply-chain model. But Nike slowly began to transform it, American style. Instead of making value through trade as translation, Nike would use American advantages in advertising and branding. When Nike's founders established their independence from their Japanese chain, they added style—in the form of the Nike "swoosh" and advertisements featuring black American sports heroes. Learning from their Japanese experience, however, it never occurred to them to manufacture shoes. "We don't know the first thing about manufacturing. We are marketers and designers," explained one Nike vice-president.[25] Instead, they contracted with the proliferating supply networks developing across Asia, making good use of the post-1985 profusion of "low-price supplier networks" mentioned above. By the early twenty-first century, the company had contracts with more than nine hundred factories, and it had become a symbol of both the excitement and the terrors of supply-chain capitalism. To speak of Nike evokes the horrors of sweatshops, on the one hand, and the pleasures of designer brands, on the other. Nike has succeeded in making this contradiction seem particularly American. But Nike's rise from a Japanese supply chain reminds us of the pervasive legacy of Japan.

That legacy is clear in the matsutake supply chain, too small and too specialized to attract the intervention of American big business. Yet the chain stretches to North America, enrolling Americans as suppliers rather than as chain directors. Nike on its head! How were Americans convinced to take on such a lowly role? As I have explained, no one in Oregon thinks of him- or herself as an employee of a Japanese business. The pickers, buyers, and field agents are there for freedom. But freedom has come to mobilize the poor only through the freeing of American livelihoods from expectations of employment—a result of the transpacific dialogue between U.S. and Japanese capital.

In the matsutake commodity chain, then, we see the history I have been describing: Japanese traders, searching for local partners; American workers, released from the hope for regular jobs; translations across aspirations, allowing American freedom to assemble Japanese inventory. I have been arguing that the organization of the commodity chain allows us to notice this history, which otherwise might be obscured by hype about U.S. global leadership. When humble commodities are al-lowed to illuminate big histories, the world economy is revealed as emerging within historical conjunctures: the indeterminacies of encounter.

If conjunctures make history, everything rests on moments of coordination—the translations that allow Japanese investors to profit from American foraging, just as pickers take advantage of Japanese wealth. How are mushrooms that are foraged for freedom transformed into inventory? I return to Open Ticket—and its commodity chain.

9
From Gifts to Commodities— and Back

IT IS TIME TO RETURN TO THE PROBLEM OF ALIENATION. In capitalist logics of commodification, things are torn from their life-worlds to become objects of exchange. This is the process I am calling "alienation," and I use the term as a potential attribute of nonhumans as well as humans. The surprising thing about the search for matsutake in Oregon is that it does not involve alienation in the relation between foragers and mushrooms. The mushrooms are indeed torn from their fungal bodies (although, as fruit, this is their goal). But instead of becoming alienated commodities, ready for conversions between money and capital, they become trophies of the hunt—even as they are sold. Foragers beam with pride while showing off their mushrooms; they can't stop narrating the pleasures and dangers of the search. The mushrooms become part of the foragers, just as if they had eaten them. This means that somehow these trophies must be converted into commodities. If mushrooms are gathered as trophies of freedom, and become part of the pickers in that process, then how do they become capitalist commodities?

My approach to this question is guided by an anthropological legacy of attention to the special qualities of gifts as a form of social exchange. This attention was catalyzed by the exchange of necklaces and arm shells made by Melanesians east of New Guinea, described by Bronislaw Malinowski as the kula ring.[1] For generations of social analysts, kula exchange has inspired thoughts about the varied ways value is created. The amazing thing about these ornaments is that they are not particularly useful, nor tokens of general exchange, nor interesting in themselves; they have value *only* because of their role in kula. As gifts, they make relations and reputations; that is their value. This kind of value upsets economic common sense—and that is why it's good to think with.

Indeed, thinking through kula has made it possible to identify alienation as a puzzling and extraordinary feature of capitalism. Kula reminds us that things as well as people are alienated under capitalism. Just as in factories workers are alienated from the things they make, allowing those things to be sold without reference to their makers, so too, things are alienated from the people who make and exchange them. Things become stand-alone objects, to be used or exchanged; they bear no relation to the personal networks in which they are made and deployed.[2] And while this situation may seem ordinary to those of us inside capitalist worlds, studying kula makes it seem strange. In kula, things and persons are formed together in gifts through which things are extensions of persons and persons are extensions of things. Kula valuables are known through the personal relations they make; people of note, in turn, are known through their kula gifts. Things, then, do not just have value in use and commodity exchange; they may have value through the social relationships and reputations of which they are part.[3]

The difference between value making in kula and capitalism seemed so striking that some analysts argued that we might divide the world into "gift economies" and "commodity economies," each with a separate logic for making value.[4] Like most dichotomies, the contrast between gift and commodity suffers when it hits the ground; most situations juxtapose and confuse these ideal types—or stretch outside them. Yet, even in its oversimplifications, it is a useful tool because it urges us to look for difference. Rather than relax into economic common sense, we stay alert for contrasts across value regimes. To explore how capitalism draws from noncapitalist value systems—and how these fare within capitalism—a tool for noticing difference is worth trying out. The gift-versus-commodity distinction can stand in for the absence or presence of alienation, the quality necessary to turn things into capitalist assets.

In considering the matsutake commodity chain, the attraction of this tool increases, too, in attending to the final destination of matsutake. Matsutake in Japan is almost always a gift. The lowest kinds of matsutake are sold at supermarkets and used as ingredients in food manufacturing, but the better kinds, through which the product is known, are quintessential gifts. Almost no one buys a fine matsutake just to eat. Matsutake build relationships, and as gifts they cannot be separated from these relationships. Matsutake become extensions of the person, the definitional feature of value in a gift economy.

Perhaps there have been times and places when the gift was direct from a picker to a consumer; when peasants gave their lords matsutake in medieval Japan, for example, the mushrooms had only to be foraged and presented to express the relation-making force of the gift. Most of the time today, however, gifts are salvaged from capitalist commodity chains. Givers buy them in high-end grocery stores or take the guests whom they want to honor to fancy restaurants to eat them; grocery stores and restaurants obtain them from a chain of wholesalers who in turn obtain them from importers or domestic agricultural cooperatives. How are gifts made from commodities? And might those commodities, in turn, have been made earlier along the chain from gifts? The rest of this chapter explores these puzzles, which take us into the heart of those translations necessary for bringing capitalism and its constitutive others together.

Let me begin in Japan with the arrival of matsutake from abroad. Surely those mushrooms, so carefully cooled, packed, and sorted, are a capitalist commodity. They are as close as we might get to alienated, stand-alone objects: labeled only by the country of the exporter, no one could have any idea under what conditions they were foraged or sold.[5] They have no connections to the people who earlier admired and exchanged them. They are inventory: assets from which importers build their firms. But almost immediately on arrival, they begin their transformation from commodities to gifts. This is the magic of translation, and dealers at every link on the Japanese end of the commodity chain are experts at it. It is worth following them.

Importers have incoming shipments of matsutake sent directly to government-licensed wholesalers, who are paid a commission to supervise further sales. Wholesalers guide imported matsutake down one of two paths: They are sold either by negotiation or by auction to intermediate wholesalers. In both cases, rather to my surprise, wholesalers do not see their job as merely the efficient transfer of goods down the commodity chain. They are active mediators; they see their job as matching the matsutake with the very best buyers for that batch. One man who managed matsutake at a wholesale house explained, "I never sleep during matsutake season." Whenever a shipment comes in, he must assess it. When he has made a judgment about the quality and special characteristics of the lot, he calls the right buyers—the ones who could use just that kind of matsutake. He has already given the mushrooms relation-making powers: the powers of quality.

After several interviews in which we heard experiences of this kind, my collaborator Shiho Satsuka explained the role of wholesalers as "matchmakers." Their job is to match goods with appropriate buyers, getting the best possible price through the match. One vegetable wholesaler spoke of how he goes to visit farmers to see the conditions under which they grow their crops; he wants to know just which buyers these crops will satisfy. Translation from commodity to gift is already happening in making the match. The wholesaler looks for relational qualities in his goods, which, in turn make them a natural match with particular buyers. From the first, then, the sale of matsutake is wrapped up with the making and maintaining of personal relationships. The mushrooms take on relational qualities; they are given the power to make personal ties.

Intermediate wholesalers who buy matsutake at auction are even more invested in making matches. Unlike wholesalers, who make a commission on sales, they make nothing if they do not find the right match. When they buy, they are often already thinking of a particular client. Their skill too is the assessment of quality, as this forges relationships. The exception here are agents who work with supermarkets, who are more concerned with quantity and reliability than quality. Supermarkets buy lower-value matsutake. But fine matsutake are the preserve of small retail businesses who buy from intermediate wholesalers, and their relations flavor the whole trade. The ability to properly assess the mushrooms is the necessary ingredient of this flavor; it allows sellers to extend personal advice—not just a generic commodity—to buyers. The advice is the gift that comes with the mushroom, stretching it beyond use or exchange value.

The best matsutake are sold in specialty grocery stores and expensive restaurants, which pride themselves on knowing their clientele. One grocer explained that he knows his best clients well: He knows when a ceremony that could use matsutake, such as a wedding, is coming up. When he buys from the intermediate wholesaler, he too is already thinking about particular clients. He contacts these clients, maintaining a relationship, not just selling a product. There is a gift in the matsutake even before it leaves the commodity sphere.

Individuals who buy matsutake are almost always thinking about building relationships.[6] A colleague told me about riding with an anxious group to a celebration that was supposed to heal an old rift in an extended family. "Will they bring out the matsutake?" his friends kept asking. If the rift would be healed, there would be matsutake. (There was.) Thus, too, matsutake is an ideal gift to give to someone with whom one needs a long-term relationship. Suppliers give matsutake to the firms that give them business. One grocer commented that religious converts had begun to purchase matsutake for presentation to their spiritual leaders. Matsutake signals a serious commitment.

The grocer told me, too, that he thinks this is key to "Japanese" ways of life. "You can understand France without knowing about truffles," he quipped, "but you can't understand Japan without knowing matsutake." He was referring to the relational quality of the mushroom. It wasn't just the smell or the taste, but the ability of the mushroom to build personal ties that made it so powerful. This is where his work as a matchmaker comes in, too; he must make matsutake relational long before they are ready to be eaten.

It is the mushroom's relational force, as well, that evokes its opposite: wild fantasies of stuffing oneself with matsutake, far beyond satiation. Several people told me mischievously of such fantasies, knowing they were impossible. It was not just the price of matsutake, but the frisson of breaking matsutake's cardinal role: to build relationships. To stuff oneself with an endless pile would be so thoroughly and deliciously bad.

The value of matsutake then derives not just from use and commercial exchange; it is made in the act of giving. And this is possible because mediators all along the chain are already giving the quality of matsutake to their clients as a personal gift. Perhaps this personalization is reminiscent of other aristocratic goods, in other places. The gentleman wants a suit made to fit him, not one off the rack. But this parallel makes the conversion between commodity and gift even more telling. Across many sectors and cultures, mediators are poised to convert capitalist commodities into other value forms. Such middlemen are engaged in the acts of value translation through which capitalism comes to cohabit with other ways of making people and things.

But there is one set of relations that is never included with matsutake gifts in Japan: the relations of foraging and buying in other countries. Neither middlemen nor consumers concern themselves with the relations through which their matsutake are procured. Foreign matsutake are ranked according to a set of Japanese preferences that have nothing to do with the conditions under which the mushrooms grew and were foraged and marketed. When they arrive at an import warehouse, they have no connections to pickers and buyers, much less ecological life-worlds. For a moment, they are fully capitalist commodities. But how did they get that way? Herein lies another tale of value translation.

Let me take you one last time, then, to the buying scene in Open Ticket, to attend to the puzzle of alienation and its alternatives in value creation. I've been arguing that, despite the diverse histories and agendas of participants, what holds them together is the spirit they call freedom. Various versions of freedom are exchanged in the buying, each augmenting the others. Pickers bring the trophies of their political freedom and their freedom in the woods to exchange with advocates of market freedom—and thus, to gain more freedom to go back to the woods again. Might freedom, as much as mushrooms and money, be what makes value in the exchange? In the Melanesian kula ring mentioned earlier, participants bring ordinary stuff such as pigs and yams to exchange alongside kula valuables; these side trades gain value through their association with the fame-making exchange of necklaces and armbands. Similarly, in Open Ticket, mushrooms and money are as much tokens and trophies of an exchange of freedom as valuables in themselves. They gain value through their connections to freedom. They are not isolated objects to own but person-making attributes. It is in this light that—despite the fact that there are no explicit "gifts" here—if I had to judge this economy in a gift-versus-commodity contrast, I would place it on the side of gifts. Personal value and object value are made together in exchanges of freedom: Freedom as personal value is made through money and the search for mushrooms, just as the value of money and mushrooms is assessed by participants through the freedom gained by buyers and searchers. Money and mushrooms have more than use value or capitalist exchange value; they are parts of the freedom that pickers, buyers, and field agents treasure.

Half a night later, however, the mushrooms and the money that surrounds them are something completely different. By the time the mushrooms are packed into crates with ice gel and are sitting on the tarmac for shipment to Japan, it would be hard to find a trace of the distinctive economy of freedom that produced them as trophies. What happened? Back in Open Ticket around 11 p.m., trucks take crated mushrooms to the warehouses of bulkers in Oregon, Washington, and Vancouver, British Columbia. There something strange happens: The mushrooms are sorted again. This is particularly odd because buyers in Open Ticket are master sorters. Sorting creates the prowess of buyers; it is an expression of their deep connection with the mushrooms. Stranger yet, the new sorters are casual laborers with no interest in mushrooms at all. They are part-time, on-call workers without benefits: people who want a little extra income but have no full-time jobs. In Oregon, I saw back-to-the-land hippies sorting under neon lights in the wee hours of the morning. In Vancouver, it was immigrant Hong Kong housewives. These are workers in the classic sense of the term: alienated labor without interest in the product. And yet they are translators, North American style. It is precisely because they have no knowledge or interest in how the mushrooms got there that they are able to purify them as inventory. The freedom that brought those mushrooms into the warehouse is erased in this new assessment exercise. Now the mushrooms are only goods, sorted by maturity and size.

Why sort again? The warehouse sorting is orchestrated by bulkers: small businessmen willing to position themselves between exporters guided by Japanese economic conventions and buyers committed to a local American gift-and-trophy economy of war and freedom. They work through field agents who join the fray among the buyers. Between the field agents and the exporters, then, they must transform the mushrooms into an acceptable export commodity. They need to recognize what they are shipping and represent it to the exporters. Re-sorting helps them *know* the mushrooms.

One detail illustrates. It is illegal to pick, buy, and export very small matsutake, known in Oregon as "babies." The reason is that the Japanese market is not interested, although U.S. authorities say conservation guides the regulation.[7] Matsutake foragers pick them anyway, and buyers claim that the pickers *make* them buy small mushrooms.[8] Babies are removed in the warehouse extra sort. Because the mushrooms are small, I doubt if this makes much weight difference. U.S. authorities never check export crates for babies. But discarding babies helps bring the mushrooms into commodity standards. No longer entangled in the exchange of freedom between pickers and buyers, the mushrooms become commodities of a particular size and grade.[9] They are ready for use or commercial exchange.

Matsutake is then a capitalist commodity that begins and ends its life as a gift. It spends only a few hours as a fully alienated commodity: the time when it waits as inventory in shipping crates on the tarmac and travels in the belly of a plane. But these are hours that count. Relations between exporters and importers, which dominate and structure the supply chain, are cemented within the possibility of these hours. As inventory, matsutake allow calculations that channel profits to exporters and importers, making the work of organizing the commodity chain worthwhile from their perspective. This is salvage accumulation: the creation of capitalist value from noncapitalist value regimes.

10
Salvage Rhythms: Business in Disturbance

A COLLEAGUE WHO STUDIES PEOPLE AND FORESTS IN Borneo told me the following story: The community he worked with lived in and around a great forest. A timber company came and cut down the forest. When the trees were gone, the company left, leaving a pile of disintegrating machines. The residents could no longer make a living either from the forest or from the company. They took apart the machines and sold the metal as scrap.[1]

The story, for me, encapsulates the ambivalence of salvage: On the one hand, I am full of admiration for the people who figured out how to survive despite the destruction of their forest. On the other hand, I can't help but worry when the scrap metal will run out, and whether there will be enough other stuff in the ruins to make continuing survival possible. And while not all of us enact such a literal figuration of living in ruins, we mostly do have to work within our disorientation and distress to negotiate life in human-damaged environments. We follow salvage rhythms, whether of the market for scrap or of the entangled histories of foraging for matsutake mushrooms. By "rhythms," I mean forms of temporal coordination. Without the singular, forward pulse of progress, the unregularized coordination of salvage is what we have.

During most of the twentieth century, many people—perhaps particularly Americans—thought that business carried forward the pulse of progress. Business was always getting bigger. It seemed to be increasing the world's wealth. It was effectively reshaping the world according to its goals and needs, so that people could be empowered by money and things for use and commercial exchange. All it seemed people had to do—even ordinary people without investment capital—was to tie their own rhythms to the forward pulse of business, and they too would move forward. This worked through scalability; people and nature could join progress by becoming units in its algorithm of expansion. Advancement, ever expanding, would move through them in tandem.

All of that now seems increasingly strange. Yet experts in the business world seem to be unable to do without this apparatus for making knowledge. The economic system is presented to us as a set of abstractions requiring assumptions about participants (investors, workers, raw materials) that take us right into twentieth-century notions of scalability and expansion as progress. Seduced by the elegance of these abstractions, few think it important to take a closer look at the world the economic system supposedly organizes. Ethnographers and journalists give us reports of survival, flourishing, and distress, here and there. Yet there is a rift between what experts tell us about economic growth, on the one hand, and stories about life and livelihood, on the other. This is not helpful. It is time to reimbue our understanding of the economy with arts of noticing.

Thinking through salvage rhythms changes our vision. Industrial work no longer charts the future. Livelihoods are various, cobbled together, and often temporary. People come to them for diverse reasons, and only rarely because they offer the stable wages-and-benefits packages of twentieth-century dreams. I have suggested we watch patches of livelihood come into being as assemblages. Participants come with varied agendas, which do their small part in guiding world-making projects. For Open Ticket mushroom hunters, these include surviving war trauma and negotiating a working relationship with U.S. citizenship. Such projects mobilize commercial foraging, drawing pickers into the forest to follow "mushroom fever." Despite differences across these projects, boundary objects have formed—and particularly a commitment to what the pickers call freedom. Through such imagined common ground, commercial picking gains coherence as a scene—and a gathering becomes a happening. Multidirectional histories become possible through its emergent qualities. Without top-down discipline or synchronization, and without expectations of progress, livelihood patches help constitute the global political economy.

In collecting goods and people from around the world, capitalism itself has the characteristics of an assemblage. However, it seems to me that capitalism *also* has characteristics of a machine, a contraption limited to the sum of its parts. This machine is not a total institution, which we spend our lives inside; instead, it translates across living arrangements, turning worlds into assets. But not just any translation can be accepted into capitalism. The gathering it sponsors is not open-ended. An army of technicians and managers stand by to remove offending parts—and they have the power of courts and guns. This does not mean that the machine has a static form. As I argued in tracing the history of Japanese-U.S. trade relations, new forms of capitalist translation come into being all the time. Indeterminate encounters matter in shaping capitalism. Yet it is not a wild profusion. Some commitments are sustained, through force.

Two have been particularly important for my thinking in this book. First, alienation is that form of disentanglement that allows the making of capitalist assets. Capitalist commodities are removed from their lifeworlds to serve as counters in the making of further investments. Infinite needs are one result; there is no limit on how many assets investors want. Thus, too, alienation makes possible accumulation—the amassing of investment capital, and this is the second of my concerns. Accumulation is important because it converts ownership into power. Those with capital can overturn communities and ecologies. Meanwhile, because capitalism is a system of commensuration, capitalist value forms flourish even across great circuits of difference. Money becomes investment capital, which can produce more money. Capitalism is a translation machine for producing capital from all kinds of livelihoods, human and not human.[2]

My ability to think with patches and translations draws from a robust body of scholarship on such issues, particularly that emerging from feminist anthropology. Feminist scholars have shown that class formation is also cultural formation: the origin of my patches.[3] They also pioneered the study of transactions across heterogeneous landscapes: my translations.[4] If I have added to the conversation, it is in drawing attention to livelihoods that are simultaneously inside and outside of capitalism. Rather than focus our attention only on the capitalist imaginary, with its disciplined workers and savvy managers, I have tried to show precarious living in scenes that both use and refuse capitalist governance. Such assemblages tell us of what's left, despite capitalist damage.

Before they arrive in the hands of consumers, most commodities journey in and out of capitalist formations. Think about your cell phone. Deep in its circuitry, you find coltan dug by African miners, some of them children, who scramble into dark holes without thought of wages or benefits. No companies send them; they are doing this dangerous work because of civil war, displacement, and loss of other livelihoods, owing to environmental degradation. Their work is hardly what experts imagine as capitalist labor; yet their products enter your phone, a capitalist commodity.[5] Salvage accumulation, with its apparatus of translation, converts the ores they dig into assets legible to capitalist business. And what of my computer? After its short useful life (as I surely must replace it with a newer model), perhaps I will donate it to a charitable organization. What happens to such computers? It seems they are burned for potential components, and children indeed, following salvage rhythms, get to pick them apart for copper and other metals.[6] Commodities often finish their lives in salvage operations for the making of other commodities, to be recouped again for capitalism through salvage accumulation. If we want our theories of the "economic system" to have anything to do with livelihood practices, we had better take note of such salvage rhythms.

The challenges are enormous. Salvage accumulation reveals a world of difference, where oppositional politics does not fall easily into utopian plans for solidarity. Every livelihood patch has its own history and dynamics, and there is no automatic urge to argue *together*, across the viewpoints emerging from varied patches, about the outrages of accumulation and power. Since no patch is "representative," no group's struggles, taken alone, will overturn capitalism. Yet this is not the end of politics. Assemblages, in their diversity, show us what later I call the "latent commons," that is, entanglements that might be mobilized in common cause. Because collaboration is always with us, we can maneuver within its possibilities. We will need a politics with the strength of diverse and shifting coalitions—and not just for humans.

The business of progress depended on conquering an infinitely rich nature through alienation and scalability. If nature has turned finite, and even fragile, no wonder entrepreneurs have rushed to get what they can before the goods run out, while conservationists desperately contrive to save scraps. The next part of this book offers an alternative politics of more-than-human entanglements.

Interlude
Tracking

MUSHROOM TRACKS ARE ELUSIVE AND ENIGMATIC; following them takes me on a wild ride—trespassing every boundary. Things get even stranger when I move out of commerce into Darwin's "entangled bank" of multiple life forms.[1] Here, the biology we thought we knew stands on its head. Entanglement bursts categories and upends identities.

Mushrooms are the fruiting bodies of fungi. Fungi are diverse and often flexible, and they live in many places, ranging from ocean currents to toenails. But many fungi live in the soil, where their thread-like filaments, called hyphae, spread into fans and tangle into cords through the dirt. If you could make the soil liquid and transparent and walk into the ground, you would find yourself surrounded by nets of fungal hyphae. Follow fungi into that underground city, and you will find the strange and varied pleasures of interspecies life.[2]

Many people think fungi are plants, but they are actually closer to animals. Fungi do not make their food from sunlight, as plants do. Like animals, fungi must find something to eat. Yet fungal eating is often generous: It makes worlds for others. This is because fungi have extracellular digestion. They excrete digestive acids outside their bodies to break down their food into nutrients. It's as if they had everted stomachs, digesting food outside instead of inside their bodies. Nutrients are then absorbed into their cells, allowing the fungal body to grow—but also other species' bodies. The reason there are plants growing on dry land (rather than just in water) is that over the course of the earth's history fungi have digested rocks, making nutrients available for plants. Fungi (together with bacteria) made the soil in which plants grow. Fungi also digest wood. Otherwise, dead trees would stack up in the forest forever. Fungi break them down into nutrients that can be recycled into new life. Fungi are thus world builders, shaping environments for themselves and others.

Some fungi have learned to live in intimate associations with plants, and given enough time to adjust to the interspecies relations of a place, most plants enter into associations with fungi. "Endophytic" and "endo-mycorrhizal" fungi live inside plants. Many do not have fruiting bodies; they gave up sex millions of years ago. We are likely never to see these fungi unless we peer inside plants with microscopes, yet most plants are thick with them. "Ectomycorrhizal" fungi wrap themselves around the outsides of roots as well as penetrating between their cells. Many of the favorite mushrooms of people around the world—porcini, chanterelles, truffles, and, indeed, matsutake—are the fruiting bodies of ectomycorrhizal plant associates. They are so delicious, and so difficult for humans to manipulate, because they thrive together with host trees. They come into being only through interspecies relations.

The term "mycorrhiza" is assembled from Greek words for "fungus" and "root"; fungi and plant roots become intimately entangled in mycorrhizal relations. Neither the fungus nor the plant can flourish without the activity of the other. From the fungal perspective, the goal is to get a good meal. The fungus extends its body into the host's roots to siphon off some of the plant's carbohydrates through specialized interface structures, made in the encounter. The fungus depends on this food, yet it is not entirely selfish. Fungi stimulate plant growth, first, by getting plants more water, and, second, by making the nutrients of extracellular digestion available to plants. Plants get calcium, nitrogen, potassium, phosphorus, and other minerals through mycorrhiza. Forests, according to researcher Lisa Curran, occur only because of ectomycorrhizal fungi.[3] By leaning on fungal companions, trees grow strong and numerous, making forests.

Mutual benefits do not lead to perfect harmony. Sometimes the fungus parasitizes the root in one phase of its life cycle. Or, if the plant has lots of nutrients, it may reject the fungus. A mycorrhizal fungus without a plant collaborator will die. But many ectomycorrhizas are not limited to one collaboration; the fungus forms a network across plants. In a forest, fungi connect not just trees of the same species, but often many species. If you cover a tree in the forest, depriving its leaves of light and thus food, its mycorrhizal associates may feed it from the carbohydrates of other trees in the network.[4] Some commentators compare mycorrhizal networks to the Internet, writing of the "woodwide web." Mycorrhizas form an infrastructure of interspecies interconnection, carrying information across the forest. They also have some of the characteristics of a highway system. Soil microbes that would otherwise stay in the same place are able to travel in the channels and linkages of mycorrhizal interconnection. Some of these microbes are important for environmental remediation.[5] Mycorrhizal networks allow forests to respond to threats.

Why has the world-building work of fungi received so little appreciation? Partly, this is because people can't venture underground to see the amazing architecture of the underground city. But it is also because until quite recently many people—perhaps especially scientists—imagined life as a matter of species-by-species reproduction. The most important interspecies interactions, in this worldview, were predator-prey relations in which interaction meant wiping each other out. Mutualistic relations were interesting anomalies, but not really necessary to understand life. Life emerged from the self-replication of each species, which faced evolutionary and environmental challenges on its own. No species needed another for its continuing vitality; it organized itself. This self-creation marching band drowned out the stories of the underground city. To recover those underground stories, we might reconsider the species-by-species worldview, and the new evidence that has begun to transform it.

When Charles Darwin proposed a theory of evolution through natural selection in the nineteenth century, he had no explanation for heritability. Only the recovery in 1900 of Gregor Mendel's work on genetics suggested a mechanism by which natural selection could produce its effects. In the twentieth century, biologists combined genetics and evolution and created the "modern synthesis," a powerful story about how species come into being through genetic differentiation. The early-twentieth-century discovery of chromosomes, structures within cells that carry genetic information, gave palpability to the story. Units of heredity—genes—were located on chromosomes. In sexually reproducing vertebrates, a special line of "germ cells" was found to conserve the chromosomes that give rise to the next generation. (Human sperm and eggs are germ cells.) Changes in the rest of the body—even genetic changes—should not be transmitted to offspring as long as they do not affect the germ cells' chromosomes. Thus the self-replication of the species would be protected from the vicissitudes of ecological encounter and history. As long as the germ cells were unaffected, the organism would remake itself, extending species continuity.

This is the heart of the species self-creation story: Species reproduction is self-contained, self-organized, and removed from history. To call this the "modern synthesis" is quite right in relation to the questions of modernity that I discussed in terms of scalability. Self-replicating things are models of the kind of nature that technical prowess can control: they are modern things. They are interchangeable with each other, because their variability is contained by their self-creation. Thus, they are also scalable. Inheritable traits are expressed at multiple scales: cells, organs, organisms, populations of interbreeding individuals, and, of course, the species itself. Each of these scales is another expression of self-enclosed genetic inheritance, and thus they are neatly nested and scalable. As long as they are all expressions of the same traits, research can move back and forth across these scales without friction. Some hint of coming problems appeared in this paradigm's excesses: when researchers took scalability literally, they produced bizarre new stories of the gene in charge of everything. Genes for criminality and creativity were proposed, sliding freely across scales from chromosome to social world. "The selfish gene," in charge of evolution, required no collaborators. Scalable life, in these versions, captured genetic inheritance in a self-enclosed and self-replicating modernity, indeed, Max Weber's iron cage.

The discovery of the stability and self-replicating properties of DNA in the 1950s was the jewel in the crown of the modern synthesis—but also the opening to its undoing. DNA, with associated proteins, is the material of chromosomes. The chemical structure of its double helix strands is both stable and, amazingly, able to replicate exactly on a newly built strand. What a model for self-contained replication! The replication of DNA was mesmerizing; it formed an icon for modern science itself, which requires the replication of results, and thus research objects that are stable and interchangeable across experimental iterations, that is, without history. The results of the replication of DNA can be tracked at every biological scale (protein, cell, organ, organism, population, species). Biological scalability was given a mechanism, strengthening the story of thoroughly modern life—life ruled by gene expression and isolated from history.

Yet DNA research has led in unexpected directions. Consider the trajectory of evolutionary developmental biology. This field was one of the many that emerged from the DNA revolution; it studies genetic mutation and expression in the development of organisms, and the implications of this for speciation. In studying development, however, researchers could not avoid the history of encounters between an organism and its environment. They found themselves in conversation with ecologists, and suddenly they realized they had evidence for a type of evolution that had not been expected by the modern synthesis. In contrast to the modern orthodoxy, they found that many kinds of environmental effects could be passed on to offspring, through a variety of mechanisms, some affecting gene expression and others influencing the frequency of mutations or the dominance of varietal forms.[6]

One of their most surprising findings was that many organisms develop only through interactions with other species. A tiny Hawaiian squid, *Euprymna scolopes*, has become a model for thinking about this process.[7] The "bob-tailed squid" is known for its light organ, through which it mimics moonlight, hiding its shadow from predators. But juvenile squid do not develop this organ unless they come into contact with one particular species of bacteria, *Vibrio fischeri*. The squid are not born with these bacteria; they must encounter them in the seawater. Without them, the light organ never develops. But perhaps you think light organs are superfluous. Consider the parasitic wasp *Asobara tabida*. Females are completely unable to produce eggs without bacteria of the genus *Wolbachia*.[8] Meanwhile, larvae of the Large Blue butterfly *Maculinea arion* are unable to survive without being taken in by an ant colony.[9] Even we proudly independent humans are unable to digest our food without helpful bacteria, first gained as we slide out of the birth canal. Ninety percent of the cells in a human body are bacteria. We can't do without them.[10]

As biologist Scott Gilbert and his colleagues write, "Almost all development may be codevelopment. By codevelopment we refer to the ability of the cells of one species to assist the normal construction of the body of another species."[11] This insight changes the unit of evolution. Some biologists have begun to speak of the "hologenome theory of evolution," referring to the complex of organisms and their symbionts as an evolutionary unit: the "holobiont."[12] They find, for example, that associations between particular bacteria and fruit flies influence fruit fly mating choice, thus shaping the road to the development of a new species.[13] To add the importance of development, Gilbert and his colleagues use the term "symbiopoiesis," the codevelopment of the holobiont. The term contrasts their findings with an earlier focus on life as internally self-organizing systems, self-formed through "autopoiesis." "More and more," they write, "symbiosis appears to be the 'rule,' not the exception. . . . Nature may be selecting 'relationships' rather than individuals or genomes."[14]

Interspecies relations draw evolution back into history because they depend on the contingencies of encounter. They do not form an internally self-replicating system. Instead, interspecies encounters are always events, "things that happen," the units of history. Events can lead to relatively stable situations, but they cannot be counted on in the way self-replicating units can; they are always framed by contingency and time. History plays havoc with scalability. The only way to create scalability is to repress change and encounter. If they can't be repressed, the whole relation across scales must be rethought. When British conservationists tried to save the Large Blue butterfly, mentioned above, they could not assume that a mating population could by itself reproduce the species, although, according to the modern synthesis, populations are formed from individuals formed by genes. They could not leave out the ants without which the larvae cannot survive.[15] Large Blue butterfly populations are thus not a scalable effect of the butterflies' DNA. They are nonscalable sites of interspecies encounter. This is a problem for the modern synthesis, because population genetics was from the early twentieth century at the core of evolution-without-history. Might population science need to step aside for an emergent multispecies historical ecology? Might the arts of noticing I discuss be at its core?[16]

Reintroducing history into evolutionary thinking has already begun at other biological scales. The cell, once an emblem of replicable units, turns out to be the historical product of symbiosis among free-living bacteria.[17] Even DNA turns out to have more history in its amino-acid sequences than once thought. Human DNA is part virus; viral encounters mark historical moments in making us human.[18] Genome research has taken up the challenge of identifying encounter in the making of DNA. Population science cannot avoid history for much longer.[19]

Fungi are ideal guides. Fungi have always been recalcitrant to the iron cage of self-replication. Like bacteria, some are given to exchanging genes in nonreproductive encounters ("horizontal gene transfer"); many also seem averse to keeping their genetic material sorted out as "individuals" and "species," not to speak of "populations." When researchers studied the fruiting bodies of what they thought of as a species, the expensive Tibetan "caterpillar fungus," they found many species entangled together.[20] When they looked into the filaments of *Armillaria* root rot, they found genetic mosaics that confused the identification of an individual.[21] Meanwhile, fungi are famous for their symbiotic attachments. Lichen are fungi living together with algae and cyanobacteria. I have been discussing fungal collaborations with plants, but fungi live with animals as well. For example, *Macrotermes* termites digest their food only through the help of fungi. The termites chew up wood, but they cannot digest it. Instead, they build "fungus gardens" in which the chewed-up wood is digested by *Termitomyces* fungi, producing edible nutrients. Researcher Scott Turner points out that, while you might say that the termites farm the fungus, you could equally say that the fungus farms the termites. *Termitomyces* uses the environment of the termite mound to outcompete other fungi; meanwhile, the fungus regulates the mound, keeping it open, by throwing up mushrooms annually, creating a colony-saving disturbance in termite mound-building.[22]

Our metaphorical language (here termite "farming") sometimes gets in the way and sometimes throws up unexpected insights. One of the most common metaphors in talk of symbiosis is "outsourcing." You could say the termites outsource their digestion to fungi, or, alternatively, that the fungi outsource food gathering and niche building to termites. There are lots of things wrong with comparing biological processes to contemporary business arrangements, too many, indeed, to catalogue. But perhaps there is one insight here. As in capitalist supply chains, these chains of engagement are not scalable. Their components cannot be reduced to self-replicating interchangeable objects, whether firms or species. Instead, they require attention to the histories of encounter that maintain the chain. Natural history description, rather than mathematical modeling, is the necessary first step—as in the economy. Radical curiosity beckons. Perhaps an anthropologist, trained in one of the few remaining sciences that values observation and description, might come in handy.

Active landscapes, Yunnan. Active landscapes are puzzles, turning nature-as-we-knew-it on its head. Here, pines, oaks, goats, humans: why does matsutake flourish in the midst of all this traffic?

Part III
Disturbed Beginnings:
Unintentional Design

WHEN KATO-SAN INTRODUCED ME TO THE WORK HE was doing for the prefectural forest-research service to restore the forest, I was shocked. As an American tutored in wilderness sensibilities, I thought forests were best at restoring themselves. Kato-san disagreed: If you want matsutake in Japan, he explained, you must have pine, and if you want pine, you must have human disturbance. He was supervising work to remove broadleaf trees from the hillside he showed me. Even the topsoil had been carted away, and the steep slope now looked gouged and bare to my American eyes. "What about erosion?" I asked. "Erosion is good," he answered. Now I was really startled. Isn't erosion, the loss of soil, always bad? Still, I was willing to listen: pine flourishes on mineral soils, and erosion uncovers them.

Working with forest managers in Japan changed how I thought about the role of disturbance in forests. Deliberate disturbance to revitalize forests surprised me. Kato-san was not planting a garden. The forest he hoped for would have to grow itself. But he wanted to help it along by creating a certain kind of mess: a mess that would advantage pine.

Kato-san's work engages with a popular and scientific cause: restoring *satoyama* woodlands. Satoyama are traditional peasant landscapes, combining rice agriculture and water management with woodlands. The woodlands—the heart of the satoyama concept—were once disturbed, and thus maintained, through their use for firewood and charcoal-making as well as nontimber forest products. Today, the most valuable product of the satoyama woodland is matsutake. To restore woodlands for matsutake encourages a suite of other living things: pines and oaks, understory herbs, insects, birds. Restoration requires disturbance—but disturbance to enhance diversity and the healthy functioning of ecosystems. Some kinds of ecosystems, advocates argue, flourish with human activities.

Ecological restoration programs around the world use human action to rearrange natural landscapes. What distinguishes satoyama revitalization, for me, is the idea that human activities should be part of the forest in the same way as nonhuman activities. Humans, pines, matsutake, and other species should all make the landscape together, in this project. One Japanese scientist explained matsutake as the result of "unintentional cultivation," because human disturbance makes the presence of matsutake more likely—despite the fact that humans are entirely incapable of cultivating the mushroom. Indeed, one could say that pines, matsutake, and humans all cultivate each other unintentionally. They make each other's world-making projects possible. This idiom has allowed me to consider how landscapes more generally are products of *unintentional design*, that is, the overlapping world-making activities of many agents, human and not human. The design is clear in the landscape's ecosystem. But none of the agents have planned this effect. Humans join others in making landscapes of unintentional design.

As sites for more-than-human dramas, landscapes are radical tools for decentering human hubris. Landscapes are not backdrops for historical action: they are themselves active. Watching landscapes in formation shows humans joining other living beings in shaping worlds. Matsutake and pine don't just grow in forests; they make forests. Matsutake forests are gatherings that build and transform landscapes. This part of the book begins with disturbance—and I make disturbance a beginning, that is, an opening for action. Disturbance realigns possibilities for transformative encounter. Landscape patches emerge from disturbance. Thus precarity is enacted in more-than-human sociality.

*Active landscapes, Kyoto
Prefecture. Satoyama
forest in December.
Sometimes the life of
the forest is most evident
as it bursts through
obstacles. Farmers chop;
winter chills: life still
breaks through.*

11
The Life of the Forest

To walk attentively through a forest, even a damaged one, is to be caught by the abundance of life: ancient and new; underfoot and reaching into the light. But how does one tell the life of the forest? We might begin by looking for drama and adventure beyond the activities of humans. Yet we are not used to reading stories without human heroes. This is the puzzle that informs this section of the book. Can I show landscape as the protagonist of an adventure in which humans are only one kind of participant?

Over the past few decades, many kinds of scholars have shown that allowing only human protagonists into our stories is not just ordinary human bias; it is a cultural agenda tied to dreams of progress through modernization.[1] There are other ways of making worlds. Anthropologists have become interested, for example, in how subsistence hunters recognize other living beings as "persons," that is, protagonists of stories.[2] Indeed, how could it be otherwise? Yet expectations of progress block this insight: talking animals are for children and primitives. Their voices silent, we imagine well-being without them. We trample over them for our advancement; we forget that collaborative survival requires cross-species coordinations. To enlarge what is possible, we need other kinds of stories—including adventures of landscapes.[3]

One place to begin is a nematode—and a thesis on livability.

"Call me *Bursaphelenchus xylophilus*. I'm a tiny, wormlike creature, a nematode, and I spend most of my time crunching the insides of pine trees. But my kin are as well-traveled as any whaler sailing the seven seas. Stick with me, and I'll tell you about some curious voyages."

But wait: who would want to hear about the world from a worm? That was, in effect, the question addressed by Jakob von Uexküll in 1934, when he described the world experienced by a tick.[4] Working with the tick's sensory abilities, such as its ability to detect the heat of a mammal, and thus a potential blood meal, Uexküll showed that a tick knows and makes worlds. His approach brought landscapes to life as scenes of sensuous activity; creatures were not to be treated as inert objects but as knowing subjects.

And yet: Uexküll's idea of affordances limited his tick to the bubble-like world of its few senses. Caught in a small frame of space and time, it was not a participant in the wider rhythms and histories of the landscape.[5] This is not enough—as the voyages of *Bursaphelenchus xylophilus*, the pine wilt nematode, attest. Consider one of the most colorful:

Pine wilt nematodes are unable to move from tree to tree without the help of pine sawyer beetles, who carry them without benefit to themselves. At a particular stage in a nematode's life, it may take advantage of a beetle's journey to hop on as a stowaway. But this is not a casual transaction. Nematodes must approach beetles in a particular stage of the beetles' life cycle, just as they are about to emerge from their piney cavities to move to a new tree. The nematodes ride in the beetles' tracheae. When the beetles move to a new tree to lay their eggs, the nematodes slip into the new tree's wound. This is an extraordinary feat of coordination, in which nematodes tap into beetles' life rhythms.[6] To immerse oneself in such webs of coordination, Uexküll's bubble worlds are not enough.

Despite this sojourn with a nematode, I have not abandoned matsutake. A major reason for the current rarity of matsutake in Japan is the demise of pines that results from the habits of pine wilt nematodes. Just as whalers catch whales, pine wilt nematodes catch pines and kill them and their fungal companions. Still, nematodes were not always involved in this way of making a living. Just as for whalers and whales, nematodes become killers of pines only through the contingencies of circumstance and history. Their voyage into Japanese history is as extraordinary as the webs of coordination they weave.

Pine wilt nematodes are only minor pests for American pines, which evolved with them. These nematodes became tree killers only when they traveled to Asia, where pines were unprepared and vulnerable. Amazingly, ecologists have traced this process rather precisely. The first nematodes disembarked at Japan's Nagasaki harbor from the United States in the first decade of the twentieth century, riding in American pine.[7] Timber was a resource for industrializing Japan, where elites were hungry for resources from around the world. Many uninvited guests arrived with those resources, including the pine wilt nematode. Soon after its arrival, it traveled with local pine sawyer beetles; its moves can be traced concentrically out from Nagasaki. Together, the local beetle and the foreign nematode changed Japan's forest landscapes.

Still, an infected pine might not die if it is living in good conditions, and this indeterminate threat thus holds matsutake, implicated as collateral damage, in suspense. Pines stressed by forest crowding, lack of light, and too much soil enrichment are easy prey to nematodes. Evergreen broadleaf trees crowd and shade Japanese pine. Blue-stain fungus sometimes grows in pine's wounds, feeding the nematodes.[8] The warmer temperatures of anthropogenic climate change help the nematodes to spread.[9] Many histories come together here; they draw us beyond bubble worlds into shifting cascades of collaboration and complexity. The livelihoods of the nematode—and the pine it attacks and the fungus that tries to save it—are honed within unstable assemblages as opportunities arise and old talents gain new purchase. Japan's matsutake enters the fray of all this history: its fate depends on the enhancement or debilitation of the Uexküllian agilities of pine wilt nematodes.

Tracking matsutake through the journeys of nematodes allows me to return to my questions about telling the adventures of landscapes, this time with a thesis. First, rather than limit our analyses to one creature at a time (including humans), or even one relationship, if we want to know what makes places livable we should be studying polyphonic assemblages, gatherings of ways of being. Assemblages are performances of livability. Matsutake stories draw us into pine stories and nematode stories; in their moments of coordination with each other they create livable—or killing—situations.

Second, species-specific agilities are honed in the coordinations of assemblages. Uexküll gets us on the right track by noticing how even humble creatures participate in making worlds. To extend his insights, we must follow multispecies attunements in which each organism comes into its own. Matsutake is nothing without the rhythms of the matsutake forest.

Third, coordinations come in and out of existence through the contingencies of historical change. Whether matsutake and pine in Japan can continue to collaborate depends a great deal on other collaborations set in motion by the arrival of pine wilt nematodes.

To put all this together it may be useful to recall the polyphonic music mentioned briefly in chapter 1. In contrast to the unified harmonies and rhythms of rock, pop, or classical music, to appreciate polyphony one must listen both to the separate melody lines and their coming together in unexpected moments of harmony or dissonance. In just this way, to appreciate the assemblage, one must attend to its separate ways of being at the same time as watching how they come together in sporadic but consequential coordinations. Furthermore, in contrast to the predictability of a written piece of music that can be repeated over and over, the polyphony of the assemblage shifts as conditions change. This is the listening practice that this section of the book attempts to instill.

By taking landscape-based assemblages as my object, it is possible to attend to the interplay of many organisms' actions. I am not limited to tracking human relations with their favored allies, as in most animal studies. Organisms don't have to show their human equivalence (as conscious agents, intentional communicators, or ethical subjects) to count. If we are interested in livability, impermanence, and emergence, we should be watching the action of landscape assemblages. Assemblages coalesce, change, and dissolve: this *is* the story.

The story of landscapes is both easy and hard to tell. Sometimes it relaxes readers into somnolence, making us think we are not learning anything new. This is a result of the unfortunate wall we have built between concepts and stories. We can see this, for example, in the gap between environmental history and science studies. Science studies scholars, unpracticed in reading concepts through stories, don't bother with environmental history. Consider, for example, Stephen Pyne's fine work on fire in the making of landscapes; because his concepts are embedded in his histories, science studies scholars remain uninfluenced by his radical suggestions on geochemical agency.[10] Pauline Peters's trenchant analysis of how the logic of the British enclosure system came to Botswana range management—or Kate Showers's surprising findings about erosion control in Lesotho—could revolutionize our notions of normal science, but they have not.[11] Such refusals impoverish science studies, encouraging the play of concepts in a reified space. Distilling general principles, theorists expect that others will fill in the particulars—but "filling in" is never so simple. This is an intellectual apparatus that shores up the wall between concepts and stories, thus, indeed, draining the significance of the sensitivities science studies scholars try to refine. In what follows, then, I challenge readers to notice concepts and methods within the landscape histories I present.

Telling stories of landscape requires getting to know the inhabitants of the landscape, human and not human. This is not easy, and it makes sense to me to use all the learning practices I can think of, including our combined forms of mindfulness, myths and tales, livelihood practices, archives, scientific reports, and experiments. But this hodgepodge creates suspicions—particularly, indeed, with the allies I hailed in reaching out to anthropologists of alternative world makings. For many cultural anthropologists, science is best regarded as a straw man against which to explore alternatives, such as indigenous practices.[12] To mix scientific and vernacular forms of evidence invites accusations of bowing down to science. Yet this assumes a monolithic science that digests all practices into a single agenda. Instead, I offer stories built through layered and disparate practices of knowing and being. If the components clash with each other, this only enlarges what such stories can do.

At the heart of the practices I am advocating are arts of ethnography and natural history. The new alliance I propose is based on commitments to observation and fieldwork—and what I call noticing.[13] Human-disturbed landscapes are ideal spaces for humanist and naturalist noticing. We need to know the histories humans have made in these places *and* the histories of nonhuman participants. Satoyama restoration advocates were exceptional teachers here; they revitalized my understanding of "disturbance" as both coordination and history. They showed me how disturbance might initiate a story of the life of the forest.[14]

Disturbance is a change in environmental conditions that causes a pronounced change in an ecosystem. Floods and fires are forms of disturbance; humans and other living things can also cause disturbance. Disturbance can renew ecologies as well as destroy them. How terrible a disturbance is depends on many things, including scale. Some disturbances are small: a tree falls in the forest, creating a light gap. Some are huge: a tsunami knocks open a nuclear power plant. Scales of time also matter: short-term damage may be followed by exuberant regrowth. Disturbance opens the terrain for transformative encounters, making new landscape assemblages possible.[15]

Humanists, not used to thinking with disturbance, connect the term with damage. But disturbance, as used by ecologists, is not always bad—and not always human. Human disturbance is not unique in its ability to stir up ecological relations. Furthermore, as a beginning, disturbance is always in the middle of things: the term does not refer us to a harmonious state before disturbance. Disturbances follow other disturbances. Thus all landscapes are disturbed; disturbance is ordinary. But this does not limit the term. Raising the question of disturbance does not cut off discussion but opens it, allowing us to explore landscape dynamics. Whether a disturbance is bearable or unbearable is a question worked out through what follows it: the reformation of assemblages.

Disturbance emerged as a key concept in ecology at the very same time that scholars in the humanities and social sciences were beginning to worry about instability and change.[16] On both sides of the humanist/naturalist line, concerns about instability followed after the post–World War II American enthusiasm for self-regulating systems: a form of stability in the midst of progress. In the 1950s and 1960s, the idea of ecosystem equilibrium seemed promising; through natural succession, ecological formations were thought to reach a comparatively stable balance point. In the 1970s, however, attention turned to disruption and change, which generate the heterogeneity of the landscape. In the 1970s, too, humanists and social scientists began worrying about the transformative encounters of history, inequality, and conflict. Looking back, such coordinated changes in scholarly fashion might have been early warning of our common slide into precarity.

As an analytic tool, disturbance requires awareness of the observer's perspective—just as with the best tools in social theory. Deciding what counts as disturbance is always a matter of point of view. From a human's vantage, the disturbance that destroys an anthill is vastly different from that obliterating a human city. From an ant's perspective, the stakes are different. Points of view also vary *within* species. Rosalind Shaw has elegantly shown how men and women, urban and rural, and rich and poor each conceptualize "floods" differently in Bangladesh, because they are differentially affected by rising waters; for each group, the rise exceeds what is bearable—and thus becomes a flood—at a different point.[17] No single standard for assessing disturbance is possible; disturbance matters in relation to how we live. This means we need to pay attention to the assessments through which we know disturbance. Disturbance is never a matter of "yes" or "no"; disturbance refers to an open-ended range of unsettling phenomena. Where is the line that marks off too much? With disturbance, this is always a problem of perspective, based, in turn, on ways of life.

Since it is already infused with attention to perspective, I am unapologetic about my use of the term "disturbance" to refer to the distinctive ways the concept is used in varied places. I learned this layered usage from Japanese forest managers and scientists, who constantly stretch European and American conventions, even as they use them. Disturbance is a good tool with which to begin the inconsistent layering of global-and-local, expert-and-vernacular knowledge layers I have promised.

Disturbance brings us into heterogeneity, a key lens for landscapes. Disturbance creates patches, each shaped by diverse conjunctures. Conjunctures may be initiated by nonliving disturbance (e.g., floods and fires) or by living creatures' disturbances. As organisms make intergenerational living spaces, they redesign the environment. Ecologists call the effects that organisms create on their environments "ecosystems engineering."[18] A tree holds boulders in its roots that otherwise might be swept away by a stream; an earthworm enriches the soil. Each of these is an example of ecosystems engineering. If we look at the interactions across many acts of ecosystems engineering, patterns emerge, organizing assemblages: unintentional design. This is the sum of the biotic and abiotic ecosystems engineering—intended and unintended; beneficial, harmful, and of no account—within a patch.

Species are not always the right units for telling the life of the forest. The term "multispecies" is only a stand-in for moving beyond human exceptionalism. Sometimes individual organisms make drastic interventions. And sometimes much larger units are more able to show us historical action. This is the case, I find, for oaks and pines as well as matsutake. Oaks, which interbreed readily and with fertile results across species lines, confuse our dedication to species. But of course what units one uses depends on the story one wants to tell. To tell the story of matsutake forests forming and dissolving across continental shifts and glaciation events, I need "pines" as a protagonist—in all their marvelous diversity. *Pinus* is the most common matsutake host. When it comes to oaks, I stretch even farther, embracing *Lithocarpus* (tanoaks) and *Castanopsis* (chinquapin) as well as *Quercus* (oaks). These closely related genera are the most common broadleaf hosts for matsutake. My oaks, pines, and matsutake are thus not identical within their group; they spread and transform their storylines, like humans, in diaspora.[19] This helps me see action in the story of assemblage. I follow their spread, noticing the worlds they make. Rather than forming an assemblage because they are a certain "type," my oaks, pines, and matsutake become themselves in assemblage.[20]

Traveling with this in mind, I investigated matsutake forests in four places: central Japan, Oregon (U.S.A.), Yunnan (southwest China), and Lapland (northern Finland). My small immersion in satoyama restoration helped me see that foresters in each place had different ways of "doing" forests. In contrast to satoyama, humans were *not* part of forest assemblages in matsutake management in the United States and China; managers there leaped to anxieties about too much human disturbance, not too little. In contrast, too, to satoyama work, forestry elsewhere was measured on a yardstick of rational advancement: could the forest make futures of scientific and industrial productivity? In distinction, a Japanese satoyama aims for a livable here and now.[21]

But, more than comparison, I seek histories through which humans, matsutake, and pine create forests. I work the conjunctures to raise unanswered research questions rather than to create boxes. I look for the same forest in different guises. Each appears through the shadows of the others. Exploring this simultaneously single and multiple formation, the next four chapters take me into pines. Each illustrates how ways of life develop through coordination in disturbance. As ways of life come together, patch-based assemblages are formed. Assemblages, I show, are scenes for considering livability—the possibility of common life on a human-disturbed earth.

Precarious living is always an adventure.

Coming Up among Pines . . .

12
History

It was September when I first saw the pine forests of northern Finland. I rode the night train from Helsinki, past the Arctic Circle with its signs for Santa Claus's home, through smaller and smaller birches, until I found myself surrounded by pines. I was surprised. I had thought of natural forests as packed with tall and tiny trees, all jumbled together, of many species and ages. Here all the trees were just the same: one species, one age, neat and evenly spaced. Even the ground was clean and clear without a snag or a piece of downed wood. It looked exactly like an industrial tree plantation. "Ah," I thought, "How the lines have blurred." This was modern discipline, both natural and artificial. And there was contrast: I was near the border with Russia, and people told me that across the border the forest was a mess. I asked what a mess looked like, and they told me the trees were uneven and the ground full of dead wood; no one cleared it up. This Finnish forest was clean. Even lichen was cropped close by the reindeer. On the Russian side, people said, great balls of lichen grew as high as your knees.

The lines have blurred. A natural forest in northern Finland looks a lot like an industrial tree plantation. The trees have become a modern resource, and the way to manage a resource is to stop its autonomous historical action. As long as trees make history, they threaten industrial governance. Cleaning the forest is part of the work of stopping this history. But since when do trees make history?

"History" is both a human storytelling practice and that set of remainders from the past that we turn into stories. Conventionally, historians look only at human remainders, such as archives and diaries, but there is no reason not to spread our attention to the tracks and traces of nonhumans, as these contribute to our common landscapes. Such tracks and traces speak to cross-species entanglements in contingency and conjuncture, the components of "historical" time. To participate in such entanglement, one does not have to make history in just one way.[1] Whether or not other organisms "tell stories," they contribute to the overlapping tracks and traces that we grasp as history.[2] History, then, is the record of many trajectories of world making, human and not human.

Yet modern forestry has been based on the reduction of trees—and particularly pines—to self-contained, equivalent, and unchanging objects.[3] Modern forestry manages pines as a potentially constant and unchanging resource, the source of sustainable yields of timber. Its goal is to remove pines from their indeterminate encounters, and thus their ability to make history. With modern forestry, we forget that trees are historical actors. How might we remove the blinders of modern resource management to regain a feel for the dynamism so central to the life of the forest?

In what follows, I offer two strategies. First, I delve into the abilities of pines, across many times and places, to change the scene with their presence and transform the trajectories of others—that is, to make history. In this, my guide is a book, the kind of heavy tome that when it slips off your bicycle on a turn makes a great clatter and smash, stopping traffic. That book is David Richardson's edited volume, *Ecology and Biogeography of Pinus*.[4] Despite its heft and reserved title, it is an adventure story. Richardson's authors animate the variety and agility of *Pinus*, making it a lively subject across space and time, a historical subject. This provocation convinced me that all of *Pinus*, rather than a particular kind of pine, would be my subject. Following pines through their challenges is a form of history.

Second, I return to northern Finland to follow pines into interspecies encounters, and thus the assemblages of which they are architects. Industrial forestry comes back, but so too do those aggravations that reduce its success in stopping history. Matsutake helps me with this story, for, without the efforts of foresters, they help pines survive. Pine flourishes only in the encounter. Modern forest management can grasp a moment in pine's history, but it cannot stop the indeterminacy of encounter-based time.

If you ever wanted to be impressed by the historical force of plants, you might do well to start with pines. Pines are among the most active trees on earth. If you bulldoze a road through a forest, pine seedlings will likely spring up on its raw shoulders. If you abandon a field, pines will be the first trees to colonize it. When a volcano erupts, or a glacier moves back, or the wind and sea pile sand, pines may be among the first to find a foothold. Until people moved things around, pine grew only in the northern hemisphere. People carried pine and grew it in plantations in the global south. But pine jumped over the plantation fence and spread out across the landscape.[5] In Australia, pines have become a major fire hazard. In South Africa, they threaten the rare endemics of the fynbos. In open and disturbed landscapes, it's hard to keep pine down.

Pines need light. In the open they can be aggressive invaders, but they decline in the shade. Furthermore, pines are poor competitors in what are usually considered the best places for plants: places with fertile soil, adequate moisture, and warm temperatures. There, pine seedlings lose out to broadleafs, whose seedlings quickly develop the broad leaves through which we name them, shading out the pines.[6] As a result, pines have become specialists in places without those ideal conditions. Pines grow in extreme environments: cold high places; almost-deserts; sand and rock.

Pines also grow with fire. Fire shows off their diversity; there are many and varied pine adaptations to fire. Some pines go through a "grass stage," spending several years looking like tufts of grass while their root systems grow strong, and only then shooting up like crazy things until their buds might get above the coming flames. Some pines develop such thick bark and high crowns that everything can burn around them without giving them more than a scar. Other pines burn like matches—but have ways of ensuring that their seeds will be first to sprout on the burned earth. Some store seeds for years in cones that open only in fire: Those seeds will be first to hit the ashes.[7]

Pines live in extreme environments because of the help they get from mycorrhizal fungi. Fossils have been found from 50 million years ago that show root associations between pines and fungi; pines have evolved with fungi.[8] Where no organic soil is available, fungi mobilize nutrients from rocks and sand, making it possible for pines to grow. Besides providing nutrients, mycorrhizas protect pines from harmful metals and other, root-eating, fungi. In return, pines support mycorrhizal fungi. Even the anatomy of pine roots has been formed in association with fungi. Pines put out "short roots," which become the site of mycorrhizal association. If no fungi encounter them, the short roots abort. (In contrast, fungi do not cover at least the tips of anatomically different "long roots," specialized for exploration.) By moving across disturbed landscapes, pines make history, but only through their association with mycorrhizal companions.

Pines have made alliances with animals as well as fungi. Some pines are completely dependent on birds to spread their seeds—just as some birds are completely dependent on pine seeds for their food. Across the northern hemisphere, jays, crows, magpies, and nutcrackers have a close association with pines. Sometimes the relationship is specific: the seeds of high-altitude whitebark pines are the key food of Clark's Nutcrackers; in turn, the uneaten seed caches of the nutcrackers are the only way the pines spread their seeds.[9] Caches of small mammals such as chipmunks and squirrels also play an important role in spreading pine seeds, even for those pines whose seeds are also spread by wind.[10] But no mammal has spread pine seeds more widely than human beings.

Humans spread pines in two different ways: by planting them, and by creating the kinds of disturbances in which they take hold. The latter generally occurs without any conscious intent; pines like some of the kinds of messes humans make without trying. Pines colonize abandoned fields and eroded hillsides. When humans cut down the other trees, pines move in. Sometimes planting and disturbance go together.

People plant pines to remediate the disturbances they have created. Alternatively, they may keep things radically disturbed to advantage pine. This last alternative has been the strategy of industrial growers, whether they plant or merely manage self-seeded pine: clear-cutting and soil breaking are justified as strategies to promote pine.

In some of its most extreme environments, pine wants not just any fungal partner, but matsutake. Matsutake secretes strong acids that break down rock and sand, releasing nutrients for the mutual growth of pine and fungus.[11] In the harsh landscapes where matsutake and pine grow together, there are often few other fungi to be found. Besides, matsutake forms a dense mat of fungal filaments, excluding other fungi and many soil bacteria. Japanese farmers and, following them, scientists call this mat *shiro*, a "castle," and thinking of matsutake's castle allows us to imagine its wards and guards.[12] Its defense is also offense. The mat is water-repellent, allowing the fungus to concentrate the acids it needs to break down rock.[13] Together turning rock into food, matsutake-pine alliances stake out places with little organic soil.

Yet in the ordinary course of events, organic soil piles up over time, through the growth and death of plant and animal life. Dead organisms rot, becoming organic soil, which in turn becomes the ground for new life. In places without organic soil, this cycle of life and death has been broken by some contingent action; such action signals irreversible time, that is, history. By colonizing disturbed landscapes, matsutake and pine make history together —and they show us how history-making extends beyond what humans do. At the same time, humans create a great deal of forest disturbance. Matsutake, pines, and humans together shape the trajectories of these landscapes.

Two kinds of human-disturbed landscapes produce most of the matsutake that enters world trade. First, there are industrial pines—and some other conifers—in wood-producing forests. Second, there are peasant landscapes, where farmers have cut back broadleaf trees, sometimes denuding hillsides completely, advantaging pine. In peasant forests, pine often grows together with oak and oak relatives, and these are matsutake hosts in some places. This chapter goes on to tell of an industrial forest, where pine grows without other trees; here histories in the making involve all the apparatus of capitalist wood production, not only property but also the booms and busts of the logging industry, and of labor, as well as the state apparatus of regulation, including fire suppression. The next chapter moves to interactions between pines and oaks in peasant forests. Together, they show histories made in concert by humans, plants, and fungi.

Humans and pines (with their mycorrhizal allies) have about the same length of history in Finland: as soon as the glaciers retreated, some nine thousand years ago, both humans and pines started coming.[14] From a human point of view, that was a long time ago, hardly worth remembering. Thinking in terms of forests, however, the time line from the end of the Ice Age is still short. In this clash of perspectives, we see the contradictions of forest management: Finnish foresters have come to relate to forests as stable, cyclical, and renewable, yet the forests are open-ended and historically dynamic.

Birch was the first tree to arrive after the glaciers; but pine was close behind. Pine—with its fungi—knew how to handle the piles of rock and sand the glaciers left behind. Only one pine came, Scots pine, *Pinus sylvestris*, with short, bristly needles and red-brown bark. Behind birch and pine straggled other broadleafs, but most never made it to the far north. Finally, Norway spruce arrived, the latecomer. For those of us used to temperate or tropical forests, this is a very small number of trees. In Lapland, among forest-forming trees, there is one pine, one spruce, and two kinds of birch.[15] That's all. It's from the perspective of this small species count that the time of the glaciers seems so near. Other trees have not yet arrived. The forest might seem predestined for an industrial monocrop: Many stands were just one kind before they were managed.

Yet people in Finland have not always valued the sameness of the forest. Through the beginning of the twentieth century, swidden (fire-based shifting cultivation) was a common practice; through it farmers converted forests into ashes for their crops.[16] Swidden created pastures and uneven-aged broadleaf copses; it stimulated forest heterogeneity. This uneven peasant forest was one of the admired forms of nature-loving nineteenth-century artists.[17] Meanwhile, masses of pines had been cut to produce tar for a maritime capitalism that sourced its products from all over the world.[18] The story of a micromanaged Finnish forestry begins not with the long-durée of forest form but with the anxieties of an emerging crop of nineteenth-century experts. A German forester's 1858 report is downright belligerent:

> The destruction of forests, in which the Finns have become adept, is furthered by the careless and uncontrolled grazing of cattle, swidden practices, and destructive forest fires. In other words, these three means are used for the same main aim, namely the destruction of the forests.[19] . . . The Finns live in and from the forest, but out of stupidity and greed—like the old woman in the fairy tale—they kill the goose that lays the golden eggs.[20]

In 1866, a comprehensive forestry law was passed, and forest management began.[21]

It was not until after World War II, however, that Finland became a vast terrain of modern silviculture. Two developments turned all attention to timber. First, more than four hundred thousand Karelians came over the border from the Soviet Union after Finland ceded Karelia after the war. They needed houses and amenities, and the government built roads and opened up the forests to settle them. The roads made logging possible in new areas. Second, Finland agreed to pay U.S.$300 million to the Soviet Union in reparations for the war. Timber seemed just the way to raise the money—and jump-start Finland's postwar economy.[22] Big companies got involved in managing timberlands. But most of Finland's forests continue to be owned by small holders, and the commitment of the populace to timber as the quintessential Finnish product has helped make scientific forestry a national cause. Forestry associations came to be ruled by national standards.[23] Those standards enshrined the forest as a constant cycle of renewable timber—a static and even-sustainable resource. History making would be for humans, alone.

But how does one stop a forest in its tracks? Consider the pines. As fungi mobilize more nutrients and organic matter accumulates, the northern soils compact and sometimes become waterlogged. Spruce are likely to come in under pine, and as the pines die, succeed them. Forest management has determined to stop this process. First, there is clear-cutting, which foresters call even-aged management. In Finland, clear-cutting aims to mimic the effects of forest fires that replaced whole stands of trees every century or so in the boreal forests before humans stopped them. Pines come back after big fires because they know how to use bright open spaces and bare soils; similarly, pines colonize clear-cuts. Between clear-cuts, there are several rounds of thinning, which weed out other species as well as ensuring an open forest for fast pine growth. Decaying wood advantages spruce seedlings, so dead wood is cleared away. Finally, after the harvest, stumps are removed and the ground is harrowed to break up the soil, advantaging a new generation of pine. Through these techniques, foresters aim to create a cycle of renewal in which only pine participates, even when it isn't planted.

Such techniques are gaining critics in Finland, as elsewhere. Even pine forests, critics remind us, were not so homogeneous in the past.[24] Foresters respond defensively, touting the biodiversity they foster. *Gynomitra* "brain mushrooms," a popular edible in Finland (although considered poisonous in the United States), pop up in brochure after brochure as an icon of this biodiversity; *Gynomitra* often fruits in the disturbed soil that follows clear-cuts.[25] What might matsutake add to this conversation?

The most curious thing about matsutake in northern Finland is its boom-and-bust habit of fruiting. Some years, the ground is covered with matsutake mushrooms. Then, in following years, no matsutake will fruit at all. In 2007, a nature guide in Rovaniemi, on the Arctic Circle, claims to have personally found one thousand kilograms of matsutake. He heaped it up in great pyramids or left it lying on the ground. The next year, he found nothing, and the following year only one or two caps. This fruiting habit resembles what for trees is called "masting," in which trees allocate resources for fruiting only sporadically— but then, triggered by long-term cycles and environmental cues, fruit massively and all together across an area.[26] Masting refers to more than tracking weather changes from year to year; it requires multiyear strategic planning so that carbohydrates stored up one year might be expended in later fruiting. Furthermore, mast fruiting occurs in trees with mycorrhizal partners; the storage and expenditure necessary for masting appears to be coordinated between trees and their fungi. Fungi store carbohydrates for the future fruiting of trees. Might trees also accommodate the uneven fruiting of fungi? I know of no research that tracks how fungal fruiting is coordinated with tree masting, but there is an enticing mystery here. Might the boom-and-bust fruiting of matsutake tell us about the historicity of pine forests in northern Finland?

Pines in northern Finland do not produce seed every year. Foresters recognize this as a problem for forest regeneration; it is not always possible to expect clear-cuts to bounce back immediately into forests, despite the fact that when pines do produce seed, they produce a great deal. In northern Sweden, researchers have noted "wavelike" and "episodic" regeneration in pine forests even without fire; seed production histories become forest histories through scarce or abundant seedlings.[27] Surely mycorrhizal partners must have a hand in the timing of pine seed production. Fungal fruiting may be one indication of such complex rhythms of coordination, in which pine and fungus share resources for phased, periodic reproduction.

This is a time scale humans can understand. Certainly, we might say, pines have covered new territory since the retreat of the glaciers, but that is too slow to make a difference to us. But the historical patterns of forest regeneration are another matter: We know this kind of time. It does not follow the predictable cycles desired by forest managers. It is evidence of the strain between the eternal, cyclical forests desired by managers, and actually existing historical forests. Irregular fruiting offers a not-so-cyclical rhythm, responding to cross-year environmental differences and multiyear coordination between fungi and trees. To specify these rhythms, we find ourselves speaking in dates, not cycles: 2007 was a good year for matsutake in northern Finland. In the coordination between fungal and host tree fruiting, we might begin to appreciate the history making of the forest, that is, its tracking of irreversible as well as cyclical time. Irregular rhythms produce irregular forests. Patches develop on different trajectories, creating uneven forest landscapes. And while forceful management against irregularity can drive some species to extinction, it can never succeed in transforming trees into creatures without history.

Most mushrooms in Finland are picked in privately owned forests. However, many people besides the owners have access to those mushrooms. Pickers are allowed access to private forests under ancient common law, *jokamiehenoikeus*, translated into English as "everyman's rights." As long as one does not disturb residents, the forest is open for hiking and picking. Similarly, state forests are open to pickers. This expands the terrain in which foragers get to know mushrooms.

One day, my hosts took me to a forest reserve, where we looked at pines with three-hundred-year-old fire scars. The trees were perhaps five hundred years old. New research suggests that there were many areas in the boreal forest where stand-replacing fires were rare, and old trees flourished. Under the trees, we picked mushrooms and spoke of those that do not flourish with the younger forests of modern timber management. But matsutake is lucky. Japanese researchers suggest that matsutake fruits best—at least in central Japan—with forty- to eighty-year-old pines.[28] There is no reason that Finnish Lapland's managed pines, planned for hundred-year harvest, would not be thick with matsutake.[29] The fact that in many years they are not is itself a gift: an opening to the temporal irregularity of the histories forests make. Intermittent, spasmodic fruiting reminds us of the precarity of coordination—and the curious conjunctures of collaborative survival.

In the dilemmas generated by modern forestry's stop-history efforts, conservationists have come to believe that forests need refugia from management. But these refugia will have to be managed if they are to survive. Perhaps one skill for the Zen arts of managed nonmanagement will be to watch pine's partners rather than pine.

13
Resurgence

O NE OF THE MOST MIRACULOUS THINGS ABOUT
forests is that they sometimes grow back after they have been destroyed.
We might think of this as resilience, or as ecological remediation, and I
find these concepts useful. But what if we pushed even further by thinking through resurgence? Resurgence is the force of the life of the forest,
its ability to spread its seeds and roots and runners to reclaim places
that have been deforested. Glaciers, volcanoes, and fires have been some
of the challenges forests have answered with resurgence. Human insults
too have been met with resurgence. For several millennia now, human
deforestation and forest resurgence have responded to each other. In the
contemporary world, we know how to block resurgence. But this hardly
seems a good enough reason to stop noticing its possibilities.

Several practical habits are obstructions. First, expectations of progress: the past seems far away. Woodlands, where forests grow with human
disturbance, retreat into shadows because the peasants who work them,
as so many authors tell us, are figures from archaic times.[1] It is an em-
barrassment to bring them up; we've moved on to barcoding life and
big data. (Yet how could any catalog match the force of the forest?) Thus,

second, we imagine that—in contrast to peasants—modern Man is in control of all his work. Wilderness is the only place where nature remains sovereign; on human-disturbed landscapes, we see only the effects of that modernist caricature Man. We have stopped believing that the life of forest is strong enough to make itself felt around humans. Perhaps the best way to reverse this tide is to reclaim peasant woodlands as a figure for the here and now—not just the past.

For me to reclaim this figure, I had to visit Japan, where satoyama revitalization projects make human disturbance look good in allowing for the continual resurgence of ever-young forest. Satoyama projects reconstitute peasant disturbance to teach modern citizens to live within an active nature. This is not the only kind of forest I want to see on earth, but it is an important kind: a forest within which human household-scale livelihoods thrive. Satoyama revitalization is the subject of chapter 18. Here I follow the life of the forest, as this leads into more-than-human sociality, in and beyond Japan. The trail passes through pines and oaks. Where peasant farmers have created enclaves of tentative stability in the domains of states and empires, pines and oaks (in a broad sense) are often companions.[2] Here resurgence follows blasting: The resilience of pine-and-oak woodlands remediates the excesses of human-caused deforestation, regenerating the more-than-human peasant landscape.

Oaks and peasants have long histories in many parts of the world. Oak is useful. Above and beyond its strength as a building material, oak (unlike pine) takes its smooth time in burning; it makes some of the best firewood and charcoal. Better yet, felled oaks (unlike pines) tend not to die; they sprout back from roots and stumps to form new trees. The peasant practice of felling trees in the expectation that they will grow back from their stumps is called "coppicing," and coppiced oak woodlands are exemplary peasant forests.[3] Coppiced trees are ever young and quick growing even as they live for a long time. They outcompete new seedlings, thus stabilizing the forest's composition. Since coppice woods are open and bright, they sometimes find room for pines. Pines (with their fungi) colonize denuded spaces, and thus they also take up other parts of the continuum of peasant disturbance. Yet without human disturbance, pine may give way to oak and other broadleaf trees. It is this pine-oak-human interaction that gives the peasant forest its integrity: As the quick growth of pine on repeatedly human-denuded hillsides yields to long-living stands of coppiced oak, forest ecosystems are regenerated and sustained.

Associations of oak and pine define and anchor peasant forest diversity. The long life of coppiced oaks, together with the quick colonization of empty spaces by pines, creates a tentative stability in which many species thrive, not just humans and their domesticates, but also familiar peasant companions such as rabbits, songbirds, hawks, grasses, berries, ants, frogs, and edible fungi.[4] Like the lives in a terrarium, in which one creature produces oxygen so that another may breathe, the diversity of peasant landscapes can be self-sustaining.

Yet history is always at work, both generating the terrarium and undermining it. Might the imagined stability of peasant landscapes follow upon great cataclysms—and the devastation I call "blasted landscapes"—that bring them into existence? Yes, I think. Peasant communities are defined by their subordination within states and empires; it takes power and violence to hold them in place. The multispecies assemblages they form are creatures too of the play of imperial power, with its property forms, its taxes, and its wars. Yet this is no reason to disparage the rhythms that develop around peasant life. Peasant forests tame blasted landscapes to make them sites of multispecies life—and peasant income. Peasant living channels and taps a forest resurgence it cannot fully control. But thus it recuperates larger-scale destructive projects, bringing life to damaged landscapes.

In Japan, one place to begin is not with humans but with the Grey-faced Buzzard (*Butastur indicus*), a lover of satoyama. These buzzards are migratory, mating in Siberia, then coming to Japan for the spring and summer to raise their young before flying off to Southeast Asia. Male buzzards feed nesting females during egg incubation. They sit atop pine trees, surveying the landscape, looking for reptiles, amphibians, and insects. In May, paddy fields are flooded, and the buzzards look for frogs. When grown rice blocks hunting, the buzzards look into the peasant woodlands for insects. One study found that male buzzards are unwilling to sit on a given tree for more than fourteen minutes if they spot no food.[5] The peasant landscape must be laid out as a larder, with frogs and insects appropriately arrayed, for these birds to thrive.

Grey-faced Buzzards have adapted their migration patterns to the Japanese peasant landscape. Meanwhile, all their foods are equally dependent on this disturbance regime. Without maintenance of the irrigation system, the frog population declines.[6] And so many insects have evolved just to live with peasant trees! *Konara* oak (*Quercus serrata*) has at least eighty-five specialist butterflies that depend on it as food. One colorful butterfly, *Sasakia charonda*, requires the sap of young oaks—kept young by peasant coppicing; when coppicing is not maintained, the oaks grow old, and the butterfly declines.[7]

How is it that the ecological relations of peasant forests have come to be the subject of so much research—especially now that Japan's woodlands have been largely abandoned, as fossil fuels have replaced firewood and as the younger generation has moved to the city? Some researchers are clear: future sustainability is best modeled with the help of nostalgia. At least that was the view of Professor K, an environmental economist in Kyoto.

Professor K told me he had become an economist because he thought he could help poor people. But ten years into a successful career, he realized his research was helping no one. Worse yet, he saw the glazed eyes of his students. He spoke to them and knew it wasn't just his lectures; his students too had lost touch with questions that mattered. Professor K reconsidered his life trajectory. He remembered his visits as a boy to his grandparents' village: how alive he felt as he explored the countryside! That landscape sustained people rather than sapping their strength. So he turned his professional work toward restoring Japan's peasant landscape. He argued and pushed until his university obtained access to an area of abandoned fields and forests, and he took his students there, not just to look but also to study the skills of peasant life. Together, they learned: they re-cleared the irrigation channels, planted rice, opened up the forests, built a kiln to make charcoal, and found their way into taking care of the forest with the eyes and ears of peasants. How enthusiastic his seminars were now!

He showed me the overgrown, abandoned forest that still crowded around their reclaimed fields. There was so much work to do to make a sustainable peasant forest emerge from the tangled brush. *Moso* bamboo, he explained, had gone wild here. Brought from China some three hundred years ago for the excellence of its bamboo shoots, plantings had always been carefully trimmed around peasant households. But as peasant forests and fields have been neglected, the bamboo has become an aggressive invader, taking over the forest. He showed me how it was suffocating the remaining pines, cloaking them in the deep shade that made them vulnerable to pine wilt. But his students were cutting back bamboo and learning too to make it into charcoal.

The coppiced oaks were also in trouble. We admired the ancient stools that had regrown over and over into trees. But a wilderness of other plants now surrounded them, and since they had not been coppiced for many years, they no longer retained the always-youthful qualities that shaped the architecture of the forest. He and his students, he explained, would have to learn the art of coppice again. Only then, he said, could they attract the plants and animals of the peasant landscape: the birds, shrubs, and flowers that made Japan's four seasons so fruitful and inspiring. Because of the work they had already done, he said, these life forms were beginning to come back. But all this was an ongoing labor of love. The sustainability of nature, he said, never just falls into place; it must be brought out through that human work that also brings out our humanity. Peasant landscapes, he explained, are the proving grounds for remaking sustainable relations between humans and nature.

Peasant forests have only recently come into focus in Japan. Before the past thirty years, foresters and forest historians were obsessed with the aristocrats among trees: Japanese cedar and cypress. When they wrote about Japan's "forests," they were usually thinking about just these two trees.[8] There is good reason: these are beautiful and useful trees. *Sugi*, called "cedar" but actually a distinctive *Cryptomeria*, grows straight and tall like a California redwood, producing a glorious, decay-resistant wood for boards, paneling, posts, and pillars. *Hinoki*, Japanese cypress (*Chamaecyparis obtusa*), is even more impressive. The wood is sweetly scented and can be planed to a beautiful texture. It resists rot. It is the perfect wood for temples. Both hinoki and sugi can grow to enormous sizes, allowing awe-inspiring posts and boards. No wonder that Japan's early rulers did their best to cut down all the sugi and hinoki in the forest for their palaces and shrines.

Early aristocratic fixation on sugi and hinoki opened possibilities for peasant claims on other trees—particularly oaks.[9] In the twelfth century, wars fractured the unity of aristocrats, allowing peasants to institutionalize claims to village forests. *Iriai* rights are common-land rights shared by villagers, allowing enrolled households to gather firewood, make charcoal, and use all the products of village lands. In contrast to common forest rights in many other places, iriai rights in Japan were codified and enforceable in courts of law. Yet it was unlikely to find a sugi or hinoki in Japan's premodern iriai forests; those trees were claimed by aristocrats, even if they grew on village lands. But sometimes peasants could claim oaks even on the lord's land; iriai can operate as a layer of use rights on land owned by others. Lords, provided for by others, didn't need oak.[10] Still, it is not surprising that elites have tried very hard to cut back on iriai rights. After the nineteenth-century Meiji Restoration, many commonly held lands were privatized or claimed by the state. Amazingly, despite all odds, some iriai forest rights have been maintained through to the present—to fall into difficulty from the late-twentieth-century abandonment of village forests as rural people flocked into cities.

What trees defined the iriai village forest? Japanese are proud of their location at the crossroads of temperate and subtropical suites of plants and animals: Japan has four seasons *and* is green all year round. Subtropical plants and insects are shared with Japan's southern neighbors in Taiwan; a cold-weather flora and fauna are shared with the northeast Asian mainland. Oaks stretch across this divide. Deciduous oaks, with large, translucent leaves that turn color and fall off in winter, form part of the northeastern flora. Evergreen oaks, with smaller and thicker leaves that are green all year, come from the southwest. Both kinds of oaks are useful for fuel and charcoal. But in some important, tradition-setting parts of central Japan, deciduous oaks are preferred to evergreens. Peasants weeded out evergreen oak seedlings, along with the rest of the underbrush and grass that grew under the trees, privileging the deciduous species. This choice made a difference for the oak-pine relationship—and the architecture of the forest: unlike evergreen oaks, which offer constant shade, deciduous oaks leave bright spaces in the winter and spring where pines, as well as temperate herbaceous plants, might have a chance. Furthermore, peasants continually opened up and cleaned out the forest, letting pines and other temperate species in among the oaks.[11]

Unlike premodern European peasants, premodern peasants in Japan did not raise milk or meat animals, and so they could not fertilize their fields with manure as Europeans did. Gathering plants and forest duff for green manure was a major occupation of peasant life. Everything on the forest floor was taken, leaving it cleared to the bare mineral soils favored by pine. Some areas were opened up to favor grass. The pillars of this disturbed forest were coppiced oaks; the most common was *Quercus serrata*, known as *konara*. Oak wood was useful for all kinds of things, from firewood to growing cultivated *shiitake* mushrooms. Periodic coppicing kept the oak trunk and branches young, allowing oaks to dominate the forest, as they grew back faster than other species could become established. On ridges, in open meadows, and on denuded hillsides grew *akamatsu* red pine, *Pinus densiflora*, with its partner matsutake.

Japanese red pine is a creature of peasant disturbance. It cannot compete with broadleaf trees, which both shade it out and create rich and deep humus layers that only add to their advantage. Paleobotanists have found that several thousand years ago, when humans first began to deforest the Japanese landscape, red pine pollen increased dramatically, from previous levels of almost nothing.[12] Pine thrives with peasant disturbance: the bright sunshine of clearing and coppicing; the bare, raked mineral soils. Oak can drive out pine on peasant hillsides. But the practices of coppicing and the gathering of green manure created complementary spaces for konara oak and akamatsu pine. Matsutake grew with the pine, helping it to find a footing on ridges and eroded slopes. In particularly denuded areas, flush with pine, matsutake was the most common forest mushroom.

In the nineteenth and twentieth centuries, members of Japan's burgeoning urban middle class began to visit the countryside on outings associated with the search for matsutake. This had once been an aristocratic prerogative, but now many could participate. Villagers designated areas of pine and matsutake as "guest mountains" and charged urban visitors for the privilege of a morning's mushroom picking followed by a sukiyaki lunch in the refreshing outdoors. This practice wove an affective bundle in which matsutake hunting wraps all the pleasures of rural biodiversity into the escape from ordinary cares. Like childhood visits to one's grandparents' farm, matsutake outings scent the rural with nostalgia, and this scent has continued to influence present-day appreciation of rural landscapes.

Contemporary advocates of the restoration of Japanese peasant landscapes may aestheticize the peasant forest as the planned result of traditional knowledge, creating nature and human needs in harmony. Yet many scholars suggest that these harmonious forms developed out of moments of deforestation and environmental destruction. Kazuhiko Takeuchi, an environmental historian, stresses the extensive deforestation associated with Japan's industrialization in the mid-nineteenth century.[13] He argues that historical changes have been key to the peasant forests that today's advocates have come to imagine, the forests of the first half of the twentieth century. In the late nineteenth century, Japan's modernization put pressure on peasant forests, leading to massive deforestation in central Japan. Visitors noted the array of "bald mountains" visible along the roads. By the turn of the century, these bare hillsides were growing back in akamatsu pine. In some cases, pine was planted, for example, for watershed management; but akamatsu seeds spread everywhere, and the pine, with the help of matsutake, came up by itself. In the first part of the twentieth century, matsutake was as common and abundant as the pine forests. With growing demands for firewood and charcoal, oak coppicing was also active. The pine-oak woodlands of contemporary nostalgic views were in full flower.

Fumihiko Yoshimura, a mycologist and pine-forest advocate, emphasizes a later deforestation: the disturbance of the forests leading up to and during World War II.[14] Trees were cut down not only for peasant uses but also as fuel and building supplies for the military buildup. The peasant landscape was significantly denuded. After the war, these landscapes experienced regreening: Pines grew up on bare landscapes. Dr. Yoshimura would like to restore the pine forests to a 1955 baseline, a time of regrowth. After that, instead of renewal, the forests deteriorated.

I save the story of the post-1950s transformations that changed the forest for later chapters. Here I want to spotlight the question of how great historical disturbances may open possibilities for the comparatively stable ecosystem of the ever-young and open peasant forest. It is ironic that these episodes of deforestation gave rise to the forests that have become the very image of stability and sustainability in much contemporary Japanese thought. This irony does not make the peasant forest less useful or desirable, but it shifts our appreciation of the work of living with forest resurgence: everyday peasant efforts are often responses to historical shifts far out of their control. Small disturbances eddy within the currents of big disturbances. To appreciate this point, it seems useful to turn away from the nostalgia-driven reconstructions of Japanese advocates and volunteers, which lull us out of history by their aesthetic perfection.

In central Yunnan, in southwest China, peasant forests are not nostalgic reconstructions but are actively used by peasants. They are not considered objects of ideal beauty but disasters that need to be cleaned up. They do not look like reconstructions. They are messy at best, and sometimes provocatively so. This is the peasant landscape in motion, not recreated through nostalgia. Despite its offending disorder, in many ways this ever-young and open forest has a striking resemblance to central Japan's peasant woods. Although the species are different, coppiced oak and pine form the forest's architecture.[15] Yunnan matsutake has different proclivities than its Japanese sibling: it grows with oaks as well as pines. But this makes the peasant-oak-pine-matsutake complex even more evident. Perhaps here, too, it is great cataclysms rather than only peasant ingenuity that allowed this forest resurgence.

In central Japan, I was offered attractively potted peasant forest histories not just by scholars but also by foresters and rural residents. Once trained inside this discourse, my work was easy; all I had to do was look and listen. Thus trained, I was surprised in Yunnan when the very idea of a peasant forest history provoked confusion and defensiveness. Everyone wanted peasants to be good forest managers, but it was through their skills as modern entrepreneurs, not traditional stewards, that they would know how to manage. Peasant forests were a modern object—a result of decentralization—not an old one, and the goal of forest experts was to make modern rationality possible. If the forests were in bad shape, it was because mistakes were made in the past. History was the story of those mistakes.[16]

Michael Hathaway and I spoke to foresters and even forest historians. They explained how the state had enclosed forests, and how, in this time of reform, they had passed them back to the peasants via household contracts. They spoke of the 1998 logging ban, which was meant to stop the damage, and of the model projects through which new forms of forest management were tried. When I turned the conversation to forest histories, they spoke again of the state, and its mistakes. Individually contracted household forests were the new way to organize forests, and they would have to grow in places damaged by earlier collective management. The key, they thought, was to sort out tenure and incentives, allowing entrepreneurs, not bureaucrats, to manage. In these new times, the forests would be remade with the market. We spoke of laws, incentives, and model projects. I hadn't yet touched the trees. I missed the aesthetic objects I had come to know in Japan, even as I now saw their strangeness.

When I arrived in rural Chuxiong Prefecture, people were equally unhappy with my Japan-taught questions. Village officials recapitulated national stories of changing administrative categories; but ordinary residents didn't know what to do with those categories. Finally, one elderly man made a comment that started a more productive comparison moving in my mind. During China's Great Leap Forward, he said, the landscape was deforested by the need for "green steel." Wasn't Japan's Meiji-era deforestation also about green steel?

The forest in central Yunnan is mainly sparse and young. It *looks* disturbed. Tracks run through the eroded hillsides. Despite the ban on commercial timber, everything is used, from the ground to the treetops. Evergreen oaks dominate the landscape, ranging from shrubs to coppiced trees. Yet the forest is open; pines mix with the oaks. Pine, like oak, has many uses. Pine resin is sometimes tapped. Pine pollen is gathered to sell to the cosmetics industry; some pines also produce commercially valuable edible seeds. Pine needles are gathered for bedding for the pigs each household raises; pig feces held together by pine needles are a major fertilizer for crops. Herbaceous plants are gathered for food for the pigs—as well as for food and medicine for people. Pig food is cooked every day with firewood on an outdoor stove; thus, even where households have other fuel sources for human cooking, every household gathers great stacks of firewood. Shepherds bring cattle and goats to browse wherever land is not obviously under crops. Commercial picking of wild mushrooms, not just matsutake but many species, creates foot traffic in the forest. In some places, groves of serious trees are still available for a vigorous if illegal timber trade, but in most areas the trees are thin and small. Exotic eucalyptus, first planted for a village-based oil industry, spreads along the roads. This is a hard forest to promote as timeless peasant wisdom, although brave Chinese scholars have tried.[17]

The messy peasant forest does little to satisfy foreign conservationists, who have flocked to Yunnan to save endangered nature, and they are quick to blame the excesses of communism for deviations from their wilderness dreams. Young Chinese scholars and students follow the foreign lead. More than one young city person told me that Yunnan's hills were deforested by Red Guards during China's Cultural Revolution, although this story seems unlikely. The Cultural Revolution is an easy scapegoat for everything that seems wrong. To attribute forest damage to this period mainly indicates that the faults of this young and open forest are easy for everyone to see. It is in this context that it seems striking to note similarities between peasant forests in central Yunnan and central Honshu, Japan. Perhaps Japan's oak-pine forests, in their prime, were less aesthetically and ecologically perfect than they are imagined by advocates now. Perhaps Yunnan's oak-pine forests are better than critics imagine. Those eroded hillsides are the site of a lively regeneration in which oak, pine, and matsutake have a good thing going—not just for peasants but also for many kinds of life.

The time delays are eerily similar. Central Yunnan's forests suffered during China's Great Leap Forward of the late 1950s and early 1960s, when China mustered its resources for rapid industrialization. The "green steel" to which the old villager referred was used in part to fuel backyard furnaces in which peasants melted down their pots to contribute the metal to China's development.[18] Some forests were protected, but in the next decade, the central government cut lumber from these forests for export to raise foreign currency. Forty to fifty years later, pines had colonized bare spaces, and oak stools had sprouted into trees. The peasant forest was in full flower, and matsutake mushrooms were one sign of its success.

Similarly, central Japan's forests suffered during Japan's rapid industrialization in the decades after the Meiji Restoration of 1868. Forty to fifty years later, peasant oak-pine forests achieved the perfection for which they are remembered today. After the initial disturbance, as in China, peasants learned to make the regrowing trees work for them. The interlocking uses of the forest fit together; the landscape became recognizable and seemed increasingly stable and thus harmonious. Oak supplied building materials, firewood, and charcoal; pine supplied matsutake mushrooms as well as wood, turpentine, needles, and fast-burning fuel. Perhaps the living peasant forests of early-twentieth-century Japan looked a little like today's forests in central Yunnan. Although historians rush to differentiate the modernization achieved by Japan's Meiji Restoration and the failures of China's Great Leap Forward, from the perspective of a tree, there may not have been much difference. If peasant forests are viewed differently in each context, it may be in part be contrast between close and distant, and forward- and backward-looking views.

People and trees are caught in irreversible histories of disturbance. But some kinds of disturbance have been followed by regrowth of a sort that nurtures many lives. Peasant oak-pine forests have been eddies of stability and cohabitation. Yet they are often put into motion by great cataclysms, such as the deforestation that accompanies national industrialization. Small eddies of interlocking lives within great rivers of disturbance: these are surely sites for thinking about human talents for remediation. But there is also the forest's point of view. Despite all insults, resurgence has not yet ceased.

Active landscapes,
Oregon. Critics describe
the eastern Cascades
forest as "festering sores
on the back of a mangy
old dog," and even its
foresters admit that
management has been
a series of mistakes.
Yet for pickers, this forest
is "ground zero."
In the contingency
of error, sometimes
mushrooms pop.

14
Serendipity

WHEN OLD TIMERS EXPLAINED THAT OREGON'S eastern Cascades had once been a center for industrial logging, I could hardly believe them. All I saw was the highway, flanked by unhealthy-looking trees—although a few roadside signs said "Industrial Forest." People showed me where towns and mills had once flourished, but now there was nothing but brush.[1] They took me to now-vanished homes, hotels, and hobo camps. The hobos had left piles of rusting cans, but the towns were gone to scruffy stands of overcrowded pines, neither wilderness nor civilization. The folks who remained made do with this and that. On the highway, shut-down stores sagged with broken windows. Businesses mixed gun and liquor sales. Signs on driveways said uninvited guests would be shot. When a new truck stop opened, they said, no one showed up for the preemployment open meeting because they had heard about the company's drug testing and personal surveillance. "Anyone who lives out here wants to be left alone," someone explained.[2]

Resource management does not always lead to the effects it expects. One place to look for life in the forest is in those plans' undoing. Mistakes were made . . . but mushrooms popped up.

The eastern Cascades is managed for industrial pine, but it does not look like Finnish Lapland. The forest is messy. Dead wood lies and leans everywhere. Trees are often scraggly and either sparse or densely packed. Dwarf mistletoe and root rot sap their strength. In contrast to Finland, where smallholders jointly manage most of the forest, Cascades matsutake grows on national forest—or else timber company—land. There are few small forest owners to coordinate management. This is just as well for forest management dreams, because white residents and visitors tend to resent the idea of forest regulation as iconic of an overreaching federal government. They shoot holes in Forest Service signs and boast about the rules they flaunt. The Forest Service works to appeal to them, but it is an uphill battle.

Social scientists often stress the bureaucratic assertiveness of the U.S. Forest Service. Yet the foresters I met in the eastern Cascades were humble in their explanations of forest management. Their programs, they said, were a series of experiments, and most all of them had failed. How, for example, should they deal with the lodgepoles that just kept coming back in denser thickets? They tried clear-cutting, which created those dense thickets. They tried saving seed trees and shelterwood, but lone trees were blown down by the wind and snow. Should they try to save jobs at the one remaining logging mill even when it means clashing with environmentalists in court?[3] Although environmental goals have changed Forest Service rhetoric, district offices are still evaluated by the board feet of timber they generate. There was nothing to do, they said, but deal with each dilemma as it arose. Since there was no good alternative, they just kept trying.

The landscape has not made forest management easy. While, as in Finland, there were glaciers in the U.S. Pacific Northwest, pines occupy the eastern Cascades for a different reason. A volcanic eruption some 7,500 years ago covered the region with lava, ash, and pumice (the air-filled stone that results when ejected lava cools). If there was organic soil there before, it was buried. There are still blocks of lava and pumice beds where almost nothing grows. That pines grow at all on this unfriendly ground seems a miracle—and one for which matsutake can claim some credit.

Matsutake grows with many host trees in Oregon. In the wet, mixed conifer forests found at high altitudes, matsutake is abundant with Shasta red fir, mountain hemlock, and sugar pine. On western Cascade slopes, it is sometimes found with Douglas fir; on the Oregon coast, matsutake grows with tanoak. On the dry eastern slopes of the Cascades, matsutake lives with ponderosa pines. In each of these sites, there are other fungi. Where the relationship between tree and fungus starts to get exclusive is the lodgepole pine forests. Foraging in lodgepole, one only occasionally spots another mushroom species. This is not a sure sign of lack of underground diversity: many fungi rarely send up fruiting bodies. Still, it seems clear that an especially intimate companionship has formed between matsutake and lodgepole in the eastern Cascades.

Like most friendships, this one depends on chance meetings and small beginnings that later surge into significance. Both protagonists were once neglected; if now they dominate regional news, there must be a story. Deploying their own blasted-landscapes metaphor, foragers call this area "ground zero" of the American matsutake scene. What brought fungus and root together with such spectacular results?

When whites first came to the eastern Cascades in the nineteenth century, they did not notice lodgepoles. Instead, they stood in awe of the giant ponderosas that dominated the forest. According to historian William Robbins, these pine forests once were "the most impressive and spectacular" of Oregon's interior forests.[4] The trees were huge, and they were surrounded by parklike open country with little underbrush. U.S. Army Captain John Charles Fremont came through in 1834: "Today the country was all pine forest. . . . The timber was uniformly large, some of the pines measuring 22 feet in circumference, and 12 to 13 feet at six above."[5] A turn-of-the-century U.S.G.S. surveyor added, "The forest floor is often as clean as if it had been cleared, and one may ride or drive without hindrance."[6] A 1910 newspaper made the obvious connection: "No timber in the world can be logged more easily."[7]

Ponderosa timber attracted both government and industry. In 1893, President Grover Cleveland created the Cascade Forest Reserve; soon, a race was on to construct railroads to bring out the timber, and by the early twentieth century, lumbermen had obtained title to huge lots.[8] By the 1930s, Oregon timber dominated the U.S. wood industry; eastern

Cascade ponderosas, in heavy demand, were logged as fast as fellers could get to them.[9] The mix of public and private land shaped the timing of logging. Before World War II, timber companies pressured the government to keep national forests closed, to keep prices high. By the end of the war, private lands were depleted, and the same voices then called for opening the national forests. Only this, they said, could keep the mills open, preventing unemployment and national wood shortages. Afterward, national forests increasingly bore the brunt of logging.[10]

The impact of logging changed with postwar practices of industrial forestry. Foresters, buoyed by the optimism of new technologies as well as the boom economy, had an idea for how national forests could be opened without depleting their timber. All they had to do was replace "decadent," "overmature" old growth forests with fast-growing and vigorous young trees, which would be harvestable in predictable eighty- to one-hundred-year year intervals.[11] They might even plant superior stock, making the new forests faster-growing and more resistant to pests and diseases. New technologies were making it practical to remove all the trees, not just the most desirable ones; thus foresters turned to clear-cutting.[12] Clear-cutting would lead to renewal even as it made the forest into units of expansion. The faster the forest was cut, according to this logic, the more productive it would become. Some local foresters were not convinced, but the force of national opinion swept them along. In the 1970s, replanting after cutting became standard practice. Aerial spraying against "weeds" was also used in some areas.[13] As one eastern Cascade forester recalled, in the vision of that period, "Forests of the future would be dominated by a mosaic of 25 to 40 acre even-aged stands of healthy and intensively managed young-growth."[14]

What went wrong with the postwar vision? Ponderosa was increasingly logged out, and it did not grow back, at least not readily. It was missing fire. The great ponderosas in their open parks had emerged together with Native American fire regimes, in which frequent burning of the underbrush encouraged browse for deer and berries for fall picking. Fire burned out competing conifer species while allowing the ponderosas to thrive. But whites drove out Native Americans in a series of wars and relocations. The Forest Service stopped not only their fires but all fires. Without fire, flammable species such as white fir and lodgepole grew up under the ponderosas. When the ponderosas were removed through logging, these other species took over. The open character of the landscape disappeared as small trees grew in. Pure stands of ponderosa became rare. The landscape looked less and less like the open ponderosa forests of the early twentieth century—and less and less like a landscape of interest to the timber industry.

In dispossessing Native peoples from the lands they had made so inviting, white loggers, soldiers, and foresters destroyed the parklike forests they had wanted so badly. To pause in recollection, it seems useful to tell of the last great Native dispossession by fiat: the 1954 "termination," or ending of all treaty obligations to the Klamath Tribes. As a result of termination, a chunk of ponderosa land became national forest, ready to be logged by private interests. A few decades later, what was left? The quotations that follow, from the tribe's website, help tell the story.[15]

> The prosperous and powerful Klamath, Modoc and the Yahooskin Band of Snake Paiute people (hereinafter "the Klamaths") once controlled 22 million acres of territory in south central Oregon and Northern California. Their lifestyles and economies provided abundantly for their needs and their cultural ways for over 14,000 years. Contact with invading Europeans, however, quickly decimated their numbers through disease and war and resulted in a treaty reserving to the tribes a diminished land base of 2.2 million acres. Once traditional rivals, the three tribes were forced to live in close proximity to one another on these drastically reduced reserved lands.

In the 1950s, scalability was a matter for citizenship as well as resource use. America was the melting pot, where immigrants could be homogenized to face the future as productive citizens. Homogenization allowed progress: the advance of scalability in business and in civic life. This was the climate in which legislation was passed to unilaterally abrogate U.S. treaty obligations to selected Indian tribes. In the language of the day, members of these tribes were said to be ready to assimilate into American society without special status; their difference would be erased by law.[16]

The rights of the Klamath Tribes looked ripe for termination, to lawmakers, because the tribes were well off. The railroad and the logging of adjacent forests had changed the value of the reservation; by the 1950s, the Klamath Reservation encompassed a large swath of the ponderosa pine that loggers wanted so badly. Klamath Indians were doing well from revenues from timber. They were not a burden on the government. But loggers and officials wanted what they had.

> The Klamath Tribes were by every measure not only no burden, but a significant contributor to the local economy. Their strength and wealth were, however, no match for determined efforts of the federal government to eradicate their culture and acquire their most valuable natural resources—a million acres of land and ponderosa pine. The stage was set for the dispossession of the Klamaths in the early 1950s when the Tribe was subjected to the worst of many disastrous experiments in federal-Indian policy—termination.

As termination proceeded, private companies and public agencies circled. In the end, the federal government took precedence, taking the land as national forest.[17] Klamath Tribes members were paid off.

> Much of the wealth derived from the sale of the Klamath's heritage was lost to sharp dealings by merchants; unscrupulous attorneys that mishandled, embezzled or engaged in self-dealing from trust accounts of those determined to be incompetent; to poorly considered investments— sometimes by attorneys lending themselves money from the accounts; or to exorbitant fees charged by local attorneys or banks for the handling of the beneficiaries['] affairs—which hardly ever got more sophisticated than handing out checks to the beneficiaries—a process usually handled in the most paternalistic of ways.

The dreams of progress imagined by termination advocates did not make Klamath "standard Americans" with capital and privilege. Social and personal problems followed.

> Data compiled for the years from 1966 through 1980 showed the following:
> * 28 percent died by age 25.
> * 52 percent died by age 40.
> * 40 percent of all deaths were alcohol related.
> * Infant mortality was two and one-half times the statewide average.

- 70 percent of the adults had less than a high-school education.
- Poverty levels were three times that of non-Indians in Klamath County—the poorest county in Oregon.

Finally, in 1986, U.S. recognition was restored. Since then, the tribes have pursued water rights and the return of at least some of their reservation land. The tribes have forest management plans for this now logged-over land.[18]

> The Klamaths seek return of these [lands and resources] primarily for the purpose of healing the land and its resources and restoring them to some semblance of the abundance they once reflected. They also seek to restore the spiritual integrity of the land. . . . They want their way of life back.

For the moment, some are picking matsutake mushrooms.

And what of the cut-over forest? On the landscape once known for its ponderosa, fir and lodgepole emerged in crowds. Lodgepole has many fine piney characteristics, and, by the 1960s, foresters and loggers did their best to work with it. Mills began processing lodgepole along with ponderosa.[19] In 1970s replanting schemes, lodgepole rather than ponderosa was often used, owing to its easy establishment on disturbed ground. If you look at the forest from above today on Google Earth, you see mainly swaths of lodgepole growing on old clear-cuts. It's not a pretty sight. Turn-of-the-century critics—taking foresters by surprise—described eastern Cascade timber areas as "festering sores on the back of a mangy old dog" and complained that they were "visible from outer space."[20] Lodgepole had become noticeable. It is time to make it a protagonist of the story.

Lodgepole, *Pinus contorta*, is an old resident in the eastern Cascades. It may have been the first tree to arrive after the glaciers melted.[21] After the eruption of Mt. Mazama, lodgepole was one of the few trees that could grow on pumice flats. It also flourished in cold pockets on the hillside, which were affected by summer frosts that killed other trees, even ponderosa. In the western Cascades, it gathers in old mudslides, where organic soil was swept away. Working with matsutake, lodgepole is hardy.

Selective logging advantaged lodgepole. In mixed conifer forests, loggers picked the best timber and left the rest. Stumps of sugar pines litter the high mountains, although living sugar pine has become rare. Lodgepole was one of the trees not taken. It didn't mind the disturbance. Abandoned logging roads are thick with young lodgepole.

On dry ponderosa slopes, it was the exclusion of fire that most advantaged lodgepole. Lodgepole and ponderosa have opposite piney strategies for dealing with fire. Ponderosa has thick bark and tall crowns; most ground fires won't touch it. Fire thins ponderosa stands, removing small trees and allowing survivors to dominate hillsides uncrowded by the demands of others. In contrast, lodgepole burns readily; its thick groves, live and dead trees intermingled, spread fire. But it generates more seeds than most other trees, and it is often the first to reseed burned areas. In the Rocky Mountains, lodgepoles have closed cones, releasing their seeds only in fires. In the Cascades, lodgepole release seeds every year. There are so many of them that they are quick to colonize new lands.[22]

In the open, bright clearings that follow clear-cut logging, Cascades' lodgepole seedlings colonize in thick packs, which sometimes grow into stands so dense that foresters call them "dog-hair regeneration." One old timer showed me a patch so tightly intertwined that it seemed a welded solid; he joked that we should call it "frog-hair regeneration." Thick groves are places for diseases and pests. As the trees grow up, some start to die. Dead and live wood intermix; dead trees lean across live ones. Straining under the weight, whole groups blow down. Meanwhile, a single spark can burn the whole grove—and with it the rest of the landscape, including private houses, horse camps, timber holdings, and Forest Service offices. Although a few entertain fantasies of cleaning things up this way, most foresters think this is a bad idea.

From lodgepole's perspective, burning is not so terrible, since a new crop of seedlings come up after the fire. Over the long history of the Cascades, fire is one way lodgepole kept its place on the landscape. But Forest Service fire exclusion has given lodgepole forests a new experience: living into old age. Instead of a rapid cycling of generations, together with fire, lodgepoles in the eastern Cascades are maturing. And as they mature, they have increasingly met with matsutake mushrooms.

Fungi are choosy about forest succession. Some are quick to establish themselves with new trees, while others let the forest mature before they take hold. Matsutake seems to be a mid-successional fungus. In Japan, research suggests that matsutake first begin to produce fruiting bodies in pine forests after forty years.[23] Fruiting continues for more than forty years thereafter.[24] No one has gathered clear data on this issue in Oregon, but foragers and foresters agree: matsutake does not fruit with young trees. In the first decade of the twenty-first century, pine plantations established in the 1970s and 1980s did not yet produce matsutake. In naturally regenerating forest, perhaps only forty-to-fifty-year-old trees begin to support matsutake fruiting.[25]

But forty-to-fifty-year-old lodgepole might not even exist except for Forest Service fire exclusion. The budding presence of matsutake mushrooms, their mycelia entwined with lodgepole roots, is an unintended consequence of the most famous Forest Service mistake in the interior forests of the American West: the exclusion of fire.

Meanwhile, the biggest challenge for foresters today is how to keep densely packed and aging lodgepoles from burning the forest down. This is complicated by changes in the Forest Service over the past few decades. First, environmental goals had begun to influence the Forest Service by the 1980s. As the Forest Service entered into dialogue with environmentalists, varied new experiments were tried, such as uneven-aged management. Second, timber companies moved on, and fewer federal funds were made available (see chapter 15). It became impossible for foresters to propose any initiative that was not both specifically mandated by law and incredibly cheap. All forest management would have to be subcontracted to loggers in exchange for the best remaining trees. Labor-intensive treatments were no longer an option. Without the dominance of big timber money, foresters have increasingly seen their job as one of balancing various interests—among different forest users (e.g., wildlife vs. loggers), among different forestry approaches (e.g., sustainable yield vs. sustainable ecosystem services), and among different patch ecologies (e.g., even- vs. uneven-aged management). Missing a singular path to progress, they juggle alternatives.

Foresters would like to thin the lodgepoles.[26] But here they run into the sensibilities of matsutake pickers, who have seen their favorite patches disappear as a result of Forest Service interference. Foresters appeal to pickers with Japanese research, which argues that opening up the forests is good for matsutake. But forests in Japan are different: pines suffer from shading by broadleafs; forest thinning is almost always done by hand. Pines have no broadleaf competition in the eastern Cascades, and foresters there cannot imagine thinning without heavy mechanical equipment. Pickers in the Cascades argue that the equipment breaks and compacts the soil, destroying the fungus. They showed me once-productive patches now marked only with the deep and persistent tracks of heavy equipment. Pickers say that fungi destroyed by soil compaction take many years to reestablish themselves, even when mature tree roots are available.

Given that a major government bureaucracy faces off here with rather powerless forest foragers, it is amazing to me that foresters listen to such complaints at all. Perhaps it is a sign of the newly equivocal Forest Service. In any case, something extraordinary happened during the matsutake season of 2008: one Forest District decided to officially experiment with lodgepole management for matsutake. What this meant was not thinning, even where other Forest Service mandates, such as fire protection, would warrant thinning. At least for a moment, matsutake had entered the Forest Service imagination, and its pact with lodgepole was noticed. To appreciate how strange this is, consider that no other nontimber forest product has attained the status of a management objective, at least in this part of the country. In a bureaucracy that sees only trees, a mushroom companion has made a splash appearance.

Mistakes were made . . . and mushrooms popped up.

15
Ruin

THE MATSUTAKE FORESTS OF JAPAN AND OREGON ARE different in almost every possible way except one: they would probably be converted to more profitable industrial forests if the price of timber were higher. This small convergence is a reminder of structures explored in part 2: the globe-spanning supply chains through which commodities are procured and the state-and-industry pacts through which capitalists gain leverage. Forests are shaped not only in local livelihood practices and state management policies but also by transnational opportunities for the concentration of wealth. Global history is at play—but sometimes with unexpected results.

This chapter asks, how are ruined industrial forests produced separately and in tandem? How do transnational conjunctures make forests? Instead of showing us one overarching frame, conjunctures show us how to follow connections snaking in and out of nations, regions, and local landscapes. These arise from common histories—but also from unexpected convergences and moments of uncanny coordination. Precarity is a globally coordinated phenomenon, and yet it does not follow unified global force fields. To know the world that progress has left to us, we must track shifting patches of ruination.

To taste the surprising force of unexpected concurrences, I begin off track, with falling timber in Southeast Asia in the last third of the twentieth century. Southeast Asian tropical wood supplied the Japanese construction boom between the 1960s and the 1990s. Deforestation was sponsored by Japanese trading companies and put in place through Southeast Asian military force. Because of these supply-chain arrangements, the wood was incredibly cheap. It depressed the global price of timber—and particularly timber used by Japanese consumers. The tropical forests of Southeast Asia were devastated.[1] So far, I imagine you are not surprised. But consider the effects on two still-standing forests: the interior pine forests of the U.S. Pacific Northwest, and the sugi "cedar" and hinoki "cypress" forests of central Japan. Both were potential sources of industrial timber for Japan's development. Both lost their ability to compete. Both fell into neglect. Both are exemplars of ruined industrial forests.[2] Each holds a separate ironic relation to the production of matsutake. Their connected difference invites me to explore global coordination in its multiple forms.

How can we peer into the history of ruination without positing just *one* forest history in which all forests are merely stops along the way? My experiment pulls threads from the contrasting histories of forests in Oregon and central Japan.[3] Since distinctive forests and management are involved, I assume their difference. What calls out for explanation, then, is when they happen to converge. In these moments of unexpected coordination, global connections are at work. But rather than homogenizing forest dynamics, distinctive forests are produced despite the convergences. It is this process of patchy emergence within global connection that a history of convergences can show. Matsutake allows my story to reflect on life in global histories of industrial ruin. In what follows, I pair convergent moments, explaining them in my own words.

Sometimes conjunctures are the result of international "winds," the term Michael Hathaway uses to describe the force of traveling ideas, terms, models, and project goals that prove charismatic or forceful and thus are

able to reshape human relations to the environment.[4] This was the case
with the nineteenth-century German forestry I mentioned as having
changed Finland's forests. One characteristic feature of this traveling expertise was categorical opposition to forest burning. This opposition became a keystone of "modern" forest management in many countries.

1929 central Japan. National law prohibits burning in national forests.[5]

1933 Oregon. At the start of America's New Deal, the Tillamook fire
places fire control at the center of public-private forest cooperation.
When the fire, starting in a private logging operation, blows up, the Civilian Conservation Corps is called to fight it. Afterwards, state foresters
facilitate private "salvage" logging and call for "concerted private and
public action." The U.S. Forest Service begins an ambitious program of
fire exclusion—unintentionally changing Oregon's forests.[6]

Because its goals were to manage forests for states, modern forestry
took hold in relation to peculiarities of state making. Early-twentieth-
century Japan and the United States had different state-making styles.
Yet in both countries, for different reasons, state foresters were concerned with how to work with private interests. In the United States,
corporations were already then more powerful than any state bureaucracy; foresters could only propose rules with which at least some timber barons agreed.[7] In Japan, Meiji-era reforms deeded more than half
of the forest to small private owners. State standards of forestry were
relayed and negotiated with forest owners through forest associations.[8]
Despite these differences, in both countries, fire exclusion became the
connecting point between public and private interests in the forest.
Within divergent forest histories, common ground emerged.

A few years after, forest bureaucracies developed governance traction through mobilization for war—with each other. Coordination
arose in their mutual opposition.

1939 central Japan. Municipality-level forest associations are listed
with other forms of mobilization for war and become mandatory under
the Amended Forest Law.[9]

1942 Oregon. A Japanese floatplane launched from a submarine unsuc-
cessfully attempts to start a forest fire in the mountains of southern

Oregon. This small incident begins an intensification of U.S. Forest Service governance in which the campaign against forest fires is pursued with military-like discipline and zeal. In 1944, as fears of Japanese fire bombs over Oregon forests circulate, Smokey Bear becomes a symbol of fire protection as homeland security.[10]

To manufacture industrial forest ruins first requires an apparatus of governance for imposing public-private dreams—to the detriment of ecological processes. In both Japan and the United States, the bureaucracies of modern forestry played this role.

After Japan's surrender, U.S. occupation tied the countries together, including in their forestry policies. For a few years, their forests could not be imagined separately; convergence derived from a common structure of authority. Postwar U.S. political culture pushed the optimism of growth, public and private, as the route to American-style democracy. In the United States, this meant opening the national forests to private loggers. In Japan, this meant converting natural forests to tree plantations. In each case, policymakers looked forward to a future of expanded business opportunities.

> **1950 Oregon.** Oregon's timber production leads the nation at 5,239 million board feet.[11] In one mill complex on the Deschutes River, loggers cut an average of 350,000 board feet of ponderosa pine every day.[12]

> **1951 central Japan.** A forest law sponsored by the U.S. occupation expands the business role of forest associations. New activities include the remaking of private persons, as forest associations invest to improve forest owners' socio-economic position.[13] The new entrepreneurial persons promoted by the law can then be groomed to make forest plantations.

This is the period in which forests designed for modern industry were promoted in both places. The new Japan that arose after American occupation was just as devoted to growth as Americans advised, but national interests were to shape growth, including a plan for self-sufficiency in wood. In both Japan and the United States, old forests were cut down and new dreams of industrially rationalized resources took their place.[14] The past would not rule the future. New forests would be scalable and rationally managed for industry; their production could be calculated, adjusted, and maintained. Still, the timing of such fantasies differed in each case. In central Japan, planting and intensive management began in the 1950s. Intensive management on private land also took off in Oregon, but in the national forests, the 1950s were devoted to cutting. Great trees were still there for the taking.

> **1953 central Japan.** Loans and tax advantages are offered for converting forests to sugi and hinoki plantations. Japan will be self-sufficient and meet rising demand for wood. Village loggers remember the call to cut timber. Even during the war they had taken out expensive woods first; now all kinds of trees are cut together. In their place, plantations are established, even on steep slopes.[15] Both sugi and hinoki are planted densely, with the government recommending 3,500 to 4,500 seedlings per hectare.[16] Labor is cheap. The trees can be hand-weeded, thinned, pruned, and harvested later. The government subsidizes half the cost and agrees to tax just one fifth of the income.[17]

> **1953 Oregon.** *Newsweek* writes, "The sweetest smell to the Oregonian is that of sawdust. Roughly 65 cents of every dollar in incomes derives from wood and wood products."[18]

Reminders occasionally popped up of other ways of making forests. Another convergence: in both regions, the value of forest land to elites owed a debt to earlier residents—and to the violence of the state. Earlier forms of forest management had *made* the forests that states and corporations now claimed.

> **1954 Oregon.** The U.S. federal government grabs the Klamath Reservation for the national forest system.

> **1954 central Japan.** The newly organized Japanese Self-Defense Forces take over village forests on Mt. Fuji's north slope as practice grounds. But these forests are the common-access satoyama woodlands of eleven villages. Villagers say military practice disrupts the ecosystem and damages the trees. In the mid-1980s, perhaps even as the Klamath Tribes are being reinstated, villagers win a lawsuit for compensation to their commons.[19]

Optimism over industrial forestry did not last long. In Japan, the problem began as early as the 1960s, when enthusiasm over tree plantations ended. Wood imports had begun. Between the end of the war and 1960, the Japanese government had prohibited the importation of timber to save foreign currency in order to buy oil, which was imagined as a strategic resource. But by 1960, oil had become cheap, and the construction industry had pressured the government to open the gates to foreign wood. The first breath of coming domestic difficulties came with a new disparity between the prices of sugi and hinoki, which until the 1960s had been similar. In 1965, the entry of U.S. Pacific Northwest timber into the Japanese market changed this. Hemlock, Douglas fir, and pine competed with sugi, a softwood, but not hinoki, which could be reserved for finer uses.[20] In addition, the wage rate for forest workers rose, thus discouraging forest maintenance.[21] By 1969, Japan's measure of self-sufficiency in timber had fallen for the first time to less than 50 percent.[22]

The 1960s were, in contrast, a time of optimism in Oregon—in part because of the Japanese market for Oregon's wood. Here is how historian William Robbins described that period: "When I arrived in Oregon in the early 1960s, loggers cut trees to water's edge, 'cat skinners' drove bulldozers through streambeds, and some of the largest timberland owners were indifferent to reforesting cutover land. Willamette Valley farmers plowed from fence row to riverbank, removed hedgerows, and drained sloughs to create ever larger fields, all in the interest of economies of scale."[23] Expansion still seemed to answer all problems.

Robbins's description prefigured the concerns of the next decade: By the 1970s, environmental activists were complaining about Pacific Northwest forests. In 1970, the National Environmental Policy Act required environmental impact statements. Voices were raised against herbicide spraying of forests, which had been linked to miscarriages. Critics opposed clear-cutting. Public forest managers were pressed to attend to environmental goals. So, too, in Japan: in 1973, new national policy called for environmental goals in national forests.

But perhaps the most important events of the 1970s for both forests were happening elsewhere. In the 1960s, Philippine wood imports to Japan had increased, but easily logged Philippine wood was already running out. In 1967, Indonesia passed a new forest law that assigned all forests to the state, which then used timber to court foreign investment. In the 1970s and 1980s, logs for Japan came flooding out of Indonesia, and later out of other parts of Asia.[24] Domestic industrial timber competed with easy pickings elsewhere. By 1980, the prices of Japanese domestic wood had fallen so low that almost no one could afford to harvest trees. Although intensive management was still strongly promoted in Oregon, the end was coming. By the 1990s, the timber companies had left, the Forest Service was broke, and the dream of intensive public management was in ruin.

I wrote of Oregonian ruin in the previous chapter. What of Japanese forests? As mentioned above, sugi and hinoki were planted densely on steep slopes, with the expectation of manual weeding, thinning, and pruning, followed by manual harvesting. The fact that everyone's trees were the same age did not help prices. It became too expensive to weed, thin, and prune, and even too expensive to harvest these forests. Crowding led to pests and diseases; the timber became less and less saleable.

Many Japanese came to dislike these forests. The pollen of sugi drifted over the countryside in clouds, causing allergies and stopping some families from leaving the city for fear of affecting their children. Hikers avoided these dark and monotonous places. The young plantings had encouraged herbaceous weeds, which in turn had encouraged a spike in the deer population; as the trees grew up and shaded out undergrowth, the deer had nothing to eat and became pests in villages and towns. The quest for controlled abundance that once had foreigners calling Japan "the green archipelago" had led to ruined forests.[25]

As Mitsuo Fujiwara put it: "[M]ost forests will remain uncut and will progress from middle to old age because forest owners have lost interest in silviculture. . . . If forests are simply left to age without being tended, they will not produce good-quality timber, nor will they perform the environmental function expected of well-maintained, mature forests."[26]

The effect of industrial ruins on living things depends on which living things we follow. For some insects and parasites, ruined industrial forests proved a bonanza. For other species, the rationalization of the forest itself—before ruination—proved disastrous. Somewhere between these extremes lie the world-building proclivities of matsutake.

The decline in matsutake in Japan resulted from the loss of actively maintained village woodlands since the 1950s, particularly owing to their conversion to sugi and hinoki plantations. After the 1970s, it was too expensive for owners to maintain them; the making of new plantations stopped. That there are significant patches of pine and broadleaf forest left at all, then, derives from this change in prices and resulting forestry practices. If there is still matsutake forest, it is because not all that forest was felled to make way for sugi and hinoki. In this sense, the matsutake forest is in debt to the violent deforestation of Southeast Asia—at least if one takes for granted Japan's inflamed pursuit of plantations beforehand. Although matsutake do not grow in Japan's ruined plantations, they grow because of their ruin, which saved other forests from conversion.

This is the spot of common ground with Oregon forests where matsutake flourish. At the height of the postwar logging boom in Oregon, in the 1960s and 1970s, the most important market for Oregon's timber was Japan. But emerging Southeast Asian wood was so cheap that Oregon eventually could not compete. It was this problem as much as the more-heralded rise of environmental lawsuits that drove the timber companies out of Oregon. With prices low, the companies wanted cheaper wood, and they saw it first in the regrowing pines of the U.S. South and then, with the continuing mobility of capital, in supply-chain timber around the world, wherever local strongmen make deforestation cheap. With the departure of the timber companies, the Forest Service lost both goals and resources. Intensive management for timber was no longer either necessary or possible. Replanting with superior stock, systematic thinning and selection, spraying poisons to kill insects and weeds: none of these were worth discussing. Had such programs been put into place, matsutake would have suffered. Intensively managed plantations have not suited matsutake. Besides, foragers might not have been welcome among expensive timber; certainly, no one would have devised management plans to suit them. Oregon's matsutake forests, then, also owe their flourishing to the low price of global timber. Matsutake forests in Oregon and central Japan are joined in their common dependence on the making of industrial forest ruin.

Perhaps you imagine that I am trying to dress up this ruin or to make lemonade from lemons. Not at all. What engages me is the wholesale, interconnected, and seemingly unstoppable ruination of forests across the world such that even the most geographically, biologically, and culturally disparate forests are still linked in a chain of destruction.

It is not just forests that disappear that are affected, as in Southeast Asia, but also the forests that manage to remain standing. If all our forests are buffeted by such winds of destruction, whether capitalists find them desirable or throw them aside, we have the challenge of living in that ruin, ugly and impossible as it is.

And yet heterogeneity remains important; it is impossible to explain the situation through the actions of a single hammer striking every nail with the same stroke. The difference between disappearing forests, forests plagued by overcrowding and pests, and forests left to grow when conversions to plantations prove uneconomic, matters. Intersecting historical processes produced forest ruins in Oregon and Japan, but it would be preposterous to argue that forest-making forces and reactions are therefore everywhere the same. The singularity of interspecies gatherings matters; that's why the world remains ecologically heterogeneous despite globe-spanning powers. The intricacies of global coordination also matter; not all connections have the same effects. To write a history of ruin, we need to follow broken bits of many stories and to move in and out of many patches. In the play of global power, indeterminate encounters are still important.

. . . in Gaps and Patches

16
Science as Translation

AS WITH CAPITALISM, IT IS USEFUL TO CONSIDER science a translation machine. It is machinic because a phalanx of teachers, technicians, and peer reviewers stands ready to chop off excess parts and to hammer those that remain into their proper places. It is translational because its insights are drawn from diverse ways of life. Most scholars have studied the translational features of science only as they contribute to the machinic ones.[1] Translation helps them watch the elements of science come together into a unified system of knowledge and practice. There has been less attention to the messy process of translation as jarring juxtaposition and miscommunication. In part this is because science studies has only too rarely been willing to stray outside of that imagined entity, the West. Science studies needs postcolonial theory to extend itself beyond the common sense of this self-imposed box. In postcolonial theory, translation shows us misfits as well as joins.[2] Thus Shiho Satsuka watches *nature* emerge in just this kind of mixed-up, unresolved translation. In transnational practices for interpreting nature, she shows, shared training can go hand and hand with the eruption of difference.[3]

Translation in this sense creates patches of incoherence and incompatibility in science. To the extent that there are separate bodies of research, review, and reading, such patches may persist despite crosscutting forms of training and communication. These patches are neither closed nor isolated; they shift with new materials.[4] Their distinctiveness is not prior logic but an effect of the convergence. Watching them returns me to the open-ended gatherings I am calling assemblages. Here layered, inconsistent, and jumbled ontologies form even within the domain of the machine. Matsutake science and forestry are vivid examples; this chapter explores messy translation and the formation of knowledge patches through it.

To begin with, if science is an international enterprise, why might there be *national* matsutake sciences? The answer requires attention to the infrastructure of science, which segregates even as it draws together. Matsutake science is national to the extent that it is tied to state-sponsored forestry institutes. Forestry emerged as a science of state governance and continues a close relationship. Even in its cosmopolitan reach, forestry is national. Already, we are on the road to divergent assemblages. But the situation is even more peculiar. Why has established research had so little influence across national borders? Why are the gaps so great, despite common training, international conferences, and public-domain publication? The answers here begin with the exclusion of Japan from North American and European common sense. Matsutake science and forestry are well established in Japan. Everywhere else, they are new, emerging with the commercialization of matsutake. One might expect that Japanese matsutake science would be the mother tradition that inspires new science elsewhere. Except in Korea, this is not the case.[5] Scientists in matsutake-exporting countries are busy inventing their own matsutake sciences. This is not the universal science we are taught to expect. Following its uneven development shows us science as postcolonial translation.

Alternative performances of "nature" are at stake. Consider their different takes on human disturbance. Drawing from satoyama research, Japanese scientists argue that matsutake forests are threatened by too little human disturbance. Abandoned village forests shade out pines, losing matsutake. In contrast, in the United States, scientists argue that matsutake forests are threatened by too much human disturbance.

Reckless harvesting kills off species. This is not a debate: despite the fact that both groups of scientists circulate internationally, there has been almost no communication about these positions. Furthermore, scientists in Japan and in the United States tend to use contrasting investigative strategies—particularly on issues of site selection and scale. This removes the possibility of direct comparisons across their respective results. In this process, segregated patches of knowledge and research practice are formed.

That divergences matter is particularly evident when alternative sciences arrive in the same place. In China, matsutake science and forestry are caught between Japanese and U.S. trajectories. In the matsutake forests of China's northeast, Japanese scientists have sturdy collaborations with Chinese counterparts.[6] But in Yunnan, U.S. experts in conservation and development have arrived in droves, and matsutake science has been drawn into their sphere of influence. Chinese scholars see their job as catching up with "international," that is, English-language science. As one young scientist explained, the young and ambitious never read Japanese sources because out-of-date older scholars who have no command of English can read them. U.S. approaches have had the power to set policy in Yunnan: Yunnan matsutake have been entered on the CITES list of endangered species; regulations against uncontrolled pickers and picking have been drawn up.[7] Yet Yunnan's forests are nothing like U.S. matsutake forests. As I argued in chapter 13, they have affinities to Japan's satoyama. American experts do not recognize the landscape dynamics of such forests. But I am jumping ahead of myself. How did Japanese and U.S. knowledge patches develop, and then spread?

Modern matsutake science began in Japan in the early twentieth century; after World War II its champion was Kyoto University's Minoru Hamada.[8] Dr. Hamada saw how matsutake could enlarge science through its position at key intersections between applied and basic research—and between vernacular and expert knowledge. Matsutake's economic value generated government and private support; it also opened barely explored biological research trajectories involving interspecies interactions. To explore those interactions, Dr. Hamada was willing to listen to peasant experience. For example, he used the folk term *shiro* ("castle," "white," or "plant bed") to refer to the mycelial mats—indeed, white, defense-oriented growth beds—in which matsutake fungus grows. He learned from peasant knowledge about shiro, including early attempts to cultivate the fungus.[9] Meanwhile, he explored the implications of the shiro's interspecies relationships with trees, even as it raised philosophical questions. Might we think, he asked, of mutualisms as a form of love?[10]

Dr. Hamada's students—and their students—spread and deepened matsutake research. One, Makoto Ogawa, initiated a program for matsutake research in prefectural forestry offices across Japan. Prefectural forest researchers addressed applied questions with simple equipment and field-based methods; they kept the dialogue between vernacular and expert knowledge lively and productive.[11] Even university- and institute-based researchers in this legacy have continued to address farmers, writing popular books and field manuals as well as professional articles.[12] At the heart of their questions is the decline of matsutake since the 1970s—and the possibility of reversing this decline. On the one hand, they have worked to cultivate matsutake in the laboratory; on the other, they have explored the conditions most conducive to its growth in forests. Thus some have become involved with initiatives to save Japan's satoyama forests. Matsutake cannot flourish in Japan without revitalizing pine forests.

Thinking of matsutake in relation to the decline of satoyama led the researchers of this school to emphasize matsutake's relationality, not only with other species but also with the nonliving environment.[13] Researchers investigated the plants, slopes, soils, light, bacteria, and other fungi in matsutake environments. Matsutake is never seen as self-contained, but always in relation—and thus site specific. To promote matsutake, these researchers advise attention to the site—and to a regime of human disturbance to favor pine. In neglected forests, *more* disturbance is needed. One pair of researchers called this the "orchard method."[14] Through favoring pine, matsutake becomes a hoped-for weed.

Meanwhile, both private companies and university-based researchers have been busy trying to cultivate matsutake in laboratories. As long as prices remain high, what a prize that would be! For a decade starting in the mid-1990s, Kazuo Suzuki gathered a high-profile research team at the University of Tokyo to investigate the conditions of matsutake cultivation. The Suzuki lab brought in international postdoctoral fellows, adding to the cosmopolitanism of Japanese matsutake science. This research turned away from field-based methods to explore biochemistry and genomic studies. Results have not so far included successful cultivation of mushrooms.[15] However, many insights have been gained, especially about fungus-tree relations: relations remain central here. At one point, Dr. Suzuki brought mature pine trees into his laboratory, constructing basement cages in which root symbioses could be observed and measured in detail.

Why hasn't this research been influential in the United States? The separation between U.S. and Japanese approaches to matsutake science was not ingrained from the start. When matsutake first came to the attention of forestry researchers in the U.S. Pacific Northwest in the 1980s, they set out to find out about it—from Japanese research.[16] Central Washington University's David Hosford went to Japan to work with Hiroyuki Ohara, who had trained with Dr. Hamada. Dr. Hosford also had a number of scientific articles translated from Japanese. His work resulted in an extraordinary publication, coauthored with American colleagues: *Ecology and Management of the Commercially Harvested American Matsutake*.[17] The publication is as close to Japanese research as anything published in the United States. The opening summarizes the history of matsutake in Japan, and it proceeds to Japanese-style research in Washington State, which Dr. Ohara helped supervise. It even describes site-specific vegetation patterns in U.S. matsutake areas. However, it also includes a caveat: "American foresters . . . are likely to view the Japanese methods for enhancing matsutake production in a different context . . . [because] forest management goals differ greatly."[18] This caveat turned out to be fateful. All subsequent U.S. Forest Service research on matsutake takes Japanese studies into account only by citing Hosford.

What was the block? One Pacific Northwest researcher told me that Japanese studies are not very useful because they are "descriptive." In untangling what "descriptive" might mean, and what is wrong with it, the cultural and historical specificity of U.S. forestry research comes into focus. Descriptive means site-specific, that is, attuned to indeterminate encounters and thus nonscalable. U.S. forestry researchers are under pressure to develop analyses compatible with the scalable management of timber trees. This requires that matsutake studies scale up to timber. Site selection in Japanese research follows patches of fungal growth, not timber grids.

Forest Service–sponsored matsutake research has addressed one big question: Can matsutake as an economic product be managed sustainably?[19] This question takes shape within the history of Forest Service efforts at timber management. In this history, nontimber forest products cannot be seen unless they make themselves compatible with timber. Thus the stand—the unit of manageable timber—is the basic landscape unit U.S. foresters can see.[20] The fungal patch ecologies studied by Japanese scientists just do not register on this grid. The scale of U.S. forestry research on matsutake is adjusted accordingly. Some studies use random transects to sample matsutake on a scale that is compatible with timber stands.[21] Others build models through which fungal patches can be scaled up.[22] These studies devise monitoring techniques to make matsutake visible on the scale of timber's rationalization.

One of the key questions of U.S. matsutake research concerns pickers: Are pickers destroying their resource? This question draws from U.S. forestry history, with its central query: Are loggers destroying their resource? This legacy suggested research on pickers' techniques. As with loggers, the point of impact is imagined as the harvest. Studies have found that raking the ground lessens future mushroom production; if mushrooms are gently removed, future production is unharmed.[23] Pickers must be trained to harvest properly. The effect of other forms of human disturbance on mushroom harvests—e.g., thinning, fire suppression, or silviculture—has not been studied; it does not jump to the minds of researchers worried about overharvesting. This is U.S. sustainability: a defense against greed-based popular destruction.

In contrast to Japan, in the U.S. foresters are concerned about dangerous human disturbance. Too much, not too little human activity destroys the forest. By chance, "raking" is symbolic of disturbance in both sciences—but with opposite valences. Raking destroys matsutake forests in the U.S. by disturbing underground fungal bodies. Raking makes productive matsutake forests in Japan by uncovering mineral soil for pine. These are very different forests, with different challenges. Advocacy for pine is unnecessary in the conifer forests of the U.S. Pacific Northwest (although opening the national forests to citizens' thinning groups might be great). The contrast, however, raises issues other than which approach is right: it shows the productivity of basic questions and assumptions. Cosmopolitan science is made in emerging patches of research, which grow into or reject each other in varied encounters.

Returning to Yunnan, the influence of U.S. approaches should now be clearer. This would be prime country in which to ask about relations between matsutake, oaks-and-pines, and people: How might people sustain oak-pine forests for matsutake? Instead, researchers imagine matsutake, American style, as a self-contained, scalable product, whose accounting requires no attention to relations with other species. The questions that follow about sustainability ask not about relational forests but about picker practices: Are pickers destroying their own resource? When researchers ask villagers about declines in matsutake harvests, they do not ask about forests. The question of decline is addressed as if mushrooms inhabited the landscape alone.[24] This is the American question, the question learned from the experience of rationalizing timber in the hopes of saving it from greedy loggers. But mushroom pickers are not loggers.[25]

Despite the hegemony of American frameworks among scientists, there are audiences for Japanese matsutake research in Yunnan. Matsutake export businesses have ties to Japan because that is where the mushrooms go. Furthermore, Japanese science explores how humans can manage forests to increase the yield of matsutake mushrooms. In contrast, Americans explore how the mushroom harvest should be regulated to keep harvesters from destroying their resource. Japanese forest management promises more mushrooms for the market; American science promises fewer. Yunnan matsutake businesses have reason to prefer the Japanese paradigm. When a prominent Japanese scientist had his book on matsutake management translated into Chinese, it was the matsutake business association in Yunnan, not the scientists, who translated it, and even after its translation, the scientists did not know about it.[26]

All of this brings me to the first international matsutake studies conference held in Kunming in September 2011. The Yunnan matsutake business association organized it in concert with a team of Japanese scientists. Also in attendance were a group of North Korean matsutake scientists—and the North American–based Matsutake Worlds Research Group. Communication was made difficult by the fact that translators were provided only for the ceremonial opening session, and even then the translators were overwhelmed by discussion in an unfamiliar field. The rest of the conference was supposed to be in English, but participants struggled with that standard. Still, language was only part of the problem. We each had completely different ideas about the point of matsutake studies. Most of the Chinese participants hoped to promote Chinese matsutake, and so they spoke of cultural values, new processing techniques, and efforts by the government to protect the mushroom. The Japanese participants, in contrast, were excited by the opportunity to see non-Japanese varieties of matsutake, which might have better potential for cultivation. (Some Chinese objected; they didn't want to be data.) The North Koreans begged for copies of international scientific articles, blocked to them at home. And dancing around this were the North American anthropologists, with our metacommentary on science and society.

We had different agendas. Yet in two days of joint fieldwork before the papers, we watched each other watching the forest. It was an amazing opportunity to see several kinds of science-in-action performed simultaneously. Chinese participants witnessed to the diversity of the forest's fungal life and the newly cordial relations between peasants and international experts. Japanese scholars savored the rare chance to work with foreign fungus–host tree relations. North Koreans were eager to learn new techniques. No one thought this meeting was unproductive. We practiced arts of listening: the recognition of differences as the beginning of work together.

There were also silences. Consider who did not attend. U.S. Forest Service research had been curtailed several years before by cuts in federal funding; no U.S. foresters would be sent. Just across town, a Chinese research institution boasted several matsutake researchers, and they also were not in attendance. This was a different crowd, assembled by Chinese businesses and Japanese scientists. In the confused translations and missing persons of meetings such as this, gaps and patches are maintained.

Sometimes individuals make a difference in translating across patches, fertilizing new developments. The Kunming meeting emerged only because of the efforts of an individual. As a child, Yang Huiling met a Japanese anthropologist studying her Bai community in Yunnan. She went to study in Japan and became involved in the matsutake trade. She facilitated the ties with Japanese scientists that made the Kunming meeting possible. Bringing together research traditions, she had the opportunity to begin a new patch formation.

Cosmopolitan science is composed of patches—and is richer for it. Yet individuals and events sometimes make a difference. Like mushroom spores, they may germinate in unexpected places, reshaping patch geographies.

Reading forests, Yunnan. Identifying an evergreen oak. Oaks form interbreeding hybrid swarms, and yet distinctions are somehow maintained. Names only open the mystery.

17
Flying Spores

All of this is, of course, speculation.

—*Mycologist Jianping Xu, discussing matsutake evolution*

LANDSCAPES AND LANDSCAPE KNOWLEDGE DEVELOP in patches. Matsutake shiro (mycelial mats) model the process: Patches spread, mutate, merge, reject each other, and die back. The hard work—and the creative, productive play—of science, as well as emerging ecologies, happens in patches. But one might also sometimes wonder: What moves beyond them, making them? For matsutake, there are also flying spores.

Both in forests and in science, spores open our imaginations to another cosmopolitan topology. Spores take off toward unknown destinations, mate across types, and, at least occasionally, give rise to new organisms—a beginning for new kinds. Spores are hard to pin down; that is their grace. In thinking about landscapes, spores guide us to in-population heterogeneity. In thinking about science, spores model open-ended communication and excess: the pleasures of speculation.

Why spores?

Koji Iwase first started me thinking about spores. We were having lunch in Kyoto with Shiho Satsuka and Michael Hathaway; the tape recorder wasn't on. I was curious about why matsutake is so cosmopolitan: How did it spread around the northern hemisphere? Dr. Iwase is generous with foreigners and willing to guide them. So he mentioned that the stratosphere is full of fungal spores; at those high altitudes they blow around the earth. It's not clear, he continued, how many of these spores survive to germinate in distant places. Ultraviolet radiation kills, and most spores are viable only for a short time, perhaps a few weeks. He didn't know if a matsutake spore could survive to germinate on another continent. Even if it did, he explained, it would have to find another germinating spore; without fusing, it would die in a few days. Still, over the course of millions of years, one might imagine that spores could spread the species.[1]

There is something about the stratosphere that inspires airy dreams. Imagine, spores circling the globe! My thoughts took off with drifting spores, chasing my protagonist across eons, across continents. I took my questions to mycologists here and there around the world, chasing their thoughts, too, through the stratosphere. I found a cosmopolitan science of speculation about origins and the making of kinds across space and time. Unlike the discontinuous patches of applied forestry, the science of matsutake speciation is not patchlike. There are strong winds of international consensus about methods; the materials—mushroom samples and DNA sequences—circulate across borders. Individuals and sometimes labs develop stories, bits of expertise, and even biases. But there are no schools, no patches. All this work is off the clock: no one gives out grants to study the eon-crossing travels of a mushroom. Scientists turn to these questions out of love—and because the methods and materials are there. Perhaps one day the combined results and speculations will lead us, like spores, to something new, they reason. For now, it is just the pleasure of thinking: the spore-filled airy stratosphere of the mind.

What are these materials and methods that circulate?

Henning Knudsen showed me the University of Copenhagen Botanical Garden's fungal collection, of which he is curator.[2] Type specimens arc stored here: drawers and drawers of folded envelopes, each guarding a dried fungus. When a new species is named, the namer sends a sample to the herbarium, and those specimens become the "type" for that species. Researchers from around the world can ask to see the type; the herbarium sends the original material. The herbarium system emerged with the northern European passion for identifying plants, which also resulted in Latin binomial names. It was a feature of European conquest; it also created the basis for transnational communication through the circulation of specimens. Researchers around the world know species through type specimens collected in herbaria.

Dr. Knudsen does not think matsutake spread through spores in the stratosphere; it's just too improbable that they would find mates. Instead, their distribution followed the forests: they spread together with the trees. This took a long time, but across the northern half of the earth, many species spread—ever so slowly—together. Some, such as *Boletus edulis*, may have spread across the top, from Alaska to Siberia. But the homogeneity of northern species is overstated. Many species that used to be seen as uniformly found across the global north turn out to be different species, he said.[3]

The rejection of uniform cosmopolitan species draws not from the circulation of herbarium samples but from a revolutionary new technology, DNA sequencing, which offers a new way to define "species." Mycologists examine particular DNA sequences—e.g., the internal transcribed spacer (ITS) region—that tend to be conserved within species but show variations across them. Jean-Marc Moncalvo, Dr. Knudsen's counterpart at the Royal Ontario Museum in Toronto, explained that more than a 5 percent divergence in the ITS sequence indicates a new species.[4] DNA sequencing does not reject the materials and methods of herbaria; most comparisons across species use herbarium samples. But there is a new material here in circulation: the DNA sequences themselves. Databases have made it possible for scientists around the world to consult DNA sequenced by others. The simple precision of DNA sequencing has taken the scientific world by storm: there are no alternatives. It seems so powerful that scientists keep making up questions based on the availability of this answer.

Of course, there are still pockets of difference. Dr. Moncalvo explained that, as recently as the 1980s, Chinese mycologists had trouble communicating freely with Europeans and North Americans. One Chinese mycologist sent him samples of fungi hidden between the pages of reprints. As a result of isolation, he said, Chinese taxonomies are strange. Internationally, there are no rules for naming a genus (the first name in a Latin binomial), so Chinese taxonomers have added "China" to genus names, assembling *Sinoboletus* instead of *Boletus*, and confusing foreign counterparts. Furthermore, they recognize species indiscriminately. They claim to have twenty-one species of oyster mushrooms in Yunnan, but there are only fourteen species recognized in the world. Tiny morphological differences are given too much attention. But this is changing now, he said, as young scientists with international training take over.

What do these materials and methods tell us about "kinds"?

Species has always been a slippery concept, and DNA sequencing—despite its precision—has not made it easier to handle. Classically, species boundaries were defined by the inability of individuals on each side to mate and produce fertile offspring. That's easy enough to figure for horses and donkeys. (They mate but do not produce fertile offspring.) But what about fungi? Dr. Moncalvo walks me through what it would take to find out if two different fungal strains were species according to this definition. You would need to germinate one single spore of each in culture, get those spores to mate, somehow force them to produce a mushroom, then get its spores to mate and produce mushrooms. For a fungus such as matsutake, for which no one has succeeded in producing a single mushroom in culture, and whose spores don't even germinate if alone, such experiments are hardly worth conceiving. Besides, Dr. Moncalvo added, imagine the hapless graduate student who devoted a dissertation to finding a species boundary of even the easiest-to-handle mushroom. Where would he or she get a job?

All this matters in getting to know matsutake across its diasporic locations. Twenty years ago, there were many, many species of matsutake scattered around the northern hemisphere, with more emerging constantly as scientists found them. Now there are just a few—and growing fewer. This is not because of extinction. DNA sequencing in the ITS region has allowed scientists to argue that most of those kinds of matsutake are really just one kind: *Tricholoma matsutake*. *T. matsutake* now appears to spread across most of the northern hemisphere, not just across Eurasia but into North and Central America. Only *Tricholoma magnivelare*, the matsutake of the North American Pacific Northwest, is continuing to stand clearly as a separate species, and even it is very close, in its DNA signature, to *T. matsutake*.[5]

The precision of DNA sequencing, which allows such determinations, also undermines confidence in the species as the basic category for understanding kinds. I first met Kazuo Suzuki, now president of Japan's Forestry and Forest Products Research Institute, when new results were coming in about the identity of China's oak-loving matsutake, at that time called *Tricholoma zangii*.[6] In Japan, matsutake are associated with pines; only false matsutake are found with broadleafs. The association between matsutake and conifers seemed part of its species definition. DNA studies showing the close relation between China's oak-loving matsutake and Japan's exclusively pine-loving ones caught researchers by surprise. Dr. Suzuki brought his younger colleague from Tokyo University, Dr. Matsushita, to our meeting to tell me the news himself: His examination of the ITS sequence had shown no species difference between oak and pine lovers.[7] But Dr. Suzuki, who had worked with matsutake for many years, did not accept this finding as the whole story. "It depends on what question you ask," he explained. He told me about Armillaria root rot, a complex of species in which clear species boundaries may not be relevant. Armillaria root rot spreads across whole forests, stimulating boasts of "the largest organism in the world." Differentiating "individuals" becomes difficult, as these individuals contain many genetic signatures, helping the fungus adapt to new environmental situations.[8] Species are open-ended when even individuals are so molten, so long-lived, and so unwilling to draw lines of reproductive isolation. "Armillaria root rot is fifty species in one species," he said; "it depends on what you are dividing species for."

I remember the discussion vividly: I was at the edge of my seat. Dr. Suzuki was treating species in the way cultural anthropologists treat their units: as frames that must be continually questioned to retain their use. The kinds we know, he implied, develop at that fragile junction between knowledge-making and the world. Kinds are always in process because we study them in new ways. This makes them no less real, even as they seem more fluid and beckoning of questions.

Ignatio Chapela, a forest pathologist at the University of California, Berkeley, was even more adamant that the idea of "species" limits the stories we can tell about kinds. "This binomial system of naming things is kind of quaint, but it is a complete artifact," he told me. "You define things with two words and they become an archetypal species. In fungi, we have no idea what a species is. No idea. . . . A species is a group of organisms that potentially can exchange genetic material, have sex. That applies to organisms that reproduce sexually. So already in plants, where out of a clone you can have change as time goes by, you have problems with species. . . . You move out of vertebrates to the cnidarians, corals, and worms, and the exchange of DNA, and the way groups are made, are very different from us. . . . You go to fungi or bacteria, and the systems are completely different—completely crazy by our standards. A long-lived clone can all of a sudden go sexual: you can have hybridization in which whole big chunks of chromosomes are brought in; you have polyploidization or duplication of chromosomes, where a completely new thing comes out; you have symbiotization, the capture of, say, a bacterium that allows you to either use the whole bacterium as part of yourself or use parts of that bacterium's DNA for your own genome. You've become something entirely different. Where do you break down the species?"

To compare different kinds of matsutake, Dr. Chapela used herbarium specimens as well as fresh samples and sequenced ITS-region DNA. But he refused to imagine his results as fixed species. "You start getting these groupings that you can only name relative to each other. You can't call them a species. . . . In the old taxonomic approach you say, 'this is my ideal'—it's completely Platonic—and everything is going to compare as a missed approximation to that ideal. Nobody will be the same as this, but you compare and see how close they are to this ideal. . . . If it becomes too different—by whatever measure, and the measures are completely arbitrary—you say, 'oh this must be a different species.'" To avoid a false "scientific cover," he speaks of "matsutakes" as all the varied kinds that enter the Japanese trade. His study did, however, find distinct genetic groupings by region. That means, he said, that genetic materials are not freely exchanged across those regions. "If you see good patterning, if you see good separation, that tells you that there is not much exchange between these groups." These data show that cross-regional exchange of spores is unlikely on a regular basis.

One down for the long-distance travel of spores. But other possibilities have just become more thrilling. How then do kinds travel?

Dr. Chapela, working with his colleague Dr. Garbelotto, has a story to tell about matsutake's travel.[10] The Eocene ancestral population, he argues, developed in North America's Pacific Northwest, where *T. magnivelare* continues to associate with both broadleafs and conifers, in resonance with that broadleaf-loving ancestor. The rest of the matsutake group jumped to conifers and has followed conifer forests ever after around the northern hemisphere. When conifers retreated into refugia, matsutake followed, especially with pine. Wherever the pine forest went, matsutake went too. Migrating across the Bering Straits, matsutake colonized Asia, and then Europe. The Mediterranean Sea blocked gene exchange between southern Europe and North Africa; populations on each side are independent extensions of the vast Eurasian trek. Meanwhile, Chapela and Garbelotto imagine that southeastern North America was colonized by matsutake from the rich pine-oak refugia in Mexico.

Their story was shocking, in part, because at the time they published, most people thought of matsutake as an "Asian" species complex. After all, only Japanese and Koreans loved matsutake—and thought of it as their own. How could it be a North American mushroom that came late to Asia—even if millions of years ago? (Chapela and Garbelotto date the separation of *T. magnivelare* and other matsutake as having occurred 28 million years ago, with the rise of the Rocky Mountains.) Indeed, not everyone agrees with the story they tell; this is an open-ended field. Dr. Yamanaka of the Kyoto Mycological Institute argues for a Himalayan origin for matsutake.[11] Many new species came into being with the rise of the Himalayas, which forcefully threw old kinds into new environments, stimulating difference. At the time of Chapela and Garbelotto's research, the evidence of host differentiation among matsutake in southwest China was not readily available, at least in California. It turns out that Chinese matsutake associate not just with conifers but with *Quercus* as well as *Castanopsis* and *Lithocarpus*, which find their center of species diversity in the Himalayas. (Dr. Yamanaka reminds me that the major broadleaf host of North America's *T. magnivelare* is tanoak, the only non-Asian *Lithocarpus*.[12] Might this be a clue?) Dr. Yamanaka found matsutake shiro in China associating with both conifer and broadleaf hosts. He argues for Himalayan origins, based in part on the sheer variety of mycorrhizal arrangements in that area. Diversity is often a sign of time in place.

Yet even newer research has shown that southwest China's matsutake are not particularly genetically diverse, at least in the ITS region most commonly sequenced by researchers. They are a whole lot less diverse than Japanese matsutake, which everyone agrees to be latecomers on the evolutionary scene. But this does not mean they are a newer population. Jianping Xu of Canada's McMaster University suggests that Chinese matsutake just fill up more of the available space than in Japan.[13] This "saturation," he points out, can lead to longer-living clones with less genetic competition. The stress of industrial pollution might also lead to genetic competition in Japan. Southwest China is far less industrialized. Diversity is not just about time in place.

Dr. Xu brings back the question of spores. "Many mushroom species are widespread. They are opportunistic; whenever there is food they can survive. Dispersal is not such a significant barrier for most of them." He brings up the "panspermia" hypothesis, which posits that spores are everywhere, traveling even in outer space. "For most microbial species, you can find them everywhere. Dispersal is not the barrier. It's whether they are able to survive in those environments." He jokes, "It's like Chinese now, they are everywhere. If there are business opportunities, you are probably going to find Chinese; if there's a small town, you'll probably find a Chinese restaurant." We laugh together. He talks of how well spores are dispersed. "For many species, there are limited genetic differences among populations from very different geographic areas." One example is the bacteria in our mouths: he says that the bacteria in the mouths of middle-class urban Chinese are vastly different from those of their peasant neighbors—but just the same as the bacteria of North Americans on a similar diet. It is the environment, not the location, that matters. For many fungi, too, he confirms, "dispersal is not the problem—especially since humans emerged."

There's a new thought. Humans?

Dr. Xu is not the only one who thinks that human trade and travel have dispersed fungal spores. Dr. Moncalvo finds that very significant, although he disagrees with the idea that spore clouds are everywhere.

("Mushroom populations are restricted and well defined. The same morphology on two different continents is usually separated by genetic distance.") There is exchange through spores, he argues, but it is occasional, not constant. But "exchange may be much more common now because there is more trade and more travel." For example, *Amanita muscaria* was transferred to New Zealand in the 1950s and is now spreading. It is not even out of the question that matsutake spread across the Atlantic with human contact. "There are a lot of Scots pines here. [Scots pine is a major north Eurasian matsutake host, but it is not native to the New World.] Canadians, they still have the Queen on the coin, right? So they think the pine seedlings that are coming from Her Majesty's garden must be better quality than native pine." He shakes his head in mock horror, but it is a serious point. Perhaps matsutake traveled to eastern Canada on the roots of pine seedlings. Dr. Moncalvo does not dismiss the possibility of spread without humans, but he does think the spread must be recent, because eastern North American matsutake are so very similar to Eurasian ones. And, he adds, shocking me: who knows which way the spread went? "Especially if we find the two species [western America's *T. magnivelare* and cosmopolitan *T. matsutake*] coexisting in Central America and possibly in the southern Appalachians, that might be the origin. One [*T. magnivelare*] has been stuck on the west coast, the other [*T. matsutake*] has moved. That is something a phylogenetic study should be able to tell."

"How might both species have come to Mexico?" I ask. "It was a southern refugia during the glaciation," he explains. "It's a well-known phenomenon. The southern limit of oaks and pine are the mountains in Central America. You don't find them in South America. And you find them with altitude: When it gets cold, everything moves south. When it gets warm again, they move up to a higher altitude. Three thousand meters in Mexico is like sea level here. This can also explain some shuffling. Populations will grow back from local refugia, but they are not salmon, swimming back to the stream in which they were born. There is no reason that one goes one way or the other way. It's the ecosystem that moves; it's not the fungus that moves."

It's the ecosystem that moves: No wonder humans move so many other species without meaning to; we create new ecosystems all the time. And it's not just humans that change things.

"I rather think it can sometimes be events," Dr. Moncalvo explains to my repeated questions about how kinds spread. "That's something that many people cannot grasp. The time frame is huge. The tectonic separation between the southern and the northern hemisphere is 100 million years. So we find different species in the southern hemisphere and the northern hemisphere. Australia is a great example. So people say, 'Oh, they separated 100 million years ago.' But it's not true. Now that we have molecular data, we see it's incorrect in most cases. They are isolated, but there is sometimes transfer. But the transfer is not all the time, so we don't have something homogeneous. There could be one transfer per million years, or per ten million years. That transfer could be anything; it could be a tsunami wave, starting from the Philippines and crossing the equator—they don't usually cross the equator, but in 100 million years—and carried on the top of the wave, some soil and some wood with some animals hanging. It could also be wind. It could be anything." Once mycologists thought that southern and northern hemisphere mushrooms had been isolated for 100 million years, but DNA sequences now show that this could not possibly be true. For *Amanita*, for example, there are many groups with north-south ties, rather than just a single hemispheric dichotomy. Assumptions about slow and constant mutations in place are being displaced by attention to unusual events, indeterminate encounters.

How do kinds emerge, then, in local populations?

Dr. Xu explains it: Scale matters. One cannot use the same tools to study cross-continental and local diversity. The ITS region of fungal DNA is fine for studying big blocks of regional difference, but it is useless to study local populations. There, a completely different clump of DNA is needed to judge the variations that separate one group from another. Dr. Xu has found that single nucleotide polymorphisms (SNP) are good for population-level differentiations.[14] With this tool, he studied matsutake populations in China, finding little genetic difference between oak- and pine-loving matsutake but a significant geographic separation across sampled regions. Most important, perhaps, this separation added evidence that sexual reproduction is important in matsutake populations. *Spores rise again.*

In the world of fungi this is not at all self-evident. Fungi propagate through many mechanisms, and sexual reproduction through the mating of germinated spores is just one. A good deal of fungal propagation is clonal; some clones—including those of the famous Armillaria root rot— are large and very, very old. Fungi also propagate through asexual spores, which are produced in times of stress; with their thick walls, they withstand hard times to germinate when better conditions return. For some species, sexual reproduction is absent or rare. For matsutake, however, the evidence suggests that sexual spores are important. This is investigated by examining the genetic composition of clonal patches: Are they mutating independently or exchanging genetic materials? For example, do you find more genetic diversity in older forests rather than in younger ones, where you would expect a "founder effect" rather than free spore dispersal? For matsutake, the answer to this last question is yes; spores appear to be exchanged among patches of mycelial growth.[15] However, landscape features can block the exchange of spores; researchers found that ridges, for example, block genetic exchange among matsutake populations.[16]

This seems familiar enough—but don't relax. Matsutake does something strange and wonderful that can turn your idea of sexual reproduction upside down. *It was another meal—tea this time, in Tsukuba City, with Hitoshi Murata of the Forestry and Forest Products Research Institute and Matsutake Worlds team member Lieba Faier.*[17] *I was so excited when I understood that I spilled tea all over my tray.* Dr. Murata had been studying the genetics of matsutake populations. It was a painstaking process, since matsutake is not an easy research subject. Figuring out how to get spores to germinate was itself a problem; they germinated, he found, in the presence of other matsutake parts, for example, mushroom gills. This suggested that spores might germinate best on living shiros, that is, mycelial mats, including that of the parental body that gave rise to the mushroom.[18] And what happened then, when they germinated? This is where his research revealed something wondrous. Matsutake spores are haploid, that is, bearing only one series of chromosomes, rather than paired sets. We might expect them to mate with other haploid spores, thus making full pairs; they do. Human eggs and sperm join that way. But matsutake spores are capable of something else. They can join with body cells that already have chromosomal pairs. This is called "di-mon" mating, from the prefixes for "two"—the number of chromosome copies in fungal body cells—and "one"—the number in the germinating spore.[19] *It's as if I decided to mate with (not clone) my own arm: how queer.*

The spore brings new genetic material into the shiro, even if it is the shiro's offspring, because the shiro itself is a mosaic, a combination of multiple genomes. Even emerging from the same shiro, different mushrooms might have different genomes. Even emerging on the same mushroom, different spores might have different genomes. The genetic apparatus of the fungus is open-ended, able to add new material. This adds to its ability to adapt to environmental shifts and to mend internal damage. Evolution in one body: the fungus can discard less competitive genomes to pick up others. Diversity emerges right there inside the patch.[20]

Dr. Murata explains that he was able to ask these questions because of his unusual background for a mycologist: He was originally trained in bacteriology. Most mycologists come from botany, where they see one organism at a time, or ecology, where they see interactions across organisms. But bacteria are too small to care about one at a time; we know them in patterns and masses. As a bacteriologist, he knew about "quorum sensing," the ability of each bacterium to chemically sense the presence of others and to behave differently en masse. From his very first studies of fungi he found quorum sensing there: in fungal mosaics, each cell line can sense the others, forming mushrooms in unison. By examining fungi differently, a new object came into sight: the genetically diverse fungal body, the mosaic.

Mushrooms with genetically diverse spores! Mosaic bodies! Chemical sensing that creates communal effects! How strange and wonderful the world.

I struggle: Isn't it time to come back to patches, incompatible scales, and the importance of history? Shouldn't I return to multiple rhythms, the tempos through which patches emerge in both landscape and science? But how happy it feels to fly with spores and to experience cosmopolitan excess. For the moment, the reader must make do with hasty conclusions:

Spores vitalize matsutake populations through adding new genetic materials. Mushrooms produce many, many spores, and only a few of them germinate and mate, but it is enough to keep populations cosmopolitan and diverse. Some of that diversity is within the parental bodies that produced the spores. No "one" fungal body lives self-contained, removed from indeterminate encounters. The fungal body emerges in historical mergings—with trees, with other living and nonliving things, and with itself in other forms.

Scientists speculate about open-ended questions, including the evolution and spread of matsutake, in a sporelike way. Most of those thoughts never make a difference, but the few that do can revitalize the field. Cosmopolitan knowledge develops out of historical mergings—with research subjects, living and nonliving, and with itself in other forms.

Patches are productive, but there are also spores.

Interlude
Dancing

FORAGERS HAVE THEIR OWN WAYS OF KNOWING THE matsutake forest: they look for the lines of mushroom lives.[1] Being in the forest this way might be considered dance: lines of life are pursued through senses, movements, and orientations.. The dance is a form of forest knowledge—but not that codified in reports. And, although every forager dances in this sense, not all the dances are alike. Each dance is shaped by communal histories, with their disparate aesthetics and orientations. To lead you into the dance, then, I step back into the Oregon forest. First I go alone, then with a Japanese American elder, and then with two middle-aged Mien.

To find a good mushroom, I need all my senses. For there is a secret to matsutake mushroom picking: one rarely looks for mushrooms. Every now and then one spots a whole mushroom—probably discarded by animals or so old that worms have consumed it. Good mushrooms, however, are under the ground. Sometimes I pick up the pungent aroma before I find any mushrooms. Then my other senses are alert. My eyes sweep the ground, "like windshield wipers," as one picker explained. Sometimes I get down on the ground to look at a better angle, or even to feel.

I am searching for the signs of the mushroom's growth, its activity line. Mushrooms move the ground slightly as they grow, and one must look for that movement. People call it a bump, but that implies a well-defined hillock, very rare. Instead, I think of sensing a heave, an effect like the inhalation of breath in the chest. The heave is easy to imagine as the breath of the mushroom. There may be a crack, as if the mushroom's breath escaped. Mushrooms do not breathe like that—and yet this recognition of common life forms the basis of the dance.

There are lots of lumps and cracks in any forest floor, and most of them have nothing to do with mushrooms. Many of them are old, static, and without indication of life's movement. The matsutake picker searches for those that signal a living thing slowly, slowly pushing. One then feels the ground. The mushroom may be several inches below the surface, but a good picker knows, having sensed its liveliness, its life line.

Searching has a rhythm, both impassioned and still. Pickers describe their eagerness to get into the forest as a "fever." Sometimes, they say, they didn't plan to go, but the fever catches you. In the heat of the fever, one picks in the rain or snow, even at night with lights. One gets up before dawn to be there first, lest others find the mushrooms. Yet no one can find a mushroom by hurrying through the forest: "slow down," I was constantly advised. Inexperienced pickers miss most of the mushrooms by moving too fast, for only careful observation reveals those gentle heaves. Calm but fevered, impassioned but still: the picker's rhythm condenses this tension in a poised alertness.

Pickers also study the forest. They can name host trees. But tree classification only opens the door, determining the area a picker might search; it is not so helpful in actually finding mushrooms. Pickers do not waste much time looking up into trees. Our gaze is directed below, where the mushrooms rise through the heaving earth. Some pickers mention that they pay attention to the dirt, favoring areas where the soil looks right. But when I press for specifications, they always demur. One picker was probably tired of my asking, and so he explained: the right kind of soil is the soil where matsutake grows. So much for classification. Discourse has its limits here.

Rather than a class of soils, the picker scans for lines of life. It is not just the tree that is relevant but the story that the area around it tells. Matsutake is unlikely to be found in fertile, well-watered places; other fungi will grow there. If there are dwarf huckleberries, the ground is probably too wet. If heavy machinery has been through, this spells death for the fungus. If animals have left droppings and tracks, this is a place to look. If moisture has found a place to hide next to a rock or a log, this too is good.

There is one little plant on the forest floor that depends on matsutake for far more than minerals. Candy cane (*Allotropa virgata*) forms a red-and-white striped stalk adorned by flowers but completely without the chlorophyll that would allow it to make its own food. Instead, the plant drains sugars from matsutake, which in turn takes them from the trees.[2] Even after the flowers fade, candy cane's dry stalks can be seen in the forest, and they are an indicator of matsutake—whether fruiting, or just a ball of fungal threads underground.

Life lines are entangled: candy cane and matsutake; matsutake and its host trees; host trees and herbs, mosses, insects, soil bacteria, and forest animals; heaving bumps and mushroom pickers. Matsutake pickers are alert to life lines in the forest; searching with all the senses creates this alertness. It is a form of forest knowledge and appreciation without the completeness of classification. Instead, searching brings us to the liveliness of beings experienced as subjects rather than objects.

Hiro is an elder in an urban Japanese American community.[3] Now in his late eighties, he has led an exemplary working-class life. When World War II broke out, Hiro was a young man living on a farm with his parents. His parents lost the farm when the authorities moved them to a livestock yard and then into an internment camp. Hiro joined the U.S. Army and served in the Nisei 442nd Regimental Combat Team, famous for the sacrifices it made to rescue whiter troops. Afterward, he worked in a forge, making heavy equipment. For that long life of work, he receives $11 a year in pension.

From this history of discrimination and loss, Hiro has helped to build an active Japanese American community. One component is matsutake: a symbol of both fellowship and memory. For Hiro, giving away matsutake is one of the greatest pleasures of picking. Last year he gave matsutake to sixty-four people, mainly older folks who couldn't get to the mountains to pick for themselves. Matsutake builds a sense of enjoyment through sharing. As such too, it has become a gift that elders can give to the young. Before one even gets to the woods, then, matsutake conjures memory.

During the drive to the forest with Hiro, memory gets personal. He points out the window, "That's Roy's matsutake hunting place; over there it's Henry's special spot." Only later do I realize that both Roy and Henry are deceased. But they live on in Hiro's map of the forest, recalled every time he passes their spots. Hiro teaches younger people how to hunt for mushrooms, and with the skill comes the memory.

As we walk into the forest, memory gets specific. "Under that tree, I once found nineteen mushrooms, a whole row, stretching halfway round the tree." "Over there I found the biggest mushroom I've ever found, four pounds it was, and still a bud." He shows me where storms have felled a once good mushroom tree; there will be no mushrooms there. We look at the places where a flood wiped off the topsoil, and where pickers have undermined a bush by digging. Once those were good mushroom places: no more.

Hiro walks with a cane, and it is amazing to me that he can still clamber over fallen logs, through brush, and up and down slippery ravines. But Hiro does not try to cover ground. Instead, he goes from one of his remembered mushroom spots to another. The best way to find matsutake is to look where one has found it before.

Of course, if that spot is in the middle of nowhere, under a random bush near a random tree, it's pretty hard to remember that place from year to year. It would be impossible to catalog all the places one has found a mushroom. But, Hiro explains, one doesn't have to. When one arrives in the spot, the memory washes over one, making every detail of that time come suddenly clear—the angle of a leaning tree, the smell of a resinous bush, the play of light, the texture of the soil. I have often experienced just that wash of memory. I am walking along what appears to be an unfamiliar stretch of forest, and suddenly the memory of finding a mushroom—just there—bathes my surroundings. Then I know exactly where to look, although finding is still as difficult as you can imagine.

This kind of memory requires motion and inspires an intimate historical knowledge of the forest. Hiro remembers when a road was first opened to the public: "There were so many mushrooms by the side of the road that you didn't have to go into the forest at all!" He remembers particularly good years: "I found three orange crates of mushroom, and I couldn't figure out how to carry them to the car." All of this history is layered on the landscape, threaded in and out of the spots we check for new life emerging.

The power of this dance of memory struck me particularly hard when we spoke of people who could no longer perform it. Hiro brings mushrooms to those who can no longer walk in the forest. Gifting mushrooms re-inserts the ill and the widowed into the communal landscape. Sometimes, however, memory fails, and then, for better or worse, all the world becomes mushrooms. Hiro's friend Henry told the poignant story of an elderly Nisei with Alzheimer's, confined to a nursing home. When Henry visited, the old man told him, "You should have been here last week; that hillside was white with mushroom." He pointed out the window to a clipped lawn where matsutake would never grow. Without the dance of matsutake forests, memory loses focus.

Hiro takes me to a valley where commercial pickers were not so careful with the landscape. Hiro is one of the most generous people I know, and he loves to work across racial and cultural categories. Yet after some hours, tired, he fell back into discouraged repetition: "This was a good place before the Cambodians ruined it. This was a good place before the Cambodians ruined it." Cambodians is his shorthand for Southeast Asian pickers. And no American should be shocked by the clash of racial profiling through which we stereotype each other. Without wagging a finger at either Hiro or the Cambodians, let me turn to the performance I learned from two Mien pickers. My point is not to show classificatory contrast but to sweep you into another dance.

For Moei Lin and Fam Tsoi, matsutake picking is both a livelihood and a vacation. Every matsutake season since the mid-1990s, they have made their way with their husbands from Redding, California, to the central Cascades; on weekends their children and grandchildren sometimes join them. When the season is over, Moei Lin's husband stacks crates at Wal-Mart; Fam Tsoi's husband drives a school bus. In a good year, matsutake picking is a better living than either of these alternatives. Still, they look forward to the season for multiple reasons, including the exercise and the fresh air. The women, in particular, feel released from the confinement of the cities. The neighborly shelters of their Mien encampment are the nearest they have come, in the United States, to a village in upland Laos. Mien mushroom camps are full of the bustle of village life.

There are also reasons to forget, as Fam Tsoi reminds me when I ask about memories of home. Because many Hmong pickers have told me that hiking the Oregon forests reminds them of Laos, I wonder about Mien. "Yes, of course," she says. "But if you just think about the mushroom, you can forget." Moei Lin and Fam Tsoi came to the United States with the tragedies of the U.S. war in Indochina. After spending years in Thailand, they were accepted as refugees and moved to the mild weather and agricultural wealth of central California. They had no English and no urban job experience. They grew their own foods, and their husbands forged traditional tools. When they heard that money could be made picking mushrooms in the forest, they joined the autumn harvest.

For them, pioneering new landscapes is an old skill, once necessary to migratory shifting cultivation. It is a useful skill for commercial mushroom picking, which, unlike heritage picking, requires covering a lot of ground. Unlike heritage pickers, for whom a half-bucket of mushrooms is a good day's haul, commercial pickers know that a half-bucket won't pay for gas. Commercial pickers can't afford to just check a few remembered spots. To make a living, they pick for longer days and in wider ranges and more diverse ecosystems.

Unlike refugees from cities, Moei Lin and Fam Tsoi do not fear the forest and rarely get lost. Their group feels so comfortable that there is no need to stay close together. When I pick with them, the men go off on their own, quicker trajectories, while the women forge their own way, returning to meet the men much later. "Men run off chasing big bumps," explains Fam Tsoi, "while women scratch the ground."

I scratch the ground with Fam Tsoi and Moei Lin. Everywhere we pick, other pickers have been before us. But rather than cursing their messy digs, we explore them. Moei Lin leans over and touches her stick to the area where soil has been disturbed. No heave is in evidence because the surface has already been broken. But sometimes there is a mushroom! We follow the tracks of earlier harvesters, touching their remains. Because matsutake, anchored to trees, come up again in the same spots, this is a surprisingly productive strategy. We align ourselves with invisible pickers who have gone before us but left us traces of their activity lines.

Nonhuman pickers are at least as important as humans in this strategy. Deer and elk love matsutake, eating it in preference to other mushrooms. When we find the spoor of deer or elk, it often leads us to a patch. Bears turn over logs with matsutake underneath and create quite a mess, digging up the ground. But bears—like deer and elk—never take all the mushrooms. To find a recent animal digging is a sure sign that mushrooms may be around. Following the traces of animal lives, we entangle and align our movements, searching with them.

Not all tracks guide one well. How often I find a lively bump, which, pressed, reveals just air: the tunnel of a gopher or a mole. And when I ask Moei Lin if she follows the guidance of candy cane, she frowns and says "no." "Other people will have already been there," she explains. It is too obvious a sign for the subtle entanglements we seek.

To view trash in this light is a big revelation for me. White hikers and the Forest Service hate trash. It mars the forest, they say. Southeast Asian pickers, they say, leave too much trash. Some have spoken of closing the forest to pickers because of trash. But out looking for life lines, a little trash helps. Not the mountains of beer cans white hunters leave, but a little trash tracked through the forest. A wrinkled piece of tin foil, the discarded vial of a ginseng tonic, a soggy box of Zhong Nan Hai Super Cheap Chinese cigarettes: Each of these is a sign that a Southeast Asian picker had passed through. I recognize the line; I align myself with it; it keeps me from getting lost; it puts me on the track for mushrooms. I find myself looking forward to the lines on which trash leads me.

Trash is not the only Forest Service bugaboo. Another concern is "raking," which means digging up the ground. Anti-raking spokesmen describe raking as the work of single egotistical or ignorant men. Rakers dig the ground with their big sticks, heedless of the results for others. But women pickers show me something different. Sometimes the disturbed ground labeled as raking is the work of many hands. When many hands have touched an area to find its life lines, a collectively produced trough can form. Raking is sometimes the result of many consecutive and entangled life lines.

The ground where Moei Lin and Fam Tsoi pick is not the sculpted moss and lichen carpet of Hiro's special valley. In the volcanic high desert of the eastern Cascades, the ground is dry; the trees are windblown, sickly, and sometimes sparse. Fallen trees litter the ground, their uprooted butts blocking passage. Waves of logging and Forest Service "treatments" have left a trail of stumps and roads and broken earth. It seems strange to argue that pickers are among the worst threats to the forest. Still, their tracks are there. For Moei Lin and Fam Tsoi, this is an advantage.

By following life lines and aligning their movements with them, Moei Lin and Fam Tsoi cover a lot of ground. We rise before dawn, and after a meal we are in the forest at first light. We may be out in the forest for four or five hours before we contact the men on the walkie-talkie to find out where they have gone. And although the general contours of the hills are familiar, we are always checking new places. This is not the forest of familiar attachments. We scout new territory by following the lines of life.

At lunchtime, we sit on a log and pull out plastic bags of rice. Today, our topping is carp, made into small brown nuggets, mixed with red and green bits. It's tantalizingly rich and spicy, and I ask how it's made. Fam Tsoi explains, "You have a fish. You add salt." She falters; that's it. I imagine myself in the kitchen with a raw salty fish dripping in my hand. Language has met its limit. The trick of cooking is in the bodily performance, which isn't easy to explain. The same is true for mushroom picking, more dance than classification. It is a dance that partners here with many dancing lives.

The mushroom pickers I have described are observers of others' life performances as well as performers of their own forest dances. They do not care about all the creatures of the forest; indeed, they are quite selective. But the way they notice is to incorporate others' life performances into their own. Intersecting life lines guide the performance, creating one mode of forest knowledge.

Discovering allies,
Yunnan. An itinerant
trader buying mushrooms
at a rural market
attracts a crowd.

Part IV
In the Middle of Things

IN OPEN TICKET, PICKERS ARE GATHERING FOR A meeting with the Forest Service to discuss racial profiling in stopping cars and handing out fines. Two Forest Service employees have come and some twenty pickers, a tiny fraction of those in the woods for the season. The Khmer organizer grimaces in appraisal. "Cambodian people don't come to meetings," he quips privately, "since they think someone might get killed." He is thinking of the Khmer Rouge regime, under which so many died. Our meeting, however, has other issues. It starts with lively repartee, but soon a forester drones on about regulations, and the meeting deteriorates into rules-explanation with only short questions to interrupt it. It's hard to glimpse a revolution here. Still, it is unexpected that the Forest Service is meeting with pickers at all. And there is something new, at least to me. After each statement, we hear sequential translations in Khmer, Lao, Mien, and, after a quick scramble to find someone, Guatemalan Spanish. Each presents the ear with a jarringly different cadence, and each hangs in the air, haunting. Even simple questions or explanations of rules take a *very* long time. In my discomfort, I understand that we are learning to listen—even if we don't yet know how to have a discussion.

Meetings among pickers and with the Forest Service take place because of the legacy of Beverly Brown, a tireless organizer who decided to listen to the precarious workers of the northwest forest, including mushroom pickers.[1] Brown brought pickers together through a practice of translation that, rather than resolving difference, allowed difference to disturb too-easy resolution, encouraging creative listening. Listening was Brown's starting point for political work. She had begun not with languages but with gaps across city and countryside. As she explains in a memoir recorded before her death, Brown grew up knowing that urban elites never listened to rural folks—and that she was determined to do something about this.[2] She began by listening to disenfranchised loggers and other rural whites.[3] But thus she was introduced to the commercial foragers who collect mushrooms, berries, and floral greens. These folks were more diverse than the loggers. Her work grew ever more ambitious as she set up scenes for listening across greater gulfs.

Brown's advocacy for political listening inspires me to think past a disturbance in our aspirations. Without progress, what is struggle? The disenfranchised had a common program to the extent that we could all share in progress. It was the determinacy of political categories such as class—their relentless forward motion—that brought us the confidence that struggle would move us somewhere better. Now what? Brown's political listening addresses this. It suggests that any gathering contains many inchoate political futures and that political work consists of helping some of those come into being. Indeterminacy is not the end of history but rather that node in which many beginnings lie in wait. To listen politically is to detect the traces of not-yet-articulated common agendas.

When we take this form of awareness out of formal meetings into everyday life, yet more challenges appear. How, for example, shall we make common cause with other living beings? Listening is no longer enough; other forms of awareness will have to kick in. And what great differences yawn! Like Brown, I would acknowledge difference, refusing to paper it over with good intentions. Yet we cannot rely on expert spokesmen, as we have learned in human politics. We need many kinds of alertness to spot potential allies. Worse yet, the hints of common agendas we detect are undeveloped, thin, spotty, and unstable. At best we are looking for a most ephemeral glimmer. But, living with indeterminacy, such glimmers are the political.

In this last mushroom flush, a final upsurge in the face of varied coming droughts and winters, I search for fugitive moments of entanglement in the midst of institutionalized alienation. These are sites in which to seek allies. One might think of them as latent commons. They are latent in two senses: first, while ubiquitous, we rarely notice them, and, second, they are undeveloped. They bubble with unrealized possibilities; they are elusive. They are what we hear in Brown's political listening and related arts of noticing. They require stretching concepts of the commons. Thus, I characterize them in the negative:

Latent commons are not exclusive human enclaves. Opening the commons to other beings shifts everything. Once we include pests and diseases, we can't hope for harmony; the lion will not lie down with the lamb. And organisms don't just eat each other; they also make divergent ecologies. Latent commons are those mutualist and nonantagonistic entanglements found within the play of this confusion.

Latent commons are not good for everyone. Every instance of collaboration makes room for some and leaves out others. Whole species lose out in some collaborations. The best we can do is to aim for "good-enough" worlds, where "good-enough" is always imperfect and under revision.

Latent comments don't institutionalize well. Attempts to turn the commons into policy are commendably brave, but they do not capture the effervescence of the latent commons. The latent commons moves in law's interstices; it is catalyzed by infraction, infection, inattention—and poaching.

Latent commons cannot redeem us. Some radical thinkers hope that progress will lead us to a redemptive and utopian commons. In contrast, the latent commons is here and now, amidst the trouble. And humans are never fully in control.

Given this negative character, it makes no sense to crystallize first principles or seek natural laws that generate best cases. Instead, I practice arts of noticing. I comb through the mess of existing worlds-in-the-making, looking for treasures—each distinctive and unlikely to be found again, at least in that form.

18
Matsutake Crusaders: Waiting for Fungal Action

"Let's go." "We can't." "Why not?" "We're waiting for Godot."

— *Samuel Beckett*, Waiting for Godot

Satisfaction in life comes from the fact that satoyama requires human intervention. This human intervention must, however, be in balance with natural successional forces.

— *Noboru Kuramoto, "Citizen Conservation of Satoyama Landscapes"*

HUMANS CANNOT CONTROL MATSUTAKE. WAITING to see if mushrooms might emerge is thus an existential problem. The mushrooms remind us of our dependence on more-than-human natural processes: we can't fix anything, even what we have broken, by ourselves. Yet this need not enforce paralysis. Some Japanese volunteers make themselves part of perhaps-useful landscape disturbance as they wait to see what happens. They hope their actions might stimulate a latent commons, that is, an eruption of shared assembly, even as they know they can't actually *make* a commons.

Shiho Satsuka introduced me to groups who disturb the landscape as a way of stimulating changes in multispecies gatherings—and themselves. Kyoto's Matsutake Crusaders is one. The Crusaders offer the motto: "Let's revitalize the forest so we can all eat *sukiyaki*." The meal, a meat and vegetable stew best served with matsutake, evokes the sensual pleasure that emerges from woodland revitalization. Yet, as one Crusader admitted to me, matsutake might not appear in his lifetime. The best he can do is disturb the forest—and hope that matsutake come.

Why might working the landscape evoke a sense of renewed possibilities? How might it change volunteers as well as ecologies? This chapter tells the story of woodland revitalization groups who hope that small-scale disturbance might draw both people and forests out of alienation, building a world of overlapping lifeways in which mutualistic transformation, the mode of mycorrhiza, might yet be possible.

It was a sunny Saturday in June when Shiho Satsuka and I went to see how the Matsutake Crusaders were disturbing the forest. More than twenty volunteers had come out to work. By the time we arrived, they were scattered across the hillside, digging up the roots of the broadleaf trees that had invaded what once had been a hillside of pines. They had strung a rope and pulley down the hillside, and they lowered great bags of roots and humus to a pile at the bottom of the hill. They left only red pine—lonely survivors on an otherwise empty hillside. My first reaction was disorientation. I saw a forest disappearing rather than renewal.

Dr. Yoshimura, the leader of the group, was generous enough to explain. He showed me the tangled evergreen-broadleaf brush that had developed on the hillside after its abandonment by peasant farmers. It was so dense that one could barely reach a hand through the bushes, much less a body. In the dark shade, no understory layer could develop. Light-loving species were dying out, and the lack of understory left the slope vulnerable. In all the time that peasants had cared for the hillside, Dr. Yoshimura noted, there had been no significant erosion. The road at the base of the hill was just as it had been, in local records, for several centuries. Now the dense and undisturbed forest, with its simplified structure, threatened the soil.[1]

In contrast, he showed me the next flank of the hill, where the Crusaders had finished their work. Pines greened the hillside, and spring flowers and wildlife had returned by themselves. The group was developing uses for this forest. They had built a kiln to make charcoal and made compost heaps to breed the beetles Japanese boys like to collect. There were fruit trees and vegetable gardens, fertilized by the humus they had removed, and plans for many more projects.

Many of the volunteers were retired people, but there were also students, housewives, and salaried employees willing to give up free weekends. Some had private forestland, and they were learning how to manage their own pines. One showed pictures of his satoyama forest, which had won several prizes for its beauty. In the spring, his hillsides were bedecked with the blossoms of wild cherries and azaleas. Even if no matsutake appeared, he explained, he was happy to be participating in this reconstructed woodland. The Crusaders do not aim for finished gardens; they work for still-emergent forests, which arrange themselves around the possibilities of tradition-sized disturbance. The satoyama becomes a zone where more-than-human social relations—including their own—have a chance to flourish.

At lunchtime, the volunteers gathered for introductions, jokes, and a celebratory meal. They prepared lunch: flowing somen, "noodles in the stream." A bamboo aqueduct was constructed, and I joined the line to catch the noodles flowing by. Everyone was having fun and learning as they saved the forest.

Saving an abandoned forest? As I suggested earlier, in American sensibilities an "abandoned forest" is already an oxymoron. Forests flourish without human interference. The greening of New England after its farmers moved West is a point of regional pride. Abandoned fields turn into forests; abandonment frees forests to reclaim their space. What happened in Japan to make people see abandonment as a loss to the liveliness and diversity of the forest? Several histories intertwine: forest replacement, forest neglect, forest disease, and human discontent. I turn to each.

Following World War II, U.S. occupying forces reduced land holdings, further privatizing common woodlands that had shrunk in the

Meiji reforms. In 1951, national forest planning began, which meant standardizing the timber milling industry to make wood scalable. New roads were built, allowing more harvesting. As Japan's economy revved up, the building trade demanded more of the now-scalable wood. Chapter 15 discussed the consequences. Clear-cutting was introduced; deforested lands were not allowed to grow back. By the early 1960s, what had once been peasant forests across central Japan had become sugi and hinoki tree plantations. Satoyama groups reacted to people's sense of alienation from forests, derived from the dominance of plantations.

At the edges of the flourishing cities, developers took a look at remaining peasant landscapes and grabbed them for suburban complexes and golf courses. Some satoyama conservation groups developed out of struggles against developers. Ironically, these eager volunteers were sometimes the children of migrants from the countryside, who had given up rural life. These are the satoyama defenders who call up the villages of their grandparents as the model from which rural landscapes should be reconstructed.

Even in the countryside, things were changing, and this is the second story of what happened to the forests. In the 1950s and 1960s, Japan went through a period of rapid urbanization. Farmers left the countryside behind; rural areas once used for peasant livelihoods became spaces of neglect and abandonment. Those who stayed in the countryside had less and less reason to maintain satoyama forests. Japan's abrupt "fuel revolution" meant that even remote rural farmers were using fossil fuels to heat their homes, cook, and drive tractors by the end of the 1950s. Firewood and charcoal were abandoned. (Charcoal retained a residual use for traditional practices, such as the tea ceremony.) Thus, the most important uses of the peasant forest disappeared. Coppicing was discontinued as firewood and charcoal use sharply declined. Raking for green manure disappeared with the advent of fossil-fuel-based fertilizers. Grassland maintenance and cutting for thatching also died out as grass roofs were replaced. The neglected forests changed, becoming dense with shrubs and newly established evergreen broadleaf trees. Invasive species such as *moso* bamboo crowded in. The understory of light-loving herbs was lost. Pines were smothered in the shade.

Activist farmer Kokki Goto explains the situation in his memoir.[2]

The forestlands frequently used by villagers of Ishimushiro, or what we call satoyama, were close enough that we could make four round trips a day on foot, two in the morning and two in the afternoon, carrying bundles weighing 60 kg on our back. If we walked farther into the forest, we would find it too burdensome to carry home bundles of raw wood, so we had to make them into charcoal. . . . In Ishimushiro, we have approximately 1,000 hectares of iriai [common] forestlands that cover most of the satoyama forestlands. The iriai forestlands are jointly used by 90 households that belong to the Ishimushiro Common Forest Association. . . .

In the old days when there were few ways of earning cash income, it was indispensable for villagers to have iriai rights in order to live here. We had to rely on the forestlands around the hamlet for most of the necessities of life. Those without the right to gather firewood and brushwood for use as fuel, or the right to harvest fodder in the iriai forestlands, could not have survived in the village. . . .

For a branch family like ours, which was in possession of a very small tract of forestland, the hamlet's iriai forestlands were indispensable for gathering firewood, brushwood, and other necessities for living. Sometime in the 1950s, the wave of modernization began to make an impact on Ishimushiro, changing the life-style in the hamlet at an increasing pace. Villagers began to use kerosene and electricity, replace their thatched roofs with galvanized iron sheets, and adopt tractors, rendering firewood, brushwood, fodder, and thatch grass increasingly unnecessary. Consequently, many people stopped entering the satoyama except on rare occasions. . . . Mushroom hunting is the only economically viable activity these days. Things have changed drastically from the days when the blessings of the iriai forests meant a lot to the community.

Later in his story, he speaks of his efforts, and those of others, to revitalize village landscapes. He explains group efforts to clean waterways and open forests. "When people say 'Things were better in the old days,' what they have in mind, I believe, is the joy of doing things together with many people. We have lost that joy."[3]

Pines as well as farmers no longer flourished. As described in chapter 11, pine wilt nematodes have killed off most of central Japan's red pines. This is in part because satoyama neglect and abandonment have put pines under stress. Walking through neglected satoyama forests, one sees only dead and dying pines.

These dying pines have condemned the matsutake harvest; without its host trees, matsutake cannot survive. Indeed, it is records of matsutake decline that make the loss of Japan's pine forests clearest. In the first part of the twentieth century, satoyama forests produced plenty of matsutake. Rural people took matsutake rather for granted; they formed one element of a suite of foraged autumn foods that complemented wild spring foods to mark the seasons. The big fuss only came later, when the mushroom became scarce and expensive in the 1970s. The drop was steep and abrupt. Pine trees were dying. In the 1980s, as Japan's economy continued to boom, Japanese matsutake became rare—and very valuable.

Imported matsutake crowded into the market, and even these, through the 1990s, were shockingly expensive. It is the cohort who came of age between the 1970s and the 1990s who remember the fine aroma of a thin expensive sliver in one's soup—and who react with shock and joy at the dream of plenty.

Matsutake help peasant forests remain in the working landscape. With high prices, the mushroom sales alone pay the taxes for the land and support maintenance. In areas where iriai rights still exist, villages harness matsutake benefits for communal use by auctioning off the right to harvest (and sell) the mushrooms. Auctions are held in the summer before anyone knows how good the mushroom season will be; villagers hold a feast at which, lubricated with drink, they urge each other to submit higher bids. The winner pays the village a hefty sum but later recoups by picking the mushrooms.[4] Yet despite communal and financial benefits, the work of maintaining the forest does not always get done, especially as villagers age. In neglected forests, pines die and matsutake disappears.

Satoyama movements attempt to recover the lost sociality of community life. They design activities to bring together elders, young people, and children, combining education and community building with work and pleasure. There is more involved than helping out peasants—and pines. Satoyama work, volunteers explain, remakes the human spirit.

In the economic boom that followed Japanese recovery from World War II, urban migrants left the countryside behind to pursue modern commodities and lifestyles. Yet when economic growth slowed in the 1990s, neither education nor employment seemed so easy a route to progress-based well-being. The economy of spectacles and desires flourished, but it became detached from life-course expectations. It became harder to imagine where life should lead and what, besides commodities, should be in it. One iconic figure called public attention to this problem: the *hikikomori* is a young person, usually a teenage boy, who shuts himself in his room and refuses face-to-face contact. Hikikomori live through electronic media. They isolate themselves through engagement in a world of images that leaves them free from embodied sociality—and mired in a self-made prison. They capture the nightmare of urban anomie for many: there is a little bit of hikikomori in all of us. It is this nightmare that chapter 13's Professor K saw in the glazed eyes of his students. It sent him to the countryside as a site for remaking students—and himself; and it has sent many other advocates, educators, and volunteers there also.

Satoyama revitalization addresses the problem of anomie because it builds social relations with other beings. Humans become only one of many participants in making livability. Participants wait for trees and fungi to associate with them. They work landscapes that require human action yet exceed that requirement. By the turn of the century, several thousand satoyama revitalization groups had emerged across Japan. Some focus on water management, nature education, the habitat of a particular flower—or matsutake mushrooms. All are engaged in remaking persons as well as landscapes.

To rebuild themselves, citizens' groups mix science and peasant knowledge. Scientists often take leadership roles in satoyama revitalization. But they aim to incorporate vernacular knowledge; here, urban professionals and scientists consult elderly farmers for their advice. Some volunteer to help farmers with their work or interview elders about disappearing ways of life. Their goal is to restore working landscapes, and for this they need working knowledge.

Mutual learning is also an important goal. Groups are candid about making mistakes—and learning from them. One report about satoyama work by a group of volunteers includes all the problems and mistakes of their efforts. Without coordination, they cut down too many trees. Some of the areas they cleared grew back even thicker with undesirable species. In the end, the report's authors argue, the group developed a "do, think, observe, and do again" principle, elevating collective trial and error to an art. Since one of their goals was participatory learning, allowing themselves to make and observe mistakes was an important part of the process. The authors conclude, "To be successful, volunteers have to participate in the program at all levels and stages."[5]

Groups such as Kyoto's Matsutake Crusaders take advantage of the mushroom's allure to make it the symbol for their commitments to renewing the working relations of people and forests. If matsutake do emerge—as they did in a Crusader's well-worked hillside in the fall of 2008—they bring a surge of excitement to the volunteers. Nothing could be more thrilling than this unexpected entanglement with other participants in forest making. Pines, humans, and fungi are renewed in a moment of co-species being.

No one thinks matsutake will bring Japan back to its pre-bubble glory. Rather than redemption, matsutake-forest revitalization picks through the heap of alienation. In the process, volunteers acquire the patience to mix with multispecies others without knowing where the world-in-process is going.

Discovering allies,
Yunnan. Chatting at
market. Privatization
cannot wipe out the
latent commons because
it depends on it.

19
Ordinary Assets

SOMETIMES COMMON ENTANGLEMENTS EMERGE NOT from human plans but despite them. It is not even the undoing of plans, but rather the unaccounted for in their doing that offers possibilities for elusive moments of living in common. This is the case for the making of private assets. Assembling assets, we ignore the common—even when it pervades the assembly. Yet the unnoticed, too, can be a site for potential allies.

Contemporary Yunnan is a place to consider this problem because, in the wake of the communist experiment, international and national elites are in a frenzy to make private assets everywhere. Yet much asset making is strange and raw; the juxtaposition between privatization and other ways people relate to things pops into view.[1] Matsutake forests, and the matsutake trade, are a case in point. Whose forests, and whose trade?

Forests—with their unbounded spaces and diverse ecologies—are everywhere a challenge for privatizers. For the past sixty years, Yunnan forests have ricocheted across multiple tenure arrangements, and the forest experts Michael Hathaway and I spoke with worried that peasants had become disheartened and confused in their management.[2]

Still, they were hopeful about one recent tenure category: the contracting of forests to individual peasant households.

While not the free right of American private property, such contracts, experts hoped, might rationalize peasant landscapes. Powerful international overseers imagine individual tenure as a form of conservation because it offers incentives for wise use.[3] In Yunnan, it also opens populist hopes: after an intense history of top-down impositions, here at last is a chance for local farmers to have some say in managing their own forests. Yunnan researchers, in dialogue with cosmopolitan developments in the field of political ecology, show how social justice goals may be possible through local control of forests, made possible by household contracts.[4] Thus, too, researchers are alert to the creativity and insight of farmers who learn how to use the privileges of contracts to solve local problems. One researcher reports on the ways villagers reallocate forest tracts to equalize the potential gains from each. She documents the work of adult brothers, for example, who switch forest plots sequentially to make sure each has a chance for benefits.[5]

But what are these imagined benefits? Yunnan has been under a logging ban for some years, and, at least officially, timber is to be harvested only with permission, and for domestic use. Yet there are other potential assets. In the mountains of Chuxiong Prefecture in central Yunnan, matsutake is the most valuable forest product. Experts are excited about household contracts because of it; without this step toward privatization, they say, the pickers might destroy the resource. Foresters told us of the horrors of other Yunnan areas, where village pickers spread out before dawn, combing the commons with flashlights. This is chaos, they said. Besides, small mushrooms are picked before they achieve their highest market value. Contracts, in contrast, order the forest, blocking such wildness and inefficiency. Chuxiong forests offer a model for making private assets: an example for forest reform for Yunnan and for all China.[6]

One widely praised arrangement for matsutake management is the village auction. What is auctioned is access to villagers' contracted forests during the matsutake season. The system is reminiscent of Japan's iriai forest auctions. The right to harvest and sell the matsutake on villagers' lands goes to the auction winner. In the area we visited in Yunnan, the money gained from the auction is distributed to each household and forms an important part of its cash income. Without the press of competition from other pickers, the auction winner should be able to pick each mushroom when its market price is highest, thus maximizing his or her income as well as that of the compensated villagers. Advocates of household contracts also argue that the resource—matsutake—will grow better without the pressures of chaotic overharvesting. But can matsutake thrive in private forests? Let me approach this question in steps.

Within the rural economy, auction winners are exemplary figures of the search to gather private assets. "Boss" L is one; he has won the contract to harvest matsutake in his home village of eleven households, and he has also become a major local buyer. His relationships with government foresters and researchers are good. About fifteen years ago, the foresters asked him to create a matsutake showcase forest. He fenced off several hectares of forest and built a boardwalk meandering through so that visiting foresters and researchers could look at a model forest without disturbing it. Without peasant disturbance, the trees in the showcase forest have grown big and beautiful. The ground, undisturbed by peasant rakes, has built up a thick duff—that is, a layer of leaves and needles over ever-richer humus. It is refreshing to walk through this forest, with its gracefully arching trees and its rich earth smells. When one spots a mushroom, it is a thrill; and since no one picks the matsutake here, they rise out of the duff into neat umbrellas. Visitors come from many places to admire this matsutake forest. But foresters know enough to worry: there is too much duff. The humus is too rich. The matsutake are still coming, but perhaps not for long. Matsutake prefer more goings on.

Certainly, there is plenty going on elsewhere. Outside the showcase forest, matsutake forests are much used and abused. Everywhere Michael Hathaway and I went, broadleaf trees showed signs of extensive pruning for firewood; many were reduced to much-hacked bushes. Pines too are cut and cut, as peasants remove branches to collect pollen or pine nuts, depending on species. Pine needles are raked for bedding for the pigs, which later becomes fertilizer for the fields. Goats are ubiquitous, eating everything, including young pines, which seem to have developed a "grass-stage"-like adaptation to survive the heavy grazing. People are everywhere, too, collecting medicinal plants, pig food, and commercially salable mushrooms—not only matsutake but many kinds, from acrid *Lactarius* that must be dried or boiled to questionably edible *Amanita*. Far from serene and graceful, the forest is a busy inter-section of traffic both for human needs and for the benefit of their plant and animal domesticates.

Yet these forests are the much-praised model of individual-access en-closure! How can they also be the sites of so much traffic? I was con-fused by the dissonance between traffic and enclosure until I spent the day with "Little" L, another matsutake forest auction winner, but one who works smaller forest holdings than Boss L. He took our team to his forest and introduced us to its plants and mushrooms. Like the other matsutake forests I had seen in the area, it was a badly scarred young forest, marked with traces of grazing and cutting. Little L did not mind; he showed us the richness of the forest's mushroom harvest, emerging in the midst of all that traffic. And he explained the interplay between traffic and enclosure, clearing up my confusion. During the matsutake season, he paints blazes where his forest borders on roads and trails. People know they should not enter, and, in general, they do not, al-though there are some problems with poaching. The rest of the year, they are free to come, to gather firewood, to graze their goats, and to look for other forest products. Of course! Despite his pride at matsutake enclosure, Little L did not see this as subterfuge. How else would people get their firewood, he explained, if they could not enter the forests?

This is not an official plan. Provincial foresters and experts do not talk about seasonal enclosure; if they know about it, they put it out of their minds as something international authorities would surely cen-sure. Seasonal enclosure would defeat the program of the "privatization-is-conservation" creed, because local residents are using resources in common in just the way those experts frown upon. Besides, those ex-perts would hate the way this forest looks: young, scarred, full of traffic. This is not the plan. And yet, might not this way of enacting privatiza-tion be the saving grace for matsutake? The traffic keeps the forests open, and thus welcoming to pine; it keeps the humus thin and the soils poor, thus allowing matsutake to do its good work of enriching trees. In this area, matsutake pairs with oaks and oak relatives as well as pine; the whole young and scarred forest works with matsutake to survive on mineral soils. Without all the traffic, the duff builds up, the soil be-comes rich, and other fungi and bacteria crowd out matsutake. It is the traffic, then, that privileges matsutake, making this one of the great areas for matsutake production. Yet the traffic must take place under the radar of contracts, which were introduced to this area with the explicit purpose of *saving* matsutake. Matsutake thrives in this fugitive commons. It is only matsutake incomes that can be raised through individual access.[7]

A detour through the issue of matsutake incomes can help me generalize the point that private assets most always grow out of unacknowledged commons. This point is not just about wily Yunnan peasants. Privatization is never complete; it needs shared spaces to create any value. That is the secret of property's continuing theft—but also its vulnerability. Consider again matsutake as a commodity, ready to be sent from Yunnan to Japan. What we have is mushrooms, that is, fruiting bodies of underground fungi. The fungi require the traffic of the commons to flourish; no mushrooms emerge without forest disturbance. The privately owned mushroom is an offshoot from a communally living underground body, a body forged through the possibilities of latent commons, human and not human. That it is possible to cordon off the mushroom as an asset without taking its underground commons into account is both the ordinary way with privatization and a quite extraordinary outrage, when you stop to think about it. The contrast between private mushrooms and fungi-forming forest traffic might be an emblem for commoditization more generally: the continual, never-finished cutting off of entanglement.

This brings me back to my earlier concern with alienation as an attribute of nonhumans as well as humans. To become a fully private asset, matsutake mushrooms must be torn not only from their lifeworlds but also from the relations involved in their procurement. Picking the mushroom and transporting it outside the forest can take care of the first of these. But in central Yunnan, as in Oregon, the second rupture takes longer.

In the small town where Michael Hathaway and I based our rural Yunnan research, three men were recognized as the key matsutake "bosses" (*laoban*), that is, the merchants who bought most of the area's matsutake and sold it in bigger towns. There were also mushroom buyers who came to the town's periodic markets, but they managed to buy only a small fraction of the matsutake. As the bosses explained, visiting buyers did not have enough local ties.

In watching the work of the bosses and their agents, I was struck particularly by the lack of negotiation over prices and grades, which I had come to expect from my fieldwork in Oregon. One boss sent his driver into the mountains to buy matsutake from villagers there; the pickers handed over the mushrooms without a word, receiving a bundle of cash wordlessly in exchange.[8] In other transactions, there was talk, but the pickers never asked the price offered for the mushrooms, instead just taking whatever they were given. I watched one of the bosses receive a box of mushrooms delivered by a bus driver passing by; the boss explained that he would pay the picker later. I also saw pickers work through their own mushrooms, discarding those with insect damage, rather than trying to pass what the buyer did not notice.

All this seemed utterly exotic given my experience in Oregon, where competitive market negotiation took center stage from the moment pickers entered buyers' space. It was also quite different from what happened just downstream on the Yunnan commodity chain. In dedicated mushroom markets in bigger towns and cities, price and grade negotiations were constant and intense.[9] Many wholesale buyers competed against each other, and the scramble to determine the best prices and the most appropriate grade selections took up everyone's attention. Upstream, in contrast, the buying was quiet.

Everyone we spoke with in the rural margin explained that buying without haggling occurs because of long-term relationships and the trust that goes with them. The bosses would give the pickers their best price, people said. There are community, family, and ethnic-and-linguistic ties between the bosses and the pickers.[10] They are local guys, part of the small town scene. Pickers trust them.

This "trust" is not a quality that works to everyone's equal advantage. I do not believe anyone confused "trust" with consensus or equality. Everyone knew that bosses were getting rich off of matsutake; everyone wanted to emulate their success in gaining personal wealth. Still, it is a form of entanglement with reciprocal obligations; as long as the matsutake are embedded in it, they are not fully alienated commodities. The exchange of matsutake in the small town requires the recognition of appropriate social roles. It is only in the mushroom markets of the larger towns that the mushrooms break free, becoming fully alienated creatures of exchange.

In the relation between small-town bosses and pickers, we see, again, how private assets depend on common living spaces. The bosses are able to buy local mushrooms on their own terms because they are entangled with the pickers; they can then transport the mushrooms to bigger towns where they can be converted into private wealth. It is in this light, too, that the project of issuing forest contracts can be understood as a project for redirecting wealth, rather than saving forests.[11] In household forest contracts, contractors can extract the value of the mushrooms, which in turn is drawn from an unacknowledged and fugitive commons. How wealth gets redirected is, however, still somewhat up for grabs. Here, the work of socially conscious Yunnan researchers is pressing. Their job is to turn promising local practices for keeping the wealth in villages and small towns into models for society and conservation.

The conservation part of the equation is the trickiest part, however, because the lust for private wealth only occasionally benefits the forest. Often, instead, it sponsors unexpected destruction. One auction winner proudly showed me how he had learned to milk more wealth out of the matsutake forests he had won the right to harvest. He had his men dig up rare species of flowering trees from the village forest covered under his matsutake contract. The fact that these were rare and little known species, he said, made them even more valuable. Since the city managers of Kunming, Yunnan's capital, demanded that mature trees suddenly grace what had been treeless streets, he and other entrepreneurs shipped full-grown trees into the city. Most of the trees died from the shock of removal and transport. But those that lived long enough to garner payment fetched a tidy profit. As for the forest, at the very least it lost its diversity—and the beauty of its flowering trees.

Such entrepreneurial stunts are part of the scramble for wealth in today's China. In them, we can see something about the re-making of humans in conjunction with the salvaging and savaging of landscapes. Matsutake bosses are much-admired figures in Yunnan's countryside. Bosses are pioneers in the new search for private assets; so many I spoke with wanted to be bosses—if not for matsutake, for some other product extracted from the countryside. One matsutake boss had a plaque in his living room, awarded by the local government, proclaiming him a leader in making money.[12] Rural bosses are replacements for socialist heroes;

they are models for human aspirations. Bosses are embodiments of the entrepreneurial spirit. In contrast to earlier socialist dreams, they are supposed to make themselves, not their communities, wealthy. They dream of themselves as self-made men. Yet their autonomous selves bear comparison to matsutake mushrooms: the visible fruit of unrecognized, elusive, and ephemeral commons.

Bosses privatize the wealth of collaboratively produced mushroom growth and collection. Such privatization of common wealth might characterize all entrepreneurs. The Yunnan countryside at this historical moment is good to think with because interest in rationalizing natural resource management extends only to property law and accounting. Privatization takes place merely by claiming the fruits of scavenging—not by reorganizing labor or landscape. I'm not trying to argue that such rationalization would be better; certainly, it would not help matsutake. However, there is something peculiar and frightening in this dedication to salvage, as if everyone were taking advantage of the end of the world to gather up riches before the last bits are destroyed. It is in this feature, too, that rural Yunnan is neither particular nor parochial. It is hard not to see all our enterprises in this same apocalyptic light. In rural Yunnan bosses, we see close-focus models for how to salvage fortunes from the ruin.

Most commentators on China's new wealth, both Chinese and otherwise, write about millionaires in the cities; but the scramble for private assets is equally intense in the countryside. Farmers, landless migrants, small town bosses, and fancy companies all participate in an "Everything must go" sale. It is hard to know how to think about conservation in such a social climate. However we begin, I don't think we can afford to forget the connection between value and latent commons. There are no matsutake mushrooms without such evanescent mutualities. There are no assets at all without them. Even as entrepreneurs concentrate their private wealth through building alienation into commodities, they continue to draw from unrecognized entanglements. The thrill of private ownership is the fruit of an underground common.

20
Anti-ending: Some People
I Met along the Way

WHEN I VISITED MATSIMAN IN 2007, HE WAS LIVING in a small house on top of a hill with his girlfriend and a large number of cats. ("Matsi" is American slang for matsutake.) I had wanted to see matsutake growing in the tanoak forests of coastal Oregon, and he showed me some of his places, where the stumps of once-inspiring Douglas fir, lost through logging, provided encouraging habitat. Tanoak leaves covered the ground like a rug; it seemed impossible to find a mushroom emerging under that. But he showed me how to get down on the ground and to feel the leaves with my hands until I found a promising texture, a lump. We were looking for mushrooms by feel alone—for me, a new way to learn the forest.

This method works only if you know the spots where matsutake are likely to emerge. One needs to know particular plants and fungi, not just generic types. This combination of intimate knowledge and feeling through the duff focuses my attention back on the here and now, the middle of things. We trust our eyes too much. I looked at the ground and thought, "There's nothing there." But there was, as Matsiman found with his hands. Getting by without progress requires a good deal of feeling around with our hands.

In this spirit, I let this chapter wander again through my research sites, recouping moments when I glimpsed the kinds of boundary confusions that mark the edges of alienation—and thus, perhaps, latent commons. Muddling through with others is always in the middle of things; it does not properly conclude. Even as I reiterate key points, I hope a whiff of the adventure-in-process comes through.

Matsiman assumed that name in his excitement for matsutake mushrooms. He picks commercially, and, as an amateur scientist, he studies with fervor. Tracking his patches, he has made an extraordinary record of matsutake production over time in relation to temperature and precipitation. Matsiman is also the name of his website, which is full of information about the mushroom, gathered from many sources; it has also become a space for discussion, particularly among white pickers and buyers.[1] Matsiman's passion also brings him into dialogue with the Forest Service, which has used his services for its matsutake research.

Although Matsiman is devoted to his mushrooms, he does not assume they will be enough to support his needs. He has many other dreams and enterprises. When I visited, he showed me specks of gold he had panned from the river and a smoked matsutake powder, which he was trying to sell as a spice. He was experimenting with growing medicinal fungi. He has collected firewood commercially. Matsiman is well aware that he has chosen forms of livelihood at the very edge of capitalism. He hopes never again to work for a wage—and to find places to live in the woods that involve neither owning nor renting. (He was the caretaker for a private mountain on which he lived; later he took an unpaid position as a campground host.) Like many mushroom pickers, he has explored the limit spaces of capitalism, neither properly inside nor outside, where the inability of capitalist forms of discipline to fully capture the world is especially obvious.

Matsiman navigates the possibilities as well as the problems of precarity. Precarity means not being able to plan. But it also stimulates noticing, as one works with what is available. To live well with others, we need to use all our senses, even if it means feeling around in the duff. Matsiman's own words about noticing, from his matsutake website, seem particularly apt. "Who is Matsiman?" he asks. "Anyone who loves hunting, learning, understanding, protecting, educating others, and respects matsutake mushroom and its habitat is matsiman. Those of us who can't get enough understanding, constantly trying to determine what caused this or that to happen, or not happen. We are not limited to nationality, gender, education, or age group. Anyone can be a matsiman." Matsiman calls up a latent commons of matsutake lovers. What holds his imagined matsipeople together is the pleasure of noticing.

Although I have devoted most of this book to living beings, it is useful to remember the dead. The dead, too, are part of social worlds. Lu-Min Vaario nudged me in this direction when she showed me slides of matsutake hyphae (the stringlike cells of fungal bodies) gathering around bits of charcoal. Although matsutake is known for its relations with living trees, it can get some nutrients from dead ones too, her research showed.[2] This finding inspired her to begin a research project on matsutake's "good neighbors," both living and dead. Here charcoal joins living trees, fungi, and soil microbes. She investigates how neighborliness—that is, social relations across differences of both vitality and species—is essential to good living.[3]

Dr. Vaario has thought a lot about neighborliness in this meaning—mutuality across difference—for humans as well. Although she was born and first educated in China, her research has spanned many important sites of matsutake science, and she has had to work across both hidden and overt national conventions in building neighborly matsutake studies. She trained as a postdoctoral fellow in the influential laboratory of Kazuo Suzuki at the University of Tokyo. It was there that she first tested matsutake's ability as a saprobe, an eater of the dead, which she hoped might lead to cultivation techniques. (While the hyphae do grow on nonliving materials, no one has yet seen a mushroom produced from mycelia without a live host.) When she took a research position in China, she was thrilled by the chance to explore a different matsutake landscape, yet frustrated at the lack of understanding of her research. A few years later, she married and followed her Finnish husband to his country, where she received funding to pursue the "good neighbors" research through the Finnish Forest Research Institute. The study of neighborliness turns difference into a resource for collaboration. Imagining the interactions among roots, hyphae, charcoal, and bacteria—as well as among Chinese, Japanese, and Finnish scientists—is as good a way as any to refigure our understanding of survival as a collaborative project.

Dr. Vaario is lucky to have received research funding, since, as an itinerant scientist, she has no institutional job security. The problem of living without a regular job is keener for those without advanced degrees. Consider Tiia, who lives in the Finnish countryside above the Arctic Circle. On the way to her place, she showed me the corner where the unemployed hang out, drinking and waiting for a government check. Since cheap foods became available from the European Union, she complained, farming in northern Finland has closed down, and there are no other jobs. But she is enterprising. She cofounded a cooperative marketing outlet for local products, including jams made from local berries, wooden crafts, knitted scarves—and matsutake. She learned about matsutake from a traveling seminar that showed people how to identify and pick, and she is waiting for a good year to find more. She is also interested in the possibilities of matsutake tourism.

Others in her area have trained themselves as nature guides, taking urban visitors into the woods for sports and hobbies, including mushroom picking.[4] I had the chance to pick with one exuberant young man, who promised he would be the "king of matsutake" next good year. He had learned mushrooms in a class; this was not traditional heritage. It represented a hope for him, an opening, an enthusiasm on which he would ride should a rising tide arrive. If the mushrooms came, he said, he would pick all night with lights. Matsutake were his dream not just for getting by, but for getting by with verve.

Here again is that edge, both inside and outside capitalism. When a new commodity chain arrives, this man grasps it not through industrial discipline but through personal talents—and as one of many precarious possibilities. On the one hand, this *is* capitalism; everyone wants to be an entrepreneur. On the other hand, entrepreneurship is shaped by the rhythms of the Finnish countryside, with its mixture of silent deprivations and enthusiasms to improve. Any commodity that moves downstream along that chain will have to be disembedded from those connections in a messy process of translation. There is room here for imagining other worlds.[5]

Imagining other worlds was very much on the mind of the satoyama advocates I met in Japan. I think particularly of Tanaka-san, who, like Tiia, had put together a display center for local natural products and crafts. Unlike Tiia, however, he was not concerned with making a living. He was comfortably retired, and this was his own land. His personal nature center is an attempt to build a culture of care for satoyama landscapes and a gift to neighbors and visitors. In his town, he said, children had started going to school on a bus; now that they did not walk to school, they hardly went outside. He brought children to his land to show them how to notice the forest—and to play. We walked through the forest's special places, which he hoped the children, too, might discover: here two trees (and of different species!) have grown together, knotted into a single trunk; here some crumbling Buddhist statues emerged from the brush when he cleaned it back; here a natural stone split in two reminds him of a woman. He took us to see the pines he was caring for, which otherwise would die from pine wilt disease, now rampant in this area. The treatment is expensive, and his wife does not approve of the cost. But this is his commitment to the forest.

Tanaka-san had built a small hut on the hillside, and he served tea to Shiho Satsuka and me while we sat looking down through the trees. The hut was full of curious things he had found in the forest, from lacquered conks to unusual wild fruits. After a while, his brother-in-law, a forest worker, came by, and he told us stories of how the forest was once logged by lowering trees down wires. This was before the mountain was left to brushy regrowth. Tanaka-san's family had lived in the area for five generations, working in the mountains, but he became a public servant, serving at the post office. He used the lump sum from his retirement to buy the land. Despite the expense, he feels that working in the forest has a good influence on him. It makes him no money, but the forest's ability to inspire visitors means a lot. Reinvigorating people's sense of nature, he said, makes a world worth living. If matsutake appeared, this would be an unexpected gift.

Without meaning to, most of us learn to ignore the multispecies worlds around us. Projects for rebuilding curiosity, like that of Tanaka-san, are essential work for living with others. It helps, of course, to have adequate funds and time. But that is not the only way to be curious.

I first met Xiaomei when she was nine and her mother worked at a rural hotel where Michael Hathaway and I stayed in central Yunnan. She was brave, charming, and clever—and she loved to show us things. Her parents had a good relationship with one of the matsutake bosses, who owned the hotel, and her family sometimes went up into the mountains, where they looked for mushrooms and picnicked. Once Michael and I went along, and Xiaomei and I became distracted by tiny wild strawberries with a taste so intense that I closed my eyes when they went into my mouth. Xiaomei then ran around gathering red-topped *Russula*, worthless but beautiful things. Xiaomei's enthusiasm was contagious, and I loved them too.

The next time I came, two years later, I was pleased to see she had not lost her sense of the deliciousness of life. She dragged Michael and me to see vegetable gardens along the road, and then further into the uncultivated verges where the wild plants of disturbed places grow. This was the latent commons of weeds, the "vacant places" of progress narratives, so often imagined as without value. Yet it was full of interest for us. We stuffed ourselves with berries from the brambles and searched for tiny mushrooms. We followed goat trails and examined flowers. She explained what everything was and how people used it. It was just the kind of curiosity Tanaka-san wanted to nurture in his town's children. Multispecies living depends on it.

Without stories of progress, the world has become a terrifying place. The ruin glares at us with the horror of its abandonment. It's not easy to know how to make a life, much less avert planetary destruction. Luckily there is still company, human and not human. We can still explore the overgrown verges of our blasted landscapes—the edges of capitalist discipline, scalability, and abandoned resource plantations. We can still catch the scent of the latent commons—and the elusive autumn aroma.

Elusive life, Oregon.
Remembering Leke
Nakashimura. Leke
worked to keep matsutake
memory alive by
encouraging old and
young to follow him into
the forest, looking for
mushrooms.

Spore Trail
The Further Adventures
of a Mushroom

ONE OF THE STRANGEST PROJECTS OF PRIVATIZATION and commodification in the early twentieth-first century has been the movement to commoditize scholarship. Two versions have been surprisingly powerful. In Europe, administrators demand assessment exercises that reduce the work of scholars to a number, a sum total for a life of intellectual exchange. In the United States, scholars are asked to become entrepreneurs, producing ourselves as brands and seeking stardom from the very first days of our studies, when we know nothing. Both projects seem to me bizarre—and suffocating. By privatizing what is necessarily collaborative work, these projects aim to strangle the life out of scholarship.

Anyone who cares about ideas is forced, then, to create scenes that exceed or escape "professionalization," that is, the surveillance techniques of privatization. This means designing research that requires playgroups and collaborative clusters: not congeries of individuals calculating costs and benefits, but rather scholarship that emerges through its collaborations. Thinking through mushrooms, once again, can help.

What if we imagined intellectual life as a peasant woodland, a source of many useful products emerging in unintentional design? The image calls up its opposites: In assessment exercises, intellectual life is a plantation; in scholarly entrepreneurship, intellectual life is pure theft, the private appropriation of communal products. Neither is appealing. Consider, instead, the pleasures of the woodland. There are many useful products there, from berries and mushrooms to firewood, wild vegetables, medicinal herbs, and even timber. A forager can chose what to gather and can make use of the woodland's patches of unexpected bounty. But the woodland requires continuing work, not to make it a garden but rather to keep it open and available for an array of species. Human coppicing, grazing, and fire maintain this architecture; other species gather to make it their own. For intellectual work, this seems just right. Work in common creates the possibilities of particular feats of individual scholarship. To encourage the unknown potential of scholarly advances—like the unexpected bounty of a nest of mushrooms—requires sustaining the common work of the intellectual woodland.

In this spirit, the Matsutake Worlds Research Group—the group that made my matsutake research possible—has tried to build playful collaborations into our individual and collective work. This has not been simple; pressures to privatize worm their way into every scholar's life. The tempo of collaboration is necessarily sporadic. But we have coppiced and burned, and our common intellectual woodland flourishes.

This means, too, that the intellectual equivalents of forest products have become available to each of us as gatherers. This book is just one harvest of those products. It is not the last: a woodland draws us again and again to its shifting treasures. If there is one mushroom, might there yet be more? This book opens a series of forays to our matsutake woodland. There will be more, to China, to trace commerce, and to Japan, to follow cosmopolitan science. Consider the further adventures in these companion volumes:

In China, exuberance about global trade has transformed even the most remote villages, creating a "rural China" with transnational trade at its heart. Matsutake is the ideal vehicle to follow this development. Michael Hathaway's "Emerging Matsutake Worlds" traces the making of distinctive paths for global commerce in Yunnan. The book explores conflicting transnational pressures of conservation and commerce—as seen, for example, in the hard-to-explain presence of pesticides on Chinese mushrooms—showing how particular places, including matsutake forests, develop within global connections. One surprising finding is the importance of ethnic entrepreneurship: in both Tibetan and Yi areas, pickers and village-based dealers work within ethnic circuits. Hathaway examines both the cosmopolitan character and the traditionalist preoccupations of the new ethnic aspirations promoted by matsutake.

Opening science, and knowledge more generally, to cosmopolitan history is an urgent task for scholars. Matsutake science in Japan turns out to be an ideal site for understanding the intersections between science and vernacular knowledge, on the one hand, and international and local expertise, on the other. Shiho Satsuka's "The Charisma of a Wild Mushroom" delves into such intersections to show how Japanese science is always already cosmopolitan and vernacular. She develops a concept of translation in which all knowledge is based in translation. Rather than the immaculate "Japanese" knowledge of both Orientalist and nationalist imaginations, matsutake science is translation all the way down. Her work moves beyond familiar Western epistemologies and ontologics to explore unexpected forms of personhood and thingness within the poorly differentiated human-nonhuman world matsutake shows us.

What kind of book is this that refuses to end? Like the matsutake forest, each contingent gathering sponsors others in unexpected bounty. None of this would be possible without transgressing against the commodification of scholarship. Woodlands, too, offend the plantation and the strip miner. But it is hard to make woodlands fully disappear. Intellectual woodlands too: ideas born in common play still beckon.

In "The Carrier Bag Theory of Fiction," Ursula K. Le Guin argues that stories of hunting and killing have allowed readers to imagine that individual heroism is the point of a story. Instead, she proposes that storytelling might pick up diverse things of meaning and value and gather them together, like a forager rather than a hunter waiting for the big kill. In this kind of storytelling, stories should never end, but rather lead to further stories. In the intellectual woodlands I have been trying to encourage, adventures lead to more adventures, and treasures lead to further treasures. When gathering mushrooms, one is not enough; finding the first encourages me to find more. But Le Guin says it with so much humor and spirit that I give her the last word:

> Go on, say I, wandering off towards the wild oats, with Oo Oo in the sling and little Oom carrying the basket. You just go on telling how the mammoth fell on Boob and how Cain fell on Abel and how the bomb fell on Nagasaki and how the burning jelly fell on the villagers and how the missiles will fall on the Evil Empire, and all the other steps in the Ascent of Man.
>
> If it is a human thing to do to put something you want, because it's useful, edible, or beautiful, into a bag, or a basket, or a bit of rolled bark or leaf, or a net woven of your own hair, or what have you, and then take it home with you, home being another, larger kind of pouch or bag, a container for people, and then later you take it out and eat it or share it or store it up for winter in a solider container or put it in the medicine bundle or the shrine or the museum, the holy place, the area that contains what is sacred, and then next day you probably do much the same again—if to do that is human, if that's what it takes, then I am a human being after all. Fully, freely, gladly, for the first time.[1]

Notes

ENABLING ENTANGLEMENTS

1. William Cronon, *Nature's metropolis* (New York: W. W. Norton, 1992).

2. See Matsutake Worlds Research Group, "A new form of collaboration in cultural anthropology: Matsutake worlds," *American Ethnologist* 36, no. 2 (2009): 380–403; Matsutake Worlds Research Group, "Strong collaboration as a method for multi-sited ethnography: On mycorrhizal relations," in *Multi-sited ethnography: Theory, praxis, and locality in contemporary research*, ed. Mark-Anthony Falzon, 197–214 (Farnham, UK: Ashgate, 2009); Anna Tsing and Shiho Satsuka, "Diverging understandings of forest management in matsutake science," *Economic Botany* 62, no. 3 (2008): 244–256. A special issue of articles by the group is currently under preparation.

3. Elaine Gan and Anna Tsing, "Some experiments in the representation of time: Fungal clock," paper presented at the annual meeting of the American Anthropological Association, San Francisco, 2012; Gan and Tsing, "Fungal time in the satoyama forest," animation by Natalie McKeever, video installation, University of Sydney, 2013.

4. Sara Dosa, *The last season* (Filament Productions, 2014). The film follows the relationship of two matsutake pickers in Oregon: a white veteran of the U.S.-Indochina war and a Cambodian refugee.

5. Hjorleifur Jonsson's book *Slow anthropology: Negotiating difference with the Iu Mien* (Ithaca, NY: Cornell University Southeast Asia Program Publications, 2014)

emerged from the stimulus of our collaboration—and Jonsson's continuing research with Iu Mien.

Prologue. Autumn Aroma

Epigraph: Miyako Inoue kindly worked through this translation with me; we aimed for a version both evocative and literal. For an alternative, see Matsutake Research Association, ed., *Matsutake* [in Japanese] (Kyoto: Matsutake Research Association, 1964), front matter: "The aroma of pine mushrooms. The path to the hilltop of Takamatsu, Tall Pine Tree Village, has just been barred by the rings and lines of rapidly rising caps (of pine mushrooms). They emit an attractive autumnal aroma that refreshes me a great deal . . ."

1. Sveta Yamin-Pasternak, "How the devils went deaf: Ethnomycology, cuisine, and perception of landscape in the Russian far north" (PhD diss., University of Alaska, Fairbanks, 2007).

2. *Desert* (Stac an Armin Press, 2011), 6, 78.

3. Chinese matsutake traders first told me the story, which I took to be urban legend; however, a scientist trained in Japan confirmed the existence of this story in Japanese newspapers in the 1990s. I have not yet found it. Still, the timing of the bomb in August would have corresponded to the beginning of the matsutake fruiting season. How radioactive those mushrooms were is a continuing mystery. One Japanese scientist told me he planned to research the radioactivity of Hiroshima matsutake, but the authorities told him to stay away from this topic. The U.S. bomb exploded more than five hundred meters above the city; official wisdom has it that the radioactivity was carried into global wind systems, with little local contamination.

4. In this book, I use the term "humanist" to include those trained in both the humanities and the social sciences. In using this term in contrast to natural scientists, I am evoking what C. P. Snow called "the two cultures." Charles Percy Snow, *The Two Cultures* (1959; London: Cambridge University Press, 2001). Among humanists, I include, too, those who call themselves "posthumanists."

5. Marx used "alienation" particularly to speak of the separation of the worker from the processes and products of production, as well as other workers. Karl Marx, *Economic and philosophical manuscripts of 1844* (Mineola, NY: Dover Books, 2007). I stretch the term from this use to consider the separation of nonhumans as well as humans from their livelihood processes.

6. Alienation was also intrinsic to the state-led industrial socialism of the twentieth century. Because it is increasingly obsolete, I do not discuss it here.

7. This section draws on Okamura Toshihisa, *Matsutake no bunkashi* [*The cultural history of matsutake*] (Tokyo: Yama to Keikokusha, 2005). Fusako Shimura kindly translated the book for me. For other discussions of mushrooms in Japanese culture, see R. Gordon Wasson, "Mushrooms and Japanese culture," *Transactions of the Asiatic Society of Japan* 11 (1973): 5–25; Neda Hitoshi, *Kinoko hakubutsukan* [*Mushroom museum*] (Tokyo: Yasaka Shobô, 2003).

8. Quoted in Okamura, *Matsutake*, 55 (trans. Fusako Shimura and Miyako Inoue).

9. Haruo Shirane calls this "second nature"; see *Japan and the culture of the four seasons: Nature, literature, and the arts* (New York: Columbia University Press, 2012).

10. Quoted in Okamura, *Matsutake*, 98 (trans. Fusako Shimura and Miyako Inoue).

11. The question of whether southern Europe and North Africa's *T. caligatum* (which also sells as matsutake) is the same species has not yet been resolved. For the argument in favor of separate species status, see I. Kytovuori, "The *Tricholoma caligatum* group in Europe and North Africa," *Karstenia* 28, no. 2 (1988): 65–77. Northwestern America's *T. caligatum* is another species entirely, but it too sells as matsutake. See Ra Lim, Alison Fischer, Mary Berbee, and Shannon M. Berch, "Is the booted tricholoma in British Columbia really Japanese matsutake?" *BC Journal of Ecosystems and Management* 3, no. 1 (2003): 61–67.

12. The type specimen for *T. magnivelare* is from the eastern United States, and it may prove yet to be *T. matsutake* (David Arora, personal communication, 2007). Northwestern American matsutake will need another scientific name.

13. For recent research on classification, see Hitoshi Murata, Yuko Ota, Muneyoshi Yamaguchi, Akiyoshi Yamada, Shinichiro Katahata, Yuichiro Otsuka, Katsuhiko Babasaki, and Hitoshi Neda, "Mobile DNA distributions refine the phylogeny of 'matsutake' mushrooms, *Tricholoma* sect. Caligata," *Mycorrhiza* 23, no. 6 (2013): 447–461. For more on scientists' views about matsutake diversity, see chapter 17.

14. Quoted in Okamura, *Matsutake*, 54 (trans. Fusako Shimura and Miyako Inoue).

PART I. WHAT'S LEFT?

1. For mushroom lovers: This was *Tricholoma focale*.

CHAPTER 1. ARTS OF NOTICING

Epigraph: Ursula K. Le Guin, "A non-Euclidean view of California as a cold place to be," in *Dancing at the edge of the world*, 80–100 (New York: Grove Press, 1989), on 85.

1. Philip Cogswell, "Deschutes Country Pine Logging," in *High and mighty*, ed. Thomas Vaughan, 235–260 (Portland: Oregon Historical Society, 1981); Ward Tonsfeldt and Paul Claeyssens, "Railroads up the Deschutes canyon" (Portland: Oregon Historical Society, 2014), http://www.ohs.org/education/oregonhistory/narratives /subtopic.cfm?subtopic_ID=395.

2. "Spotted owl hung in effigy," *Eugene Register-Guard*, May 3, 1989: 13.

3. Ivan Maluski, Oregon Sierra Club, quoted in Taylor Clark, "The owl and the chainsaw," *Willamette Week*, March 9, 2005, http://www.wweek.com/portland/arti cle-4188-1989.html.

4. In 1979, the price of Oregon timber dropped; mill closings and corporate mergers followed. Gail Wells, "Restructuring the timber economy" (Portland: Oregon

Historical Society, 2006), http://www.ohs.org/education/oregonhistory/narratives/sub
topic.cfm?subtopic_ID=579.

5. See, for example, Michael McRae, "Mushrooms, guns, and money," *Outside* 18,
no. 10 (1993): 64–69, 151–154; Peter Gillins, "Violence clouds Oregon gold rush for
wild mushrooms," *Chicago Tribune*, July 8, 1993, 2; Eric Gorski, "Guns part of fungi
season," *Oregonian*, September 24, 1996, 1, 9.

6. Donna Haraway, "Anthropocene, Capitalocene, Chthulucene: Staying with
the Trouble," presentation for "Arts of Living on a Damaged Planet," Santa Cruz, CA,
May 9, 2014, http://anthropocene.au.dk/arts-of-living-on-a-damaged-planet, argues
that "Anthropocene" gestures to sky gods; instead, she suggests we honor the "ten-
tacular ones"—and multispecies entanglements—by calling our era the Chthulucene. Indeed, Anthropocene calls up varied meanings, as the 2014 debate over plans
for a "good" Anthropocene illustrated. See, for example, Keith Kloor, who embraces
the Anthropocene through a "green modernism" in "Facing up to the Anthropocene," http://blogs.discovermagazine.com/collideascape/2014/06/20/facing-anthropo
cene/#.U6h8XBbgvpA.

7. World making can be understood in dialogue with what some scholars are
calling "ontology," that is, philosophies of being. Like those scholars, I am interested
in interrupting common sense, including the sometimes unselfconscious assumptions of imperial conquest (e.g., Eduardo Viveiros de Castro, "Cosmological deixis
and Amerindian perspectivism," *Journal of the Royal Anthropological Institute* 4, no. 3
(1998): 469–488). World-making projects, as with alternative ontologies, show that
other worlds are possible. World making, however, focuses us on practical activities
rather than cosmologies. It is thus easier to discuss how nonhuman beings might
contribute their own perspectives. Most scholars use ontology to understand
human perspectives on nonhumans; to my knowledge, only Eduardo Kohn's *How
forests think* (Berkeley: University of California Press, 2013), working through
Piercian semiotics, allows the radical claim that other beings have their own ontologies. In contrast, every organism makes worlds; humans have no special status. Finally, world-making projects overlap. While most scholars use ontology to segregate
perspectives, one at a time, thinking through world making allows layering and
historically consequential friction. A world-making approach draws ontological
concerns into the multi-scalar analysis that James Clifford's *Returns* calls "realism"
(Cambridge, MA: Harvard University Press, 2013).

8. Some social scientists use the term to refer to something more like a Fou-
caultian discursive formation (e.g., Aihwa Ong and Stephen Collier, eds., *Global
assemblages* [Hoboken, NJ: Wiley-Blackwell, 2005]). Such "assemblages" expand
across space and conquer place; they are not constituted through indeterminacy.
Because constitutive encounters are a key for me, my assemblages are what gathers
in a place, at whatever scale. Other "assemblages" are networks, as in Actor-Network
Theory (Bruno Latour, *Reassembling the social* [Oxford: Oxford University Press,
2007]). A network is a chain of associations that structures further associations; my
assemblages gather ways of being without assuming that interactional structure.

Assemblage translates philosopher Gilles Deleuze's *agencement*, and this has sponsored varied attempts to open up the "social"; my use joins this configuration.

9. Nellie Chu, "Global supply chains of risks and desires: The crafting of migrant entrepreneurship in Guangzhou, China" (PhD diss., University of California, Santa Cruz, 2014).

10. As a method, one might think of this as combining insights from Donna Haraway and Marilyn Strathern. Strathern shows us how the startle of surprise interrupts common sense, allowing us to notice different world-making projects within the assemblage. Haraway follows threads to draw our attention to the interplay across divergent projects. By taking these methods together, I trace out assemblages informed by the disconcerting interruptions of one kind of project by others. It may be useful to point out that these scholars are the source points for anthropological thinking, respectively, with ontology (Strathern) and world making (Haraway). See Marilyn Strathern, "The ethnographic effect," in *Property, substance, and effect* (London: Athlone Press, 1999), 1–28; Donna Haraway, *Companion species manifesto* (Chicago: Prickly Paradigm Press, 2003).

CHAPTER 2. CONTAMINATION AS COLLABORATION

Epigraph: Mai Neng Moua, "Along the way to the Mekong," in *Bamboo among the oaks: Contemporary writing by Hmong Americans*, ed. Mai Neng Moua, 57–61 (St. Paul, MN: Borealis Books, 2002), on 60.

1. Multicellular life was made possible by multiple, mutual contaminations of bacteria. Lynn Margulis and Dorion Sagan, *What is life?* (Berkeley: University of California Press, 2000).

2. Richard Dawkins, *The selfish gene* (Oxford: Oxford University Press, 1976).

3. Many critics have refused the "selfishness" of these assumptions and inserted altruism into these equations. The problem, however, is not selfishness but self-containment.

4. A species name is a useful heuristic with which to introduce an organism, but the name does not capture either the particularity of that organism or its position within sometimes-rapid collective transformations. An ethnic name has the same problem. But doing without these names is worse: we are left imagining that all trees, or Asians, look alike. I need names to give substance to noticing, but I need them as names-in-motion.

5. Harold Steen, *The U.S. Forest Service: A history* (1976; Seattle: University of Washington Press, centennial ed., 2004); William Robbins, *American forestry* (Lincoln: University of Nebraska Press, 1985).

6. For the related ecologies of Oregon's Blue Mountains, see Nancy Langston, *Forest dreams, forest nightmares* (Seattle: University of Washington Press, 1996). For a fuller discussion of eastern Cascades ecology, see chapter 14.

7. Interview, forester Phil Cruz, October 2004.

8. Jeffery MacDonald, *Transnational aspects of Iu-Mien refugee identity* (New York: Routledge, 1997).

9. Hjorleifur Jonsson, *Mien relations: Mountain people and state control in Thailand* (Ithaca, NY: Cornell University Press, 2005).

10. William Smalley, Chia Koua Vang, and Gnia Yee Vang, *Mother of writing: The origin and development of a Hmong messianic script* (Chicago: University of Chicago Press, 1990).

11. William Geddes, *Migrants of the mountains: The cultural ecology of the Blue Miao (Hmong Nyua) of Thailand* (Oxford: Oxford University Press, 1976).

12. Quoted by Douglas Martin, "Gen. Vang Pao, Laotian who aided U.S., dies at 81," *New York Times*, January 8, 2011, http://www.nytimes.com/2011/01/08/world/asia /08vangpao.html.

13. Sources for this history include Alfred McCoy, *The politics of heroin: CIA complicity in the global drug trade* (Chicago: Chicago Review Press, 2003); Jane Hamilton-Merritt, *Tragic mountains: The Hmong, the Americans, and the secret war in Laos, 1942–1992* (Indianapolis: Indiana University Press, 1999); Gary Yia Lee, ed., *The impact of globalization and transnationalism on the Hmong* (St. Paul, MN: Center for Hmong Studies, 2006).

14. Personal communication, 2007.

15. Hjorleifur Jonsson, "War's ontogeny: Militias and ethnic boundaries in Laos and exile," *Southeast Asian Studies* 47, no. 2 (2009): 125–149.

CHAPTER 3. SOME PROBLEMS WITH SCALE

Epigraph: Niels Bohr quoted in Otto Robert Frisch, *What little I remember* (Cambridge: Cambridge University Press, 1980), 95.

1. A rich interdisciplinary literature—comprising anthropology, geography, art history, and historical agronomy, among other fields—has gathered around the sugarcane plantation. See especially Sidney Mintz, *Sweetness and power: The place of sugar in modern history* (Harmondsworth, UK: Penguin, 1986); and Mintz, *Worker in the cane* (New Haven, CT: Yale University Press, 1960); J. H. Galloway, *The sugar cane industry* (Cambridge: Cambridge University Press, 1991); Jill Casid, *Sowing empire* (Minneapolis: University of Minnesota Press, 2005); and Jonathan Sauer, *A historical geography of crop plants* (Boca Raton, FL: CRC Press, 1993).

2. Sugarcane plantations were never as fully scalable as planters wished. Enslaved labor escaped into maroon communities. Imported fungal rots spread with the cane. Scalability is never stable; at best, it takes a huge amount of work.

3. Mintz, *Sweetness and power*, 47.

4. For introductions to matsutake biology and ecology, see Ogawa Makoto, *Matsutake no Seibutsugaku* [*Matsutake biology*] (1978; Tokyo: Tsukiji Shokan, 1991); David Hosford, David Pilz, Randy Molina, and Michael Amaranthus, *Ecology and management of the commercially harvested American matsutake mushroom* (USDA Forest Service General Technical Report PNW-412, 1997).

5. Key references include Paul Hirt, *A conspiracy of optimism: Management of the national forests since World War Two* (Lincoln: University of Nebraska Press, 1994); William Robbins, *Landscapes of conflict: The Oregon story, 1940–2000* (Seattle: Univer-

sity of Washington Press, 2004); Richard Rajala, *Clearcutting the Pacific rainforest: Production, science, and regulation* (Vancouver: UBC Press, 1998).

6. For what went wrong, see Langston, *Forest dreams* (cited in chap. 2, n. 6). For the eastern Cascades, see Mike Znerold, "A new integrated forest resource plan for ponderosa pine forests on the Deschutes National Forest," paper presented at the Ontario Ministry of Natural Resources workshop, "Tools for Site Specific Silviculture in Northwestern Ontario," Thunder Bay, Ontario, April 18–20, 1989.

7. Susan Alexander, David Pilz, Nancy Weber, Ed Brown, and Victoria Rockwell, "Mushrooms, trees, and money: Value estimates of commercial mushrooms and timber in the Pacific Northwest," *Environmental Management* 30, no. 1 (2002): 129–141.

INTERLUDE. SMELLING

Epigraph: John Cage, "Mushroom haiku," http://www.youtube.com/watch?v=XNz VQ8wRCBo.

1. See http://www.lcdf.org/indeterminacy/. For a live performance, see http:// www.youtube.com/watch?v=AJMekwS6b9U.

2. This translation is found on p. 97 of R. H. Blyth, "Mushrooms in Japanese verse," *Transactions of the Asiatic Society of Japan*, 3rd ser., 11 (1973): 93–106.

3. For Cage's discussion of the translation, see http://www.youtube.com/watch ?v=XNzVQ8wRCBo.

4. Alan Rayner, *Degrees of freedom: Living in dynamic boundaries* (London: Imperial College Press, 1997).

5. Kyorai Mukai, reproduced and translated in Blyth, "Mushrooms," 98.

6. Walter Benjamin, "On the concept of history," *Gesammelten Schriften*, trans. Dennis Redmond, (Frankfurt: Suhrkamp Verlag, 1974), sec. 6, 1:2.

7. Ibid., sec. 14. He is comparing fashion and revolution here; each harvests from the past to meet the present.

8. Verran, personal communication, 2010. Verran develops the concept of the here and now in many of her writings concerning the Yolngu. Thus, for example: "Yolngu knowledge is the intrusion of the Dreaming into the secular. The Dreaming is brought into the here and now by the doing of particular things at particular times by particular people. . . . Knowledge can only ever be a performance of the Dreaming, a bringing to life in the here and now of the elements of the other domain" (Verran quoted in Caroline Josephs, "Silence as a way of knowing in Yolngu indigenous Australian storytelling," in *Negotiating the Sacred II*, ed. Elizabeth Coleman and Maria Fernandez-Dias, 173–190 [Canberra: ANU Press, 2008], on 181).

9. David Arora, *Mushrooms demystified* (Berkeley: Ten Speed Press, 1986), 191.

10. William F. Wood and Charles K. Lefevre, "Changing volatile compounds from mycelium and sporocarp of American matsutake mushroom, *Tricholoma magnivelare*," *Biochemical Systematics and Ecology* 35 (2007): 634–636. I have not found the Japanese research but was told about it by Dr. Ogawa. I don't know if the same chemicals were isolated as the essence of the smell.

CHAPTER 4. WORKING THE EDGE

1. A commodity chain is any arrangement connecting producers and consumers of commodities. Supply chains are those commodity chains organized by lead firms' outsourcing. Lead firms may be producers, traders, or retailers. See Anna Tsing, "Supply chains and the human condition," *Rethinking Marxism* 21, no. 2 (2009): 148–176.

2. Shiho Satsuka, *Nature in translation* (Durham, NC: Duke University Press, 2015). Satsuka draws on extended meanings of "translation" in postcolonial theory and science studies; for further discussion, see chapter 16.

3. The term takes off from Marx's "primitive accumulation," the violence through which rural people destined for industrial work are disenfranchised. As in Marx's analysis, I step outside industrial formations to see how capitalism comes into being. In contrast to primitive accumulation, salvage is never complete; accumulation always depends on it. Salvage accumulation is also required for the production of labor power. Factory workers are produced and reproduced through life processes never fully controlled by capitalists. In factories, capitalists use the abilities of workers to make goods, but they cannot produce all those abilities. To transform workers' abilities into capitalist value is salvage accumulation.

4. I reserve the term "noncapitalist" for forms of value making outside capitalist logics. "Pericapitalist" is my term for *sites* that are both in and out. This is not a classificatory hierarchy but rather a way to explore ambiguity.

5. Joseph Conrad, *Heart of darkness* (1899; Mineola, NY: Dover Books, 1990).

6. Herman Melville, *Moby-Dick* (1851; New York: Signet Classics, 1998).

7. Misha Petrovic and Gary Hamilton, "Making global markets: Wal-Mart and its suppliers," in *Wal-Mart: The face of twenty-first-century capitalism*, ed. Nelson Lichtenstein, 107–142 (New York: W. W. Norton 2006).

8. "Was a high wall there that tried to stop me, A sign was painted said: Private Property, But on the back side it didn't say nothing—This land was made for you and me." Woody Guthrie, "This land," 1940, http://www.woodyguthrie.org/Lyrics /This_Land.htm.

9. Sources include Barbara Ehrenreich, *Nickled and dimed: On (not) getting by in America* (New York: Metropolitan Books, 2001); Lichtenstein, ed., *Wal-Mart*; Anthony Bianco, *The bully of Bentonville: The high cost of Wal-Mart's everyday low prices* (New York: Doubleday, 2006).

10. J. K. Gibson-Graham, *A post-capitalist politics* (Minneapolis: University of Minnesota Press, 2006).

11. Susanne Freidberg, *French beans and food scares: Culture and commerce in an anxious age* (Oxford: Oxford University Press, 2004).

12. Susanne Freidberg, "Supermarkets and imperial knowledge," *Cultural Geographies* 14, no. 3 (2007): 321–342.

13. Michael Hardt and Antonio Negri, *Empire* (Cambridge, MA: Harvard University Press, 2000).

14. The interplay between Hardt and Negri's *Commonwealth* (Cambridge, MA: Harvard University Press, 2009) and Gibson-Graham's *Post-capitalist politics* is particularly good to think with. See also J. K. Gibson-Graham, *The end of capitalism (as we knew it): A feminist critique of political economy* (London: Blackwell, 1996).

15. Jane Collins, *Threads: Gender, labor, and power in the global apparel industry* (Chicago: University of Chicago Press, 2003).

16. Lieba Faier offers a related view of the matsutake commodity chain in Japan: "Fungi, trees, people, nematodes, beetles, and weather: Ecologies of vulnerability and ecologies of negotiation in matsutake commodity exchange," *Environment and Planning A* 43 (2011): 1079–1097.

CHAPTER 5. OPEN TICKET, OREGON

1. When pickers buy Forest Service picking permits, they are given maps that show picking and no-picking zones. However, the zones are marked only in abstract space. The maps show only major thoroughfares and no topography, railroads, small roads, or vegetation. It is almost impossible for even the most determined reader to make sense of the map on the ground. Besides, many pickers cannot read maps. One Lao picker showed me a no-picking zone on his map by indicating a lake. Some pickers use the maps as toilet paper, which is scarce in the campgrounds.

2. A regulation requires buyers to record the place where matsutake are picked; however, I never saw such records being made. In other matsutake buying areas, this regulation is enforced through pickers' self-statements.

3. This is fire protection mandated by the industry-promoted Healthy Forests Restoration Act of 2003. Jacqueline Vaughn and Hanna Cortner, *George W. Bush's healthy forests* (Boulder: University Press of Colorado, 2005).

4. During the four seasons I watched the buying, I saw two buyers leave, midseason, because of quarrels with their respective field agents; another absconded. No one was forced out of business because of competition.

5. Jerry Guin's *Matsutake mushroom: "White" goldrush of the 1990s* (Happy Camp, CA: Naturegraph Publishers, 1997) offers a picker's diary from 1993.

6. For one example, see the account of Marlboro's history in Richard Barnet, *Global dreams: Imperial corporations and the new world order* (New York: Touchstone, 1995).

7. Other amazing accounts of precarious labor in the forests of the U.S. Pacific Northwest include Rebecca McLain, "Controlling the forest understory: Wild mushroom politics in central Oregon" (PhD diss., University of Washington, 2000); Beverly Brown and Agueda Marin-Hernández, eds., *Voices from the woods: Lives and experiences of non-timber forest workers* (Wolf Creek, OR: Jefferson Center for Education and Research, 2000); Beverly Brown, Diana Leal-Mariño, Kirsten McIlveen, Ananda Lee Tan, *Contract forest laborers in Canada, the U.S., and Mexico* (Portland, OR: Jefferson Center for Education and Research, 2004); Richard Hansis, "A political ecology of picking: Non-timber forest products in the Pacific Northwest,"

Human Ecology 26, no. 1 (1998): 67–86; Rebecca Richards and Susan Alexander, *A social history of wild huckleberry harvesting in the Pacific Northwest* (USDA Forest Service PNW-GTR-657, 2006).

CHAPTER 6. WAR STORIES

1. For a Vang Pao supporter's blow-by-blow account, see Hamilton-Merritt, *Tragic mountains* (cited in chap. 2, n. 13).

2. CBS News, "Deer hunter charged with murder," November 29, 2004, http://www.cbsnews.com/stories/2004/11/30/national/main658296.shtml.

3. "The Refugee Population," *A country study: Laos*, Library of Congress, Country Studies, http://lcweb2.loc.gov/frd/cs/latoc.html#la0065.

4. Susan Star and James Griesemer, "Institutional ecology, 'translations' and boundary objects," *Social Studies of Science* 19, no. 3 (1989): 387–420.

CHAPTER 7. WHAT HAPPENED TO THE STATE?

1. *Shigin* refers to classical poetry recitation in Japan. This poem was distributed, in Japanese and with an English translation, by Kokkan **N**omura, at the September 18, 2005 celebration of matsutake heritage at the Oregon Nikkei Legacy Center. Miyako Inoue helped to craft this new English translation.

2. This agreement forced Japan to stop issuing new passports for potential immigrants; it did not cover wives and family members of men already living in the United States. This exception encouraged the practice of finding "picture brides," a practice that was stopped by the "Ladies' Agreement" of 1920.

3. Pegues writes (personal communication, 2014): "Executive Order 9066 is signed on Feb. 19, 1942, with most of the relocation and internment/incarceration occurring between March–June. In August the Western Defense Commander announces that Japanese American removal and internment is complete. On the other side of things, Mexico declares war on the Axis powers on June 1st and the U.S. establishes the Bracero Program in July 1942 by executive order."

4. The term comes from Lauren Kessler, *Stubborn twig: Three generations in the life of a Japanese American family* (Corvallis: Oregon State University Press, 2008), chap. 13.

5. Many of the Southeast Asian pickers in Open Ticket receive disability checks and/or Aid to Dependent Children from the government; however, these do not cover expenses.

6. The first Christian Great Awakening of the eighteenth century was a precursor of the American Revolution. The second, of the early nineteenth century, is credited with creating the political culture of the American frontier as well as the Civil War. The third, in the late nineteenth century, sparked the social gospel of American nationalism and its worldwide missionary movement. Some call the Born-Again movement of the late twentieth century the Fourth Great Awakening. These Christian revivals are not the only kind of civic mobilizations in the United States, but it may be useful to see them as forming the *pattern* on which mobilization to shape public culture can successfully occur.

7. Susan Harding, "Regulating religion in mid-20th century America: The 'Man: A Course of Study' curriculum," paper presented at "Religion and Politics in Anxious States," University of Kentucky, 2014.

8. Thomas Pearson, *Missions and conversions: Creating the Montagnard-Dega refugee community* (New York: Palgrave Macmillan, 2009).

CHAPTER 8. BETWEEN THE DOLLAR AND THE YEN

1. U.S. whaling interests pushed this initiative, which demanded assistance for U.S. whaling ships (Alan Christy, personal communication, 2014). *Moby-Dick* haunts me.

2. The 1858 Harris Treaty opened more ports, made foreign nationals free from Japanese law, and put foreigners in charge of import-export duties. European powers then imposed similar treaties.

3. Kunio Yoshihara, *Japanese economic development* (Oxford: Oxford University Press, 1994); Tessa Morris-Suzuki, *A history of Japanese economic thought* (London: Routledge, 1989).

4. Satsuka, *Nature in translation* (cited in chap. 4, n. 2).

5. Hidemasa Morikawa, *Zaibatsu: The rise and fall of family enterprise groups in Japan* (Tokyo: University of Tokyo Press, 1992).

6. E. Herbert Norman, *Japan's emergence as a modern state* (1940; Vancouver: UBC Press, 2000), 49.

7. Some three hundred zaibatsu were listed for breakup, but only about ten were dissolved before the occupation government changed course. Still, regulations were put in place that made prewar vertical integration difficult to sustain (Alan Christy, personal communication, 2014).

8. Kenichi Miyashita and David Russell, *Keiretsu: Inside the hidden Japanese conglomerates* (New York: McGraw-Hill, 1994); Michael Gerlach, *Alliance capitalism: The social organization of Japanese business* (Berkeley: University of California Press, 1992). In *The fable of the keiretsu* (Chicago: University of Chicago Press, 2006), Yoshiro Miwa and J. Mark Ramseyer reassert neoclassical orthodoxy and call the *keiretsu* a figment of Japanese Marxist and Western Orientalist imaginations.

9. Alexander Young, *The sogo shosha: Japan's multinational trading companies* (Boulder, CO: Westview, 1979); Michael Yoshiro and Thomas Lifson, *The invisible link: Japan's sogo shosha and the organization of trade* (Cambridge, MA: MIT Press, 1986); Yoshihara, *Japanese economic development*, 49–50, 154–155.

10. When global commodity chains first came to the attention of American sociologists in the 1980s (Gary Gerrefi and Miguel Korzeniewicz, eds., *Commodity chains and global capitalism* [Westport, CT: Greenwood Publishing Group, 1994]), they were impressed by the new "buyer-driven" chains (clothes, shoes) and contrasted them with earlier "producer-driven" chains (computers, cars). Japanese economic history recommends equal attention to "trader-driven" chains.

11. Anna Tsing, *Friction* (Princeton, NJ: Princeton University Press, 2005); Peter Dauvergne, *Shadows in the forest: Japan and the politics of timber in Southeast Asia*

(Cambridge, MA: MIT Press, 1997); Michael Ross, *Timber booms and institutional breakdown in Southeast Asia* (Cambridge: Cambridge University Press, 2001).

12. On salmon in Chile, see Heather Swanson, "Caught in comparisons: Japanese salmon in an uneven world" (PhD diss., University of California, Santa Cruz, 2013).

13. Robert Castley, *Korea's economic miracle: The crucial role of Japan* (New York: Palgrave Macmillan, 1997).

14. Ibid., 326.

15. Ibid., 69.

16. Kaname Akamatsu, "A historical pattern of economic growth in developing countries," *Journal of Developing Economies* 1, no. 1 (1962): 3–25.

17. "Quality control" was a part of this transnational dialogue: an American idea that took off in Japan during the American-led rationalization of Japanese industry after World War II, it was reimported to the United States in the 1970s and 1980s. William M. Tsutsui, "W. Edwards Deming and the origins of quality control in Japan," *Journal of Japanese Studies* 22, no. 2 (1996): 295–325.

18. For an example of U.S. anti-Japanese economic journalism from this period, see Robert Kearns, *Zaibatsu America: How Japanese firms are colonizing vital U.S. industries* (New York: Free Press, 1992).

19. My analysis is inspired by Karen Ho, *Liquidated* (Durham, NC: Duke University Press, 2009).

20. For an example of U.S.-style reforms promoted by a Japanese economist, see Hiroshi Yoshikawa, *Japan's lost decade*, trans. Charles Stewart, Long-Term Credit Bank of Japan Intl. Trust Library Selection 11 (Tokyo: International House of Japan, 2002). The book argues that small- and medium-size enterprises are a drain on the economy.

21. Robert Brenner, *The boom and the bubble: The U.S. in the world economy* (London: Verso, 2003).

22. Shintaro Ishihara, *The Japan that can say no*, trans. Frank Baldwin (1989, with Akio Morita; New York: Touchstone Books, 1992).

23. Petrovic and Hamilton, "Making global markets" (cited in chap. 4, n. 7), 121.

24. According to Robert Brenner (*The boom*), the Reverse Plaza Accord of 1995, in which world powers stopped the ascent of the yen, triggered a shift in the world economy by both killing U.S. manufacturing and triggering the Asian financial crisis.

25. Quoted in Miguel Korzeniewicz, "Commodity chains and marketing strategies: Nike and the global athletic footwear industry," in *Commodity chains*, ed. Gereffi and Korzeniewicz, 247–266, on 252.

CHAPTER 9. FROM GIFTS TO COMMODITIES—AND BACK

1. Bronislaw Malinowski, *Argonauts of the Western Pacific* (London: Routledge, 1922).

2. My ability to think about objects, alienated and otherwise, draws on Marilyn Strathern, *The gender of the gift* (Berkeley: University of California Press, 1990); Amiria

Henare, Martin Holbraad, and Sari Wastell, eds., *Thinking through things* (London: Routledge, 2006); and David Graeber, *Toward an anthropological theory of value* (London: Palgrave Macmillan, 2001).

3. Capitalist commodities, unlike kula objects, cannot carry the weight of entanglement histories and obligations. It is not simply *exchange* that defines capitalist commodities; alienation is required.

4. Marilyn Strathern paraphrases Christopher Gregory: "If in a commodity economy things and persons assume the social forms of things, then in a gift economy they assume the social forms of persons" (Strathern, *Gender*, 134, citing Christopher Gregory, *Gifts and commodities* [Waltham, MA: Academic Press, 1982], 41).

5. Many matsutake foraged in the U.S. Pacific Northwest are labeled as Canadian because exporters send them from British Columbia. Exporters attach tags based on the location of the exporting airport. Japanese law forbids foreign food products from being labeled by region, a privilege saved for Japanese products. Only national origins are allowed.

6. Matsutake are not the only fine foods used in this way. Specialty melons and salmon are among the goods that enter this gift economy and, like matsutake, mark seasonality. Such gifts are commonly regarded as confirming "Japanese" ways of life; their status as gifts drives rankings and prices.

7. If all mushrooms are picked before their spores mature, there is no reason—in terms of the reproductive success of the fungus—to privilege babies.

8. Babies are conventionally sorted "number 3" grade (out of five), although the mushroom hunters sometimes intervene to get a few into the more expensive "number 1" crate.

9. Buyers in the central Cascades sort matsutake by maturity into five priced grades. Bulkers re-sort by size; exported mushrooms are packed by both size and maturity.

CHAPTER 10. SALVAGE RHYTHMS

1. Daisuke Naito, personal communication, 2010.

2. The accumulation of capital relies on translations in which pericapitalist sites are brought into capitalist supply lines. Here again are some of my key claims: (1) salvage accumulation is the process through which value created in noncapitalist value forms is translated into capitalist assets, allowing accumulation; (2) pericapitalist spaces are sites in which both capitalist and noncapitalist value forms may flourish simultaneously—thus allowing translations; (3) supply chains are organized through such translations, which link the inventory-making of lead firms with pericapitalist sites, where all kinds of practices, capitalist and otherwise, flourish; (4) economic diversity makes capitalism possible—and offers sites of instability and refusal of capitalist governance.

3. Some examples: In her influential study of electronics workers in Malaysia, Aihwa Ong (*Spirits of resistance and capitalist discipline* [Albany: State University of New York Press, 1987]) found that contingent trajectories of colonial and

postcolonial governance produced the kind of rural Malay women that factories wanted to hire. Sylvia Yanagisako (*Producing culture and capital* [Princeton, NJ: Princeton University Press, 2002]) showed how factory owners and managers based their decisions on cultural ideals. Rather than a neutral system of efficiency, she argues, capitalist business develops within cultural histories. Owners as well as workers develop class interests through cultural agendas.

4. Jane Guyer's study of West African economic transactions shows how monetary exchanges need not be a sign of already-established equivalence; money can be used to realign cultural economies and translate their logics from one patch to another (*Marginal gains* [Chicago: University of Chicago Press, 2004]). Transactions may incorporate nonmarket logics even as money is exchanged. Guyer's research shows how economic systems incorporate difference. Transnational commodity chains are a privileged place to see this: Lisa Rofel and Sylvia Yanagisako explore how Italian silk companies negotiate the making of value with Chinese producers across gaps of comprehension and practice ("Managing the new silk road: Italian-Chinese collaborations," Lewis Henry Morgan Lecture, University of Rochester, October 20, 2010). See also Aihwa Ong, *Neoliberalism as Exception* (Durham, NC: Duke University Press, 2006); Neferti Tadiar, *Things fall away* (Durham, NC: Duke University Press, 2009); Laura Bear, *Navigating austerity* (Stanford, CA: Stanford University Press, 2015).

5. Jeffrey Mantz, "Improvisational economies: Coltan production in the eastern Congo," *Social Anthropology* 16, no. 1 (2008): 34–50; James Smith, "Tantalus in the digital age: Coltan ore, temporal dispossession, and 'movement' in the eastern Democratic Republic of the Congo," *American Ethnologist* 38, no. 1 (2011): 17–35.

6. Peter Hugo, "A global graveyard for dead computers in Ghana," *New York Times Magazine*, August 4, 2010. http://www.nytimes.com/slideshow/2010/08/04/mag azine/20100815-dump.html?_r=1&.

INTERLUDE. TRACKING

1. Charles Darwin ends *On the origin of species* ([London: John Murray, 1st ed., 1859], 490) with the image of an entangled bank: "from so simple a beginning endless forms most beautiful and most wonderful have been, and are being, evolved."

2. For a sampler of introductions, see Nicholas Money, *Mr. Bloomfield's orchard* (Oxford: Oxford University Press, 2004) [general exposition]; G. C. Ainsworth, *Introduction to the history of mycology* (Cambridge: Cambridge University Press, 2009) [history]; J. André Fortin, Christian Plenchette, and Yves Poché, *Mycorrhizas: The new green revolution* (Quebec: Editions Multimondes, 2009) [agronomy]; Jens Pedersen, *The kingdom of fungi* (Princeton, NJ: Princeton University Press, 2013) [photography].

3. Lisa Curran, "The ecology and evolution of mast-fruiting in Bornean Dipterocarpaceae: A general ectomycorrhizal theory" (PhD diss., Princeton University, 1994).

4. Paul Stamets's *Mycelium running* (Berkeley: Ten Speed Press, 2005) offers this and other fungal stories.

5. S. Kohlmeier, T.H.M. Smits, R. M. Ford, C. Keel, H. Harms, and L. Y. Wick, "Taking the fungal highway: Mobilization of pollutant-degrading bacteria by fungi," *Environmental Science and Technology* 39 (2005): 4640–4646.

6. Scott Gilbert and David Epel's *Ecological developmental biology* (Sunderland, MA: Sinauer, 2008), chap. 10, details some of the most important mechanisms.

7. Margaret McFall-Ngai, "The development of cooperative associations between animals and bacteria: Establishing détente among domains," *American Zoologist* 38, no. 4 (1998): 593–608.

8. Gilbert and Epel, *Ecological developmental biology*, 18. *Wolbachia* infection also causes problems for many insects through how it shapes reproduction. John Thompson, *Relentless evolution* (Chicago: University of Chicago Press, 2013), 104–106, 192.

9. J. A. Thomas, D. J. Simcox, and R. T. Clarke, "Successful conservation of a threatened *Maculinea* butterfly," *Science* 203 (2009): 458–461. For related entanglements, see Thompson, *Relentless evolution*, 182–183; Gilbert and Epel, *Ecological developmental biology*, chap. 3.

10. Gilbert and Epel, *Ecological developmental biology*, 20–27.

11. Scott F. Gilbert, Emily McDonald, Nicole Boyle, Nicholas Buttino, Lin Gyi, Mark Mai, Neelakantan Prakash, and James Robinson, "Symbiosis as a source of selectable epigenetic variation: Taking the heat for the big guy," *Philosophical Transactions of the Royal Society B* 365 (2010): 671–678, on 673.

12. Ilana Zilber-Rosenberg and Eugene Rosenberg, "Role of microorganisms in the evolution of animals and plants: The hologenome theory of evolution," *FEMS Microbiology Reviews* 32 (2008): 723–735.

13. Gil Sharon, Daniel Segal, John Ringo, Abraham Hefetz, Ilana Zilber-Rosenberg, and Eugene Rosenberg, "Commensal bacteria play a role in mating preferences of *Drosophila melanogaster*," *Proceedings of the National Academy of Science* (November 1, 2010): http://www.pnas.org/cgi/doi/10.1073/pnas.1009906107.

14. Gilbert et al., "Symbiosis," 672, 673.

15. Thomas et al., "Successful conservation."

16 Population geneticists do study mutualisms, including those involving ectomycorrhizal fungi and trees. But the structure of the discipline urges most studies to see each organism as analytically self-contained rather than emerging in historical interaction. As one recent review explains, "Mutualisms are reciprocal exploitations that nevertheless increase the fitness of each partner" (Teresa Pawlowska, "Population genetics of fungal mutualists of plants," in *Microbial population genetics*, ed. Jianping Xu, 125–138 [Norfolk, UK: Horizon Scientific Press, 2010], 125). The goal of the study of mutualism is then to measure costs and benefits to each self-contained species, with special attention to "cheating." Researchers can ask how more or less mutualistic variants of a species emerge to exploit benefits, but they cannot see transformative synergies.

17. Margulis and Sagan, *What is life?* (cited in chap. 2, n. 1).

18. Masayuki Horie, Tomoyuki Honda, Yoshiyuki Suzuki, Yuki Kobayashi, Takuji Daito, Tatsuo Oshida, Kazuyoshi Ikuta, Patric Jern, Takashi Gojobori, John

M. Coffin, and Keizo Tomonaga, "Endogenous non-retroviral RNA virus elements in mammalian genomes," *Nature* 463 (2010): 84–87.

19. One promising edge of population genetics uses DNA sequencing techniques to differentiate variant alleles within a single population. To study allelic differences requires a different set of DNA markers than to study species. The specificity of scale matters. Nonscalability theory welcomes stories that can be told about allelic differences and notes that they do not translate easily in research methods and results to other scales.

20. Daniel Winkler, interview, 2007.

21. R. Peabody, D. C. Peabody, M. Tyrell, E. Edenburn-MacQueen, R. Howdy, and K. Semelrath, "Haploid vegetative mycelia of *Amillaria gallica* show among-cell-line variation for growth and phenotypic plasticity," *Mycologia* 97, no. 4 (2005): 777–787.

22. Scott Turner, "Termite mounds as organs of extended physiology," State University of New York College of Environmental Science and Forestry, http://www.esf .edu/efb/turner/termite/termhome.htm.

Chapter 11. The Life of the Forest

1. Reflections on this problem have emerged from science studies (e.g., Bruno Latour, "Where are the missing masses?" in *Technology and society*, ed. Deborah Johnson and Jameson Wetmore, 151–180 [Cambridge, MA: MIT Press, 2008]); indigenous studies (e.g., Marisol de la Cadena, "Indigenous cosmopolitics in the Andes: Conceptual reflections beyond 'politics'" *Cultural Anthropology* 25, no. 2 [2010]: 334–370); postcolonial theory (e.g., Dipesh Chakrabarty, *Provincializing Europe* [Princeton, NJ: Princeton University Press, 2000]); new materialism (e.g., Jane Bennett, *Vibrant matter* [Durham, NC: Duke University Press, 2010]); and folklore and fiction (e.g., Ursula Le Guin, *Buffalo gals and other animal presences* [Santa Barbara, CA: Capra Press, 1987]).

2. Richard Nelson, *Make prayers to the raven: A Koyukon view of the northern forest* (Chicago: University of Chicago Press, 1983); Rane Willerslev, *Soul hunters: Hunting, animism, and personhood among the Siberian Yukaghirs* (Berkeley: University of California Press, 2007); Viveiros de Castro, "Cosmological deixis" (cited in chap. 1, n. 7).

3. Some humanists worry about the politics of the word "landscape," because one of its genealogies leads to landscape painting, with its distance between viewer and scene. As Kenneth Olwig reminds us, however, another genealogy leads to that political unit in which moots could be convened ("Recovering the substantive nature of landscape," *Annals of the Association of American Geographers* 86, no. 4 (1996): 630–653). My landscapes are places for patchy assemblages, that is, for moots that include both human and nonhuman participants.

4. Jakob von Uexküll, *A foray into the world of animals and humans*, trans. Joseph D. O'Neil (1934; Minneapolis: University of Minnesota Press, 2010).

5. Uexküll's bubble worlds inspired Martin Heidegger's idea that nonhuman animals are "poor in world." Martin Heidegger, *The fundamental concepts of meta-*

physics: World, finitude, solitude, trans. W. McNeill and N. Walker (1938; Indianapolis: Indiana University Press, 2001).

6. Lilin Zhao, Shuai Zhang, Wei Wei, Haijun Hao, Bin Zhang, Rebecca A. Butcher, Jianghua Sun, "Chemical signals synchronize the life cycles of a plant-parasitic nematode and its vector beetle," *Current biology* (October 10, 2013): http://dx.doi.org/10.1016/j.cub.2013.08.041.

7. Kazuo Suzuki, interview, 2005; Kazuo Suzuki, "Pine Wilt and the Pine Wood Nematode," in *Encyclopedia of forest sciences*," ed. Julian Evans and John Youngquist, 773–777 (Waltham, MA: Elsevier Academic Press, 2004).

8. Yu Wang, Toshihiro Yamada, Daisuke Sakaue, and Kazuo Suzuki, "Influence of fungi on multiplication and distribution of the pinewood nematode," in *Pine wilt disease: A worldwide threat to forest ecosystems*, ed. Manuel Mota and Paolo Viera, 115–128 (Berlin: Springer, 2008).

9. T. A. Rutherford and J. M. Webster, "Distribution of pine wilt disease with respect to temperature in North America, Japan, and Europe," *Canadian Journal of Forest Research* 17, no. 9 (1987): 1050–1059.

10. Stephen Pyne, *Vestal fire* (Seattle: University of Washington Press, 2000).

11. Pauline Peters, *Dividing the commons* (Charlottesville: University of Virginia Press, 1994); Kate Showers, *Imperial gullies* (Athens: Ohio University Press, 2005).

12. While Bruno Latour has worked hard to separate the truth claims of science, on the one hand, and the practices of science, on the other, his deployment of the legacy of French structuralism to contrast structural logics has encouraged sharp dichotomies between science and indigenous thought. See Bruno Latour, *We have never been modern* (Cambridge, MA: Harvard University Press, 1993).

13. Here I evoke the "new alliance" of Ilya Prigogine and Isabelle Stengers's *La nouvelle alliance*, unfortunately translated into English as *Order out of chaos* (New York: Bantam Books, 1984). Prigogine and Stengers argue that appreciation of indeterminacy and irreversible time might lead to a new alliance between the natural and human sciences. The gauntlet they lay down inspires my efforts.

14 A most useful English language reference on satoyama is K. Takeuchi, R. D. Brown, I. Washitani, A. Tsunekawa, and M. Yokohari, *Satoyama: The traditional rural landscape of Japan* (Tokyo: Springer, 2008). For a sampling of the extensive literature, see also Arioka Toshiyuki, *Satoyama* [in Japanese] (Tokyo: Hosei University Press, 2004); T. Nakashizuka and Y. Matsumoto, eds., *Diversity and interaction in a temperate forest community: Ogawa Forest Reserve of Japan* (Tokyo: Springer, 2002); Katsue Fukamachi and Yukihuro Morimoto, "Satoyama management in the twenty-first century: The challenge of sustainable use and continued biocultural diversity in rural cultural landscapes," *Landscape and Ecological Engineering* 7, no. 2 (2011): 161–162; Asako Miyamoto, Makoto Sano, Hiroshi Tanaka, and Kaoru Niiyama, "Changes in forest resource utilization and forest landscapes in the southern Abukuma Mountains, Japan during the twentieth century," *Journal of Forestry Research* 16 (2011): 87–97; Björn E. Berglund, "Satoyama, traditional farming landscape in Japan, compared to Scandinavia," *Japan Review* 20 (2008): 53–68; Katsue Fukamachi, Hirokazu Oku,

and Tohru Nakashizuka, "The change of a satoyama landscape and its causality in Kamiseya, Kyoto Prefecture, Japan between 1970 and 1995," *Landscape Ecology* 16 (2001): 703–717.

15. For an introduction to disturbance, see Seth Reice, *The silver lining: The benefits of natural disasters* (Princeton, NJ: Princeton University Press, 2001). For an attempt to bring histories of disturbance into social theory (here psychoanalysis), see Laura Cameron, "Histories of disturbance," *Radical History Review* 74 (1999): 4–24.

16. Histories of ecological thought include Frank Golley, *A history of the ecosystem concept in ecology* (New Haven, CT: Yale University Press, 1993); Stephen Bocking, *Ecologists and environmental politics* (New Haven, CT: Yale University Press, 1997); Donald Worster, *Nature's economy: A history of ecological ideas* (Cambridge: Cambridge University Press, 1994).

17. Rosalind Shaw, "'Nature,' 'culture,' and disasters: Floods in Bangladesh," in *Bush base: Forest farm*, ed. Elisabeth Croll and David Parkin, 200–217 (London: Routledge, 1992).

18. Clive Jones, John Lawton, and Moshe Shachak, "Organisms as ecosystems engineers," *Oikos* 69, no. 3 (1994): 373–386; Clive Jones, John Lawton, and Moshe Shachak, "Positive and negative effects of organisms as physical ecosystems engineers," *Ecology* 78, no. 7 (1997): 1946–1957.

19. Consider a world with multiple interbreeding hominids; we might imagine resemblance beyond species more readily in that world. Our loneliness without closer cousins shapes our willingness to allow each species to stand apart in a biblical tableau.

20. This process is what Donna Haraway usefully calls "becoming with" (*When species meet* [Minneapolis: University of Minnesota Press, 2007]).

21. More contrasts: The matsutake I saw in the United States and Finland grew in industrial timber; in China, as in Japan, they grew in peasant woodlands. In Yunnan and Oregon, matsutake grow in forests regarded as messy mistakes; in Lapland and Japan, matsutake forests are aesthetically idealized. Two-by-two tables would be possible—but I have not wanted to set each location as a type. I am looking for how assemblages gather.

Chapter 12. History

1. As long as one does not get stuck in their stereotypes, it is possible to mix "mythology" and "history." History is not just national teleology; mythology is not just eternal return. To become entangled in history, one does not have to share a cosmology. Renato Rosaldo (*Ilongot headhunting* [Stanford, CA: Stanford University Press, 1980]) and Richard Price (*Alabi's World* [Baltimore, MD: Johns Hopkins University Press, 1990]) offer examples of the interweaving of varied cosmologies and world-making practices in making history. Morten Pedersen (*Not quite shamans* [Ithaca, NY: Cornell University Press, 2011]) shows histories in the making of cosmology. Many others, however, emphasize contrasts between mythology and history. By limiting the meaning of "history" through this contrast, however, they lose

the ability to see the hybrid, layered, and contaminated cosmologies of any history in the making—and vice versa.

2. Thom van Dooren (*Flight ways* [New York: Columbia University Press, 2014]) argues that birds tell stories through the ways they make places into homes. In this meaning of "story," many organisms tell stories. These are among the traces I watch as "history."

3. Chris Maser, *The redesigned forest* (San Pedro, CA: R. & E. Miles, 1988).

4. David Richardson, ed., *Ecology and biogeography of* Pinus (Cambridge: Cambridge University Press, 1998).

5. David Richardson and Steven Higgins, "Pines as invaders in the southern hemisphere," in *Ecology*, ed. Richardson, 450–474.

6. Peter Becker, "Competition in the regeneration niche between conifers and angiosperms: Bond's slow seedling hypothesis," *Functional Ecology* 14, no. 4 (2000): 401–412.

7. James Agee, "Fire and pine ecosystems," in *Ecology*, ed. Richardson, 193–218.

8. David Read, "The mycorrhizal status of *Pinus*," in *Ecology*, ed. Richardson, 324–340, on 324.

9. Ronald Lanner, *Made for each other: A symbiosis of birds and pines* (Oxford: Oxford University Press, 1996).

10. Ronald Lanner, "Seed dispersal in pines," in *Ecology*, ed. Richardson, 281–295.

11. Charles Lefevre, interview, 2006; Charles Lefevre, "Host associations of *Tricholoma magnivelare*, the American matsutake" (PhD diss., Oregon State University, 2002).

12. Ogawa, *Matsutake* (cited in chap. 3, n. 4).

13. Lefevre, "Host associations."

14. Pines were in Finland by nine thousand years ago (Katherine Willis, Keith Bennett, and John Birks, "The late Quaternary dynamics of pines in Europe," in *Ecology*, ed. Richardson, 107–121, on 113). The first artifact of human presence is a Karellan fishing net from 8300 BCE (Vaclav Smil, *Making the modern world: Materials and dematerialization* [Hoboken, NJ: John Wiley and Sons, 2013], 13).

15. Simo Hannelius and Kullervo Kuusela, *Finland: The country of evergreen forest* (Tampere, FI: Forssan Kirjapaino Oy, 1995). I also draw on field trips with foresters.

16. Medieval farmers in Finland ringed pine and spruce to bring landscapes into broadleaf agroforestry rotations (Timo Myllyntaus, Mina Hares, and Jan Kunnas, "Sustainability in danger? Slash-and-burn cultivation in nineteenth-century Finland and twentieth-century Southeast Asia," *Environmental History* 7, no. 2 [2002]: 267–302). For a vivid description of Finnish swidden, see Stephen Pyne, *Vestal fire* (cited in chap. 11, n. 10), 228–234.

17. Timo Myllyntaus, "Writing about the past with green ink: The emergence of Finnish environmental history," H-Environment, http://www.h-net.org/~environ/his toriography/finland.htm.

18. By the mid-nineteenth century, timber outpaced tar as an export. Sven-Erik Åstrom, *From tar to timber: Studies in northeast European forest exploitation and foreign*

trade, 1660–1860, Commentationes Humanarum Litterarum, no. 85 (Helsinki: Finnish Society of Sciences and Letters, 1988).

19. Edmund von Berg, *Kertomus Suomenmaan metsisistä* (1859; Helsinki: Metsälehti Kustannus, 1995). This translation is from Pyne, *Vestal fire,* 259.

20. Ibid. This translation is from Martti Ahtisaari, "Sustainable forest management in Finland: Its development and possibilities," *Unasylva* 200 (2000): 56–59, on 57.

21. Raw and processed timber accounted for three-quarters of the value of Finnish exports by 1913. David Kirby, *A concise history of Finland* (Cambridge: Cambridge University Press, 2006). Twentieth-century settlements dispersed in the forests, following the work, a pattern that continued until the 1970s, when mill jobs declined because of competition from tropical wood. Jarmo Kortelainen, "Mill closure— options for a restart: A case study of local response in a Finnish mill community," in *Local economic development,* ed. Cecily Neil and Markku Tykkläinen, 205–225 (Tokyo: United Nations University Press, 1998).

22. One-third of the reparations were paid directly in forestry and paper products; the other two-thirds involved agricultural products and machinery. Providing the last of these built Finland's postwar industry. Max Jacobson, *Finland in the new Europe* (Westport, CT: Greenwood Publishing, 1998), 90.

23. Hannelius and Kuusela, *Finland,* 139.

24. Timo Kuuluvainen, "Forest management and biodiversity conservation based on natural ecosystem dynamics in northern Europe: The complexity challenge," *Ambio* 38 (2009): 309–315.

25. For example, Hannelius and Kuusela, *Finland,* 175.

26. Curran, *Ecology and evolution* (cited in "Tracking" interlude, n. 3).

27. Weather and undergrowth conditions also make a difference in whether seeds will sprout and if seedlings will become established. For wavelike regeneration of northern Sweden's Scots pine, without fire, see Olle Zackrisson, Marie-Charlotte Nilsson, Ingeborg Steijlen, and Greger Hornberg, "Regeneration pulses and climate-vegetation interactions in nonpyrogenic boreal Scots pine stands," *Journal of Ecology* 83, no. 3 (1995): 469–483; Jon Agren and Olle Zackrisson, "Age and size structure of *Pinus sylvestris* populations on mires in central and northern Sweden," *Journal of Ecology* 78, no. 4 (1990): 1049–1062. The authors do not consider masting. Other researchers report: "Mast years are relatively frequent but at the boreal forest limit seed maturation is impeded by the short growing season; mast years may occur as seldom as once or twice in 100 years." Csaba Matyas, Lennart Ackzell, and C.J.A. Samuel, *EUFORGEN technical guidelines for genetic conservation and use of Scots pine* (Pinus sylvestris) (Rome: International Genetic Resources Institute, 2004), 1.

28. Hiromi Fujita, "Succession of higher fungi in a forest of *Pinus densiflora*" [in Japanese], *Transactions of the Mycological Society of Japan* 30 (1989): 125–147.

29. The study of matsutake ecology in Nordic Europe is in its infancy. For an introduction, see Niclas Bergius and Eric Darnell, "The Swedish matsutake (*Tricholoma nauseosum* syn. *T. matsutake*): Distribution, abundance, and ecology," *Scandinavian Journal of Forest Research* 15 (2000): 318–325.

Chapter 13. Resurgence

1. Scholarship on the disappearance of the peasantry begins with histories of the formation of the modern (e.g., Eugen Weber, *Peasants into Frenchmen* [Stanford, CA: Stanford University Press, 1976]). In the discussion of contemporary life, the trope is used to suggest our entry into a postmodern era (e.g., Michael Kearney, *Reconceptualizing the peasantry* [Boulder, CO: Westview Press, 1996]; Michael Hardt and Antonio Negri, *Multitude* [New York: Penguin, 2004]).

2. As discussed in chapter 11, I include *Quercus*, *Lithocarpus*, and *Castanopsis* in my use of the term "oak."

3. Oliver Rackham, *Woodlands* (London: Collins, 2006). Some biologists speculate that oaks may have developed their ability to coppice from long association with elephants, once common in the global north (George Monbiot, *Feral* [London: Penguin, 2013]). Even the suggestion speaks of the new importance of the cross-species evolutionary thinking discussed in the "Tracking" interlude.

4. For Japan: Hideo Tabata, "The future role of *satoyama* woodlands in Japanese society," in *Forest and civilisations*, ed. Y. Yasuda, 155–162 (New Delhi: Roli Books, 2001). For the coexistence of tree species in the satoyama, see Nakashizuka, and Matsumoto, *Diversity* (cited in chap. 11, n. 14).

5. Atsuki Azuma, "Birds of prey living in yatsuda and satoyama," in *Satoyama*, ed. Takeuchi et al., (cited in chap. 11, n. 14), 102–109.

6. Ibid., 103–104.

7. Larval forms of this butterfly eat *Celtis sinensis*, one of the species of the coppice woodlands. Adults eat the sap of *Quercus acutissima*, another peasant coppiced oak (Izumi Washitani, "Species diversity in satoyama landscapes," in *Satoyama*, ed. Takeuchi et al., 89–93 [cited in chap. 11 n. 14], on 90). Coppice supports a high diversity of plants as well as insects; in comparison, abandoning an area may allow a few aggressive species to dominate. See Wajirou Suzuki, "Forest vegetation in and around Ogawa Forest Reserve in relation to human impact," in *Diversity*, ed. Nakashizuka and Matsumoto, 27–42.

8. Conrad Totman following earlier Japanese historians, offers this focus in *The green archipelago: Forestry in preindustrial Japan* (Berkeley: University of California Press, 1989).

9. This paragraph draws from Totman, *Green archipelago*; Margaret McKean, "Defining and dividing property rights in the commons: Today's lessons from the Japanese past," International Political Economy Working Paper no. 150, Duke University, 1991; Utako Yamashita, Kulbhushan Balooni, and Makoto Inoue, "Effect of instituting 'authorized neighborhood associations' on communal (iriai) forest ownership in Japan," *Society and Natural Resources* 22 (2009): 464–473; Gaku Mitsumata and Takeshi Murata, "Overview and current status of the *irai* (commons) system in the three regions of Japan, from the Edo era to the beginning of the 21st century," Discussion Paper No. 07–04 (Kyoto: Multilevel Environmental Governance for Sustainable Development Project, 2007).

10. Oliver Rackham points out that aristocrats in Europe used oak for elite building; thus oak was a lords' tree. In Japan, lords had sugi and hinoki for building. Rackham, "Trees, woodland, and archaeology," paper presented at Yale Agrarian Studies Colloquium, October 19, 2013, http://www.yale.edu/agrarianstudies/colloq-papers/07rackham.pdf.

11. Tabata, "The future role of satoyama."

12. Matsuo Tsukada, "Japan," in *Vegetation history*, ed., B. Huntley and T. Webb III, 459–518 (Dordrecht, NL: Kluwer Academic Publishers, 1988).

13. Interview, 2008. Deforestation was associated with logging, shifting cultivation, the spread of intensive agriculture, and residential settlement. See Yamada Asako, Harada Hiroshi, and Okuda Shigetoshi, "Vegetation mapping in the early Meiji era and changes in vegetation in southern Miura peninsula" [in Japanese], *Eco-Habitat* 4, no. 1 (1997): 33–40; Ogura Junichi, "Forests of the Kanto region in the 1880s" [in Japanese], *Journal of the Japanese Institute of Landscape Architects* 57, no. 5 (1994): 79–84; Kaoru Ichikawa, Tomoo Okayasu, and Kazuhiko Takeuchi, "Characteristics in the distribution of woodland vegetation in the southern Kanto region since the early 20th century," *Journal of Environmental Information Science* 36, no. 5 (2008): 103–108.

14. Interview, 2008. About one well-documented Kanto forest, Wajirou Suzuki notes the acceleration of logging: "With development of domestic industries after World War I, the demand for charcoal increased dramatically, and during World War II, charcoal-burning and manufacturing equipment for military horses became the main industries in the area" (Suzuki, "Forest vegetation," 30).

15. As in central Japan, Yunnan forests without human disturbance revert to broadleaf associations, without pine. Stanley Richardson, *Forestry in communist China* (Baltimore, MD: Johns Hopkins University Press, 1966), 31. Histories of village use also show parallels. While he does not write about Yunnan, Nicholas Menzies describes village forest use in imperial China in a way quite reminiscent of the satoyama literature: "The community forests of Shanxi were known collectively as *She Shan* (village mountains).... These hillsides were unsuitable for agriculture, but they were important to their users to provide for ritual needs (such as grave sites for clan members), and as a source of forest products. Ren Chengtong noted that villages used the timber from their forests to provide funding and materials for public works within the community, and that villagers also had rights to gather nuts, fruit, wildlife (for meat), mushrooms, and medicinal herbs for their private use" (Menzies, *Forest and land management in imperial China* [London: St. Martin's Press, 1994], 80–81).

16. Forest reform, leading to several kinds of tenure categories including contracts with households, began in 1981. For an analysis of changing forest tenure, see Liu Dachang, "Tenure and management of non-state forests in China since 1950," *Environmental History* 6, no. 2 (2001): 239–263.

17. Yin Shaoting's pioneering work on shifting cultivation in Yunnan introduced the sustainability of the peasant landscape to scholars for whom peasants

were generally imagined as backward. Yin, *People and forests*, trans. Magnus Fiskesjo (Kunming: Yunnan Education Publishing House, 2001).

18. Liu ("Tenure," 244) writes of the "disastrous deforestation" of this period.

CHAPTER 14. SERENDIPITY

1. A useful description of the mills and their work is found in P. Cogswell, Jr., "Deschutes country pine logging," in *High and mighty: Selected sketches about the Deschutes country*, ed. T. Vaughn, 235–259 (Portland, OR: Oregon Historical Society, 1981). One of the stranger mill towns was Hixon, "which wandered about Deschutes, Lake, and Klamath counties, moving every few years to be close to Shelvin-Hixon's logging operations" (251). With the advent of logging roads, mill towns settled down.

2. When the company withdrew its drug policy, many people signed up.

3. The Healthy Forests Restoration Act of 2003—which mandated logging, thinning, and post-burn salvage as the route to forest health—pushed the Forest Service into a series of continuing battles with conservationists (Vaughn and Cortner, *George W. Bush's healthy forests* [cited in chap. 5, n. 3]).

4. William Robbins, *Landscapes of promise: The Oregon story, 1800–1940* (Seattle: University of Washington Press, 1997), 224.

5. Quoted in ibid., 223.

6. Quoted in ibid., 225.

7. Quoted in ibid., 231.

8. This part of the story is well documented by local historians. Two points come through in all accounts. First, private owners from the first encroached on what was supposed to be public land, creating a mix of public and private forest holdings (e.g., Cogswell, "Deschutes"). Second, the race to build a railroad up the Deschutes River encouraged land speculation and added excitement and urgency to attempts to grab the forests (e.g., W. Carlson, "The great railroad building race up the Deschutes River," in *Little-known tales from Oregon history*, 4:74–77 [Bend, OR: Sun Publishing, 2001]).

9. In 1916, two large mill complexes, Shelvin-Hixon and Brooks-Scanlon, opened along the Deschutes River (Robbins, *Landscapes of promise*, 233). Shelvin Hixon sold out in 1950, while an expanded Brooks-Scanlon continued (Robbins, *Landscapes of conflict* [cited in chap. 3, n. 5], 162). Brooks-Scanlon merged with Diamond International Corporation in 1980 (Cogswell, "Deschutes," 259).

10. Robbins (*Landscapes of conflict*, 152) quotes the *New York Times* in 1948: "More and more, lumber operators are looking to national and state-owned forests to fill out their operations." In the eastern Cascades, the fact that valuable timber remained mainly in national forests stimulated mill consolidation in 1950. Phil Brogan, *East of the Cascades* (Hillsboro, OR: Binford and Mort, 1964), 256.

11. Hirt, *Conspiracy* (cited in chap. 3, n. 5).

12. Robbins, *Landscapes of conflict*, 14.

13. Writing about ponderosa in Oregon and northern California, Fiske and Tappeiner write, "Herbicide use started in the 1950's with adaptation of agricultural

aerial application techniques of the phenoxy herbicides. Later, appropriate use of a much broader range of herbicides was established." John Fiske and John Tappeiner, *An overview of key silvicultural information for Ponderosa pine* (USDA Forest Service General Technical Report PSW-GTR-198, 2005).

14. Znerold, "New integrated forest resource plan for ponderosa pine" (cited in chap. 3, n. 6), 3.

15. Indented quotations in this section are from the Klamath Tribes website, http://www.klamathtribes.org/background/termination.html.

16. Donald Fixico's *The invasion of Indian country in the twentieth century* (Niwot: University Press of Colorado, 1998) tells the Klamath story in the context of other terminations and seizures.

17. Crown-Zellerbach, a pulp-and-paper company, was able to buy ninety thousand acres of reservation land for timber (http://www.klamathtribes.org/background /termination.html). In 1953, Crown-Zellerbach possessed the second-largest timber holdings in the West, after Weyerhaeuser (Harvard Business School, Baker Library, Lehman Brothers Collection, http://www.library.hbs.edu/hc/lehman/industry.html ?company=crown_zellerbach_corp).

18. Edward Wolf, *Klamath heartlands: A guide to the Klamath Reservation forest plan* (Portland, OR: Ecotrust, 2004). The Klamath Tribes employ specialists in forestry to monitor projects slated for reservation land. In 1997, the Tribes successfully appealed a proposed national forest timber sale, which led to a 1999 memorandum of agreement on forest management (Vaughn and Cortner, *George W. Bush's healthy forests*, 98–100).

19. Robbins (*Landscapes of conflict*, 163) notes that Brooks-Scanlon had already begun to cut some lodgepole in 1950 to augment its decreasing ponderosa supplies.

20. Znerold, "New integrated forest resource plan for ponderosa pine," 4.

21. Jerry Franklin and C. T. Dyrness, *Natural vegetation of Oregon and Washington* (Portland, OR: Pacific Northwest Forest and Range Experiment Station, U.S.D.A. Forest Service, 1988), 185.

22. This ability to quickly colonize open lands impressed novice forester Thornton Munger, who was sent by the Forest Service in 1908 to study the encroachment of lodgepole pine on ponderosa territory. Munger considered lodgepole "a practically worthless weed"; he also thought the problem for ponderosa was too many fires, which, he thought, killed ponderosa and advantaged lodgepole. He promoted the prevention of forest fires to preserve ponderosa. This is almost the opposite of what foresters argue today. Even Munger later changed his mind: "It has since struck me how audacious or naïve it was for the Washington Office to assign a forest assistant with no experience, who had not even seen the two species before" (Munger quoted in Les Joslin, *Ponderosa promise: A history of U.S. Forest Service research in central Oregon* [General Technical Report PNW-GTR-711, Portland, OR: U.S.D.A. Forest Service, Pacific Northwest Research Station, 2007], 7).

23. Fujita, "Succession of higher fungi" (cited in chap. 12, n. 28).

24. Fumihiko Yoshimura, interview, 2008. Dr. Yoshimura has seen matsutake with trees as young as thirty years old.

25. Fungal underground bodies have a more sustained presence than fruiting bodies. In boreal Europe, mycorrhizal fungi remain in the soil after fires, reinfecting pine seedlings (Lena Jonsson, Anders Dahlberg, Marie-Charlotte Nilsson, Olle Zackrisson, and Ola Karen, "Ectomycorrhizal fungal communities in late-successional Swedish boreal forests, and their composition following wildfire," *Molecular Ecology* 8 [1999]: 205–215).

26. As early as 1934, long before lodgepole was considered a commercial species, foresters in the eastern Cascades experimented with thinning lodgepoles to speed up wood production. Only after World War II, however, when lodgepole became a resource for pulp and paper, as well as for poles, box shook, and even lumber, did its silviculture become an important interest of the eastern Cascades Forest Service. In 1957, a lodgepole pulp mill was opened near Chiloquin. Joslin, *Ponderosa promise*, 21, 51, 36.

Chapter 15. Ruin

1. In viewing Japan's environment through tropical deforestation, I follow Dauvergne, *Shadows* (cited in chap. 8, n. 11). (For regulatory and conservation responses, see Anny Wong, "Deforestation in the tropics," in *The roots of Japan's international environmental policies*, 145–200 [New York: Garland, 2001].) Most scholarship on Japan's environmental problems, in contrast, focuses on industrial pollution (Brett Walker, *Toxic archipelago: A history of industrial disease in Japan* [Seattle: University of Washington Press, 2010]; Shigeto Tsuru, *The political economy of the environment: The case of Japan* [Cambridge: Cambridge University Press, 1999].)

2. I am indebted to Mayumi and Noboru Ishikawa for these insights. As researchers in Sarawak, they saw the destruction of the forest and wondered about Japan's responsibility. Back in Japan, they connected this with the ruin of the domestic forest industry. Earlier environmental historians, in contrast, saw only Japan's "green archipelago" (Totman, *Green archipelago* [cited in chap. 13, n. 8]).

3. For Japan's forest policies, I rely particularly on Yoshiya Iwai, ed., *Forestry and the forest industry in Japan* (Vancouver: UBC Press, 2002).

4. Michael Hathaway, *Environmental winds: Making the global in southwest China* (Berkeley: University of California Press, 2013).

5. Miyamato et al., "Changes in forest resource utilization" (cited in chap. 11, note 14), 90. Burning had been conventional for the maintenance of grasslands and for creating forest openings, such as for shifting cultivation (Mitsuo Fujiwara, "Silviculture in Japan," in *Forestry*, ed. Iwai, 10–23, on 12). Now some local forest associations also prohibited burning (Koji Matsushita and Kunihiro Hirata, "Forest owners' associations," in *Forestry*, ed. Iwai, 41–66, on 42).

6. Stephen Pyne, *Fire in America* (Seattle: University of Washington Press, 1997), 328–334. Pyne argues that the Tillamook fire inaugurated U.S. industrial forest plantations by making replanting standard practice.

7. Steen, *U.S. Forest Service*; Robbins, *American forestry* (both cited in chap. 2, n. 5).

8. Iwai, *Forestry*.

9. Many forest owners had less than five hectares. All had to participate in coordinated forest management, including timber control, reforestation, and the prevention of fire. Matsushita and Hirata, "Forest owners' associations," 43.

10. The incident is recalled as the Lookout air raids; in 1944 and 1945, it was followed by Japanese attempts to launch fire balloons into the jet stream (http://en.wikipedia.org/wiki/Fire_balloon). Frida Knoblock's *The culture of wilderness* (Raleigh: University of North Carolina Press, 1996) describes the militarization of the U.S. Forest Service that followed. See also Jake Kosek, *Understories* (Durham, NC: Duke University Press, 2006).

11. Robbins, *Landscapes of conflict* (cited in chap. 3, n. 5), 176.

12. Ibid., 163.

13. Matsushita and Hirata, "Forest owners' associations," 45.

14. Scott Prudham analyzes the industrialization of Oregon's Douglas fir forestry from the 1950s ("Taming trees: Capital, science, and nature in Pacific slope tree improvement," *Annals of the Association of American Geographers* 93, no. 3 [2003]: 636–656). For a prehistory of this industrial turn, see Emily Brock, *Money trees: Douglas fir and American forestry, 1900–1940* (Corvallis: Oregon State University Press, 2015).

15. Interview with forest workers conducted by Mayumi and Noboru Ishikawa, Wakayama prefecture, 2009.

16. Fujiwara, "Silviculture in Japan," 14.

17. Ken-ichi Akao, "Private forestry," in *Forestry*, ed. Iwai, 24–40, on 35. Akao further explains that after 1957, the government reduced subsidies to 48 percent for conversion of natural forest to tree plantation.

18. Quoted in Robbins, *Landscapes of conflict*, 147. The Oregon timber industry was then diversifying to plywood, particleboard, and pulp and paper. Less desirable timber had become usable, encouraging clear-cutting. Gail Wells, "The Oregon coast in modern times: Postwar prosperity," Oregon History Project, 2006, http://www.ohs.org/education/oregonhistory/narratives/subtopic.cfm?subtopic_id=575.

19. The Imperial Japanese Army had confiscated these forests in 1939, while nevertheless confirming traditional access rights. U.S. occupying forces took the area from the Japanese; Japanese Self-Defense Forces reclaimed it from the Americans. Margaret McKean, "Management of traditional common lands in Japan," in *Proceedings of the conference on common property resource management April 21–26, 1985*, ed. Daniel Bromley, 533–592 (Washington, DC: National Academy Press, 1986), 574.

20. Akao, "Private forestry," 32; Yoshiya Iwai and Kiyoshi Yukutake, "Japan's wood trade," in *Forestry*, ed. Iwai, 244–256, on 247, 249.

21. Akao, "Private forestry," 32.

22. Ibid., 33.

23. Robbins, *Landscapes of conflict*, xviii.

24. In the 1980s, Indonesia restricted exports of raw logs and built a plywood processing industry. Japanese trading companies began buying more logs from Sarawak and Papua New Guinea. Easy pickings did not last long in any place, but trading companies kept moving to new supply areas. The matsutake forests I visited in Yunnan, China, felled in the 1970s for foreign exchange, were part of this 1970s Japanese import boom. Since I do not find China on Iwai and Yukutake's table of imported logs, I assume those logs entered Japan without full papers. Iwai and Yukutake, "Japan's wood trade," 248.

25. See Totman, *Green archipelago* (cited in chap. 13, n. 8).

26. Fujiwara, "Silviculture in Japan," 20. John Knight recounts how forested villages asked for help to continue to maintain their forests. Knight, "The forest grant movement in Japan," in *Environmental movements in Asia*, ed. Arne Kalland and Gerard Persoon, 110–130 (Oslo: Nordic Institute of Asian Studies, 1998).

CHAPTER 16. SCIENCE AS TRANSLATION

1. "Translation" is a key term for the actor-network theory conceived by Bruno Latour and John Law, where it refers to articulations between humans and those nonhumans working with humans, such as technologies; through translation, in this usage, networks of action emerge that include humans and nonhumans equally. An early and influential exposition of this position is Michel Callon, "Some elements of a sociology of translation: Domestication of the scallops and the fishermen of St. Bruic Bay," in *Power, action and belief*, ed. John Law, 196–223 (London: Routledge, 1986).

2. The question of translation here forms part of a larger scholarly discussion about "modernity." European common sense, which science studies too often takes for granted, shows us a modernity formed of Western thought, which has become universal. In contrast, that postcolonial theory that emerged from Asia in the late twentieth century showed modernity formed in power-laden interchanges between the global north and south. The emergence of modernity as a project is best understood in the first instance outside the West—for example, in the kingdom of Siam or colonial India. In these places, one sees the play of power, events, and ideas in which organizational and ideational complexes are formed (Thongchai Winichatkul, *Siam mapped: A history of the geo-body of a nation* [Honolulu: University of Hawaii Press, 1994]; Dipesh Chakrabarty, *Provincializing Europe* [Princeton, NJ: Princeton University Press, 2000]). This does not mean that modernity was not taken up in Europe and North America, and with distinctive variations. But to penetrate the smokescreen of West-is-all dreams, one must learn to see Western versions as derivative and exotic. From those Other places, it is easy to grasp modernity projects as partial and contingent, rather than overdetermined by a single cultural logic. This is the insight needed for science studies. (To complicate the situation, however, a new postcolonial theory emerging from Latin America requires sharply drawn

West-versus-Other cosmological distinctions, e.g., Eduardo Viveiros de Castro, "Economic development and cosmopolitical reinvolvement," in *Contested ecologies*, ed. Lesley Green, 28–41 [Cape Town, SA: HSRC Press, 2013].)

3. Satsuka, *Nature in translation* (cited in chap. 4, n. 2).

4. Itty Abraham's *Making of the Indian atomic bomb* (London: Zed Books, 1998) shows how postwar Indian physics emerged in the political conjunctures that created "India."

5. For an example of Korean research, see Chang-Duck Koo, Dong-Hee Lee, Young-Woo Park, Young-Nam Lee, Kang-Hyun Ka, Hyun Park, Won-Chull Bak, "Ergosterol and water changes in *Tricholoma matsutake* soil colony during the mushroom fruiting season," *Mycobiology* 37, no. 1 (2009): 10–16.

6. For an example of such collaboration, see S. Ohga, F. J Yao, N. S. Cho, Y. Kitamoto, and Y. Li, "Effect of RNA-related compounds on fructification of *Tricholoma matsutake*," *Mycosystema* 23 (2004): 555–562.

7. Nicholas Menzies and Chun Li ("One eye on the forest, one eye on the market: Multi-tiered regulation of matsutake harvesting, conservation, and trade in north-western Yunnan Province," in *Wild product governance*, ed. Sarah Laird, Rebecca McLain, and Rachel Wynberg, 243–263 [London: Earthscan, 2008]) review regulations to show how flexible enforcement enters at each scale.

8. Ohara Hiroyuki, "A history of trial and error in artificial production of matsutake fruitings" [in Japanese], *Doshisha Home Economics* 27 (1993): 20–30.

9. The shiro is an alternative unit to the "genet" of non-Japanese researchers for counting "individual" fungal organisms. The shiro, the dense mycelial mat, is determined by morphological observation. The genet, the genetic individual, is sometimes described as synonymous to the shiro (e.g., Jianping Xu, Tao Sha, Yanchun Li, Zhi-wei Zhao, and Zhu Yang, "Recombination and genetic differentiation among natural populations of the ectomycorrhizal mushroom *Tricholoma matsutake* from southwestern China," *Molecular Ecology* 17, no. 5 [2008]: 1238–1247, on 1245). But the term implies genetic homogeneity, an assumption contradicted by Japanese research (Hitoshi Murata, Akira Ohta, Akiyoshi Yamada, Maki Narimatsu, and Norihiro Futamura, "Genetic mosaics in the massive persisting rhizosphere colony 'shiro' of the ectomycorrhizal basidiomycete *Tricholoma matsutake*," *Mycorrhiza* 15 [2005]: 505–512). Technical sophistication is sometimes less productive than the inclusion of peasant knowledge.

10. Timothy Choy and Shiho Satsuka, writing as Mogu-Mogu, have written about this turn in Dr. Hamada's research. "Mycorrhizal relations: A manifesto," in "A new form of collaboration in cultural anthropology: Matsutake worlds," ed. Matsutake Worlds Research Group, *American Ethnologist* 36, no. 2 (2009): 380–403.

11. Interviews, 2005, 2006, 2008. See Ogawa, *Matsutake* (cited in chap. 3, n. 4).

12. See, for example, Ito Takeshi and Iwase Koji, *Matsutake: Kajuen Kankaku de Fuyasu Sodateru* [Matsutake: Increase and nurture as in an orchard] (Tokyo: Nosangyoson Bunka Kyokai, 1997).

13. See, for example, Hiroyuki Ohara and Minoru Hamada, "Disappearance of bacteria from the zone of active mycorrhizas in *Tricholoma matsutake* (S. Ito et Imai) Singer," *Nature* 213, no. 5075 (1967): 528–529.

14. Ito and Iwase, *Matsutake*.

15. In 2004, the team stimulated a mycorrhiza in a mature pine root (Alexis Guerin-Laguette, Norihisa Matsushita, Frédéric Lapeyrie, Katsumi Shindo, and Kazuo Suzuki, "Successful inoculation of mature pine with *Tricholoma matsutake*," *Mycorrhiza* 15 [2005]: 301–305). Soon afterward, Dr. Suzuki retired, and the team disbanded. He subsequently became president of the Forestry and Forest Products Institute.

16. For a much earlier Japanese-U.S. collaboration, see S. M. Zeller and K. Togashi, "The American and Japanese Matsu-takes," *Mycologia* 26 (1934): 544–558.

17. Hosford et al., *Ecology and management* (cited in chap. 3, n. 4).

18. Ibid., p. 50.

19. There are exceptions, and if matsutake research in the U.S. Pacific Northwest had been allowed to develop, the tradition might have exploded in new directions. Research flourished only between the 1990s and 2006; after that, funding cuts ended grant opportunities, and researchers moved on. One exception to timber-scalable approaches is Charles Lefevre's dissertation on matsutake host associations in the Pacific Northwest (cited in chap. 12, n. 11). This was relational analysis, and, without any nods to Japan, it touched on common concerns. Lefevre even developed a "smell test" for matsutake mycelia; as in Japanese research, his work used and empowered nonexperts. Lefevre moved on to selling inoculated truffle trees.

20. David Pilz and Randy Molina, "Commercial harvests of edible mushrooms from the forests of the Pacific Northwest United States: Issues, management, and monitoring for sustainability," *Forest Ecology and Management* 5593 (2001): 1–14.

21. David Pilz and Randy Molina, eds., *Managing forest ecosystems to conserve fungus diversity and sustain wild mushroom harvests* (USDA Forest Service PNW-GTR-371, 1999).

22. James Weigand, "Forest management for the North American pine mushroom (*Tricholoma magnivelare* (Peck) Redhead) in the southern Cascade range" (PhD diss., Oregon State University, 1998).

23. Daniel Luoma, Joyce Eberhart, Richard Abbott, Andrew Moore, Michael Amaranthus, and David Pilz, "Effects of mushroom harvest technique on subsequent American matsutake production," *Forest Ecology and Management* 236, no. 1 (2006): 65–75.

24. Anthony Amend, Zhendong Fang, Cui Yi, and Will McClatchey, "Local perceptions of matsutake mushroom management in NW Yunnan, China," *Biological Conservation* 143 (2010): 165–172. This collaboration between American and Chinese scholars criticizes Japanese research from a U.S. point of view. The authors blame Japanese researchers' site specificity for lack of scalability, i.e., "reliance on site rather than temporal replication . . . [because] stand-level productivity is difficult to test empirically" (167).

25. Socially concerned Chinese scientists take matsutake research in a different direction, asking how land tenure might make a difference. In this discussion, matsutake is still a scalable commodity and a source of income, but this income can be distributed differently (see chapter 19). Some Americans, e.g., David Arora ("The houses that matsutake built," *Economic Botany* 62, no. 3 (2008): 278–290) are also critics.

26. Jicun Wenyan [Yoshimura Fumihiko], *Songrong cufan jishu* [The technique of promoting flourishing matsutake], trans. Yang Huiling (Kunming: Yunnan keji chubanshe [Yunnan Science and Technology Press], 2008).

CHAPTER 17. FLYING SPORES

1. Interview, 2005.

2. Interview, 2008.

3. See Henning Knudsen's and Jan Vesterholt's taxonomy, *Funga nordica* (Copenhagen: Nordsvamp, 2012).

4. Interview, 2009.

5. The name *Tricholoma caligatum* (also *T. caligata*) is used for several quite different fungi, some counted as matsutake. See prologue, n. 11.

6. Interview, 2005.

7. See also Norihisa Matsushita, Kensuke Kikuchi, Yasumasa Sasaki, Alexis Guerin-Laguette, Frédéric Lapeyrie, Lu-Min Vaario, Marcello Intini, and Kazuo Suzuki, "Genetic relationship of *Tricholoma matsutake* and *T. nauseosum* from the northern hemisphere based on analyses of ribosomal DNA spacer regions," *Mycoscience* 46 (2005): 90–96.

8. Peabody et al., "Haploid vegetative mycelia" (cited in "Tracking" interlude, n. 21).

9. Interview, 2009.

10. Ignacio Chapela and Matteo Garbelotto, "Phylogeography and evolution in matsutake and close allies as inferred by analysis of ITS sequences and AFLPs," *Mycologia* 96, no. 4 (2004): 730–741.

11. Interview, 2006; Katsuji Yamanaka, "The origin and speciation of the matsutake complex" [in Japanese with English summary], *Newsletter of the Japan Mycology Association, Western Japan Branch* 14 (2005): 1–9.

12. Manos et al., worried about how an American *Lithocarpus* might exist, have moved tanoak to a new genus, *Notholithocarpus*. Paul S. Manos, Charles H. Cannon, and Sang-Hun Oh, "Phylogenetic relations and taxonomic status of the paleoendemic Fagaceae of western North America: Recognition of a new genus *Notholithocarpus*," *Madrono* 55, no. 3 (2008): 181–190.

13. Interview, 2009.

14. Jianping Xu, Hong Guo, and Zhu-Liang Yang, "Single nucleotide polymorphisms in the ectomycorrhizal mushroom *Tricholoma matsutake*," *Microbiology* 153 (2007): 2002–2012.

15. Anthony Amend, Sterling Keeley, and Matteo Garbelotto, "Forest age correlates with fine-scale spatial structure of matsutake mycorrhizas," *Mycological Research* 113 (2009): 541–551.

16. Anthony Amend, Matteo Garbelotto, Zhengdong Fang, and Sterling Keeley, "Isolation by landscape in populations of a prized edible mushroom *Tricholoma matsutake*," *Conservation Genetics* 11 (2010): 795–802.

17. Interview, 2006.

18. According to Dr. Murata, matsutake does not have a somatic incompatibility system to restrict matings. See Murata et al., "Genetic mosaics" (cited in chap. 16, n. 9).

19. Haploid nuclei in fungal body cells may not combine until production of fruiting bodies, meanwhile producing cells with two (or more) nuclei, each with one copy of the chromosomes. The "di-" refers to fungal body cells with two haploid nuclei.

20. For an opposing view, see Chunlan Lian, Maki Narimatsu, Kazuhide Nara, and Taizo Hogetsu, "*Tricholoma matsutake* in a natural *Pinus densiflora* forest: Correspondence between above- and below-ground genets, association with multiple host trees and alteration of existing ectomycorrhizal communities," *New Phytologist* 171, no. 4 (2006): 825–836.

INTERLUDE. DANCING

1. See Timothy Ingold, *Lines* (London: Routledge, 2007).

2. Lefevre, "Host associations" (cited in chap. 12, n. 11).

3. My ethnographic present here is 2008. Hiro has since passed away.

PART IV. IN THE MIDDLE OF THINGS

1. Brown founded the Jefferson Center for Education and Research in 1994; the center folded after her death in 2005. After Brown's opening work, other organizations took over mushroom picker organizing, including the Institute for Culture and Ecology, the Sierra Institute for Community and Environment, and the Alliance of Forest Workers and Harvesters. The project hired "mushroom monitors" from among the pickers. Their job was to identify pickers' needs, to work with their forms of knowledge, and to help design empowerment programs. Even when monitors stopped being paid, some continued as volunteers. The efforts of many people and organizations came together in the project.

2. Peter Kardas and Sarah Loose, eds., *The making of a popular educator: The journey of Beverly A. Brown* (Portland, OR: Bridgetown Printing, 2010).

3. Beverly Brown, *In timber country: Working people's stories of environmental conflict and urban flight* (Philadelphia: Temple University Press, 1995).

CHAPTER 18. MATSUTAKE CRUSADERS

1. Dr. Yoshimura's concern to protect the slope from erosion thus contrasts with Kato-san's attempt to expose mineral soils through erosion, noted in the opening to part 3.

2. Kokki Goto (edited, annotated, and with an introduction by Motoko Shimagami), "'*Iriai* forests have sustained the livelihood and autonomy of villagers': Experience of commons in Ishimushiro hamlet in northeastern Japan," working

paper no. 30, Afrasian Center for Peace and Development Studies, Ryukoku University, 2007, 2–4.

3. Ibid., 16.

4. Haruo Saito, interview, 2005; Haruo Saito and Gaku Mitsumata, "Bidding customs and habitat improvement for matsutake (*Tricholoma matsutake*) in Japan," *Economic Botany* 62, no. 3 (2008): 257–268.

5. Noboru Kuramoto and Yoshimi Asou, "Coppice woodland maintenance by volunteers," in *Satoyama*, ed. Takeuchi et al., 119–129 (cited in chap. 11, n. 14), on 129.

CHAPTER 19. ORDINARY ASSETS

1. As Michael Hathaway reminds me (personal communication, 2014), privatization in Yunnan sometimes revives pre-Communist tenure relations. The abruptness of changes, rather than their absolute novelty, draws attention to property's constitutive relations.

2. For discussions of tenure, see Liu, "Tenure" (cited in chap. 13, n. 16); Nicholas Menzies, *Our forest, your ecosystem, their timber: Communities, conservation, and the state in community-based forest management* (New York: Columbia University Press, 2007). After 1981 policies took effect, most forests were divided into three categories: state-owned forest, collective forest, and forest for which individual households were to hold responsibility. In the second category, forest was also divided into individual household contracts. Rights to trees and other forest access were increasingly separated; in 1998, a logging ban was instituted in Yunnan. Regions within Yunnan varied in how things worked. Michael Hathaway and my field site in Chuxiong became known for individual-access arrangements. However, we found that the farmers we interviewed were often confused or dismissive of the niceties of these categories.

3. In the view of the IMF and the World Bank, privatization avoids the "tragedy of the commons," in which we destroy shared resources. Garrett Hardin, "The tragedy of the commons," *Science* 162, no. 3859 (1986): 1243–1248.

4. For some English-language entries, see Jianchu Xu and Jesse Ribot, "Decentralisation and accountability in forest management: A case from Yunnan, southwest China," *European Journal of Development Research* 16, no. 1 (2004): 153–173; X. Yang, A. Wilkes, Y. Yang, J. Xu, C. S. Geslani, X. Yang, F. Gao, J. Yang, and B. Robinson, "Common and privatized: Conditions for wise management of matsutake mushrooms in northwest Yunnan province, China," *Ecology and Society* 14, no. 2 (2009): 30; Xuefei Yang, Jun He, Chun Li, Jianzhong Ma, Yongping Yang, and Jianchu Xu, "Management of matsutake in NW-Yunnan and key issues for its sustainable utilization," in *Sino-German symposium on the sustainable harvest of non-timber forest products in China*, ed. Christoph Kleinn, Yongping Yang, Horst Weyerhaeuser, and Marco Stark, 48–57 (Göttingen: World Agroforestry Centre, 2006); Jun He, "Globalised forest-products: Commodification of the matsutake mushroom in Tibetan villages, Yunnan, southwest China," *International Forestry Review* 12, no. 1 (2010): 27–37; Jianchu Xu and David R. Melick, "Rethinking the effectiveness of

public protected areas in southwestern China," *Conservation Biology* 21, no. 2 (2007): 318–328.

5. Su Kai-mei, Yunnan Academy of Agricultural Sciences, interview, 2009. See also Yang Yu-hua, Shi Ting-you, Bai Yong-shun, Su Kai-mei, Bai Hong-fen, Mu Li-qiong, Yu Yan, Duan Xing-zhou, Liu Zheng-jun, Zhang Chun-de, "Discussion on management model of contracting mountain and forest about bio-resource utilization under natural forest in Chuxiong Prefecture" [in Chinese], *Forest Inventory and Planning* 3 (2007): 87–89; Li Shu-hong, Chai Hong-mei, Su Kai-mei, Zhing Ming-hui, and Zhao Yong-chang, "Resources investigation and sustainable suggestions on the wild mushrooms in Jianchuan" [in Chinese], *Edible Fungi of China* 5 (2010).

6. See X. Yang et al., "Common and privatized," and Y. Yang et al., "Discussion on management model." Very different governance over matsutake harvesting—with much more communal control—characterizes the Diqing Tibetan area of Yunnan, where most foreign researchers gravitate. Menzies, *Our forest*; Emily Yeh, "Forest claims, conflicts, and commodification: The political ecology of Tibetan mushroom-harvesting villages in Yunnan province, China," *China Quarterly* 161 (2000): 212–226.

7. Other researchers in this region usefully describe the disjunction between management policies and local practices as an issue of different scales of governance. Liu, "Tenure"; Menzies and Li, "One eye on the forest" (cited in chap. 16, n. 7); Nicholas K. Menzies and Nancy Lee Peluso, "Rights of access to upland forest resources in southwest China," *Journal of World Forest Resource Management* 6 (1991): 1–20.

8. I was unable to go on this trip; Michael Hathaway kindly described what happened.

9. David Arora ("Houses" [cited in chap. 16, n. 25]) saw matsutake change hands eight times in two hours in a Yunnan mushroom market. My experience watching matsutake in dedicated mushroom markets was similar; exchanges were constant.

10. The contrast between this buying scene and the much more competitive local matsutake markets Michael Hathaway studied in the Tibetan area of Yunnan is instructive. There, Tibetan pickers sell to Han Chinese merchants; the buying scene is intensely competitive from the first. In the area I am describing, both the bosses and the pickers are of Yi nationality. Ties of kinship and residence also link pickers and buyers.

11. Brian Robinson's account of "the tragedy of the commons" for Yunnan matsutake admits that picking mushrooms in the commons may not hurt the fungus. He focuses instead on the problem of reduced income. Brian Robinson, "Mushrooms and economic returns under different management regimes," in *Mushrooms in forests and woodlands*, ed. Anthony Cunningham and Xuefei Yang, 194–195 (New York: Routledge, 2011).

12. I am in debt to Michael Hathaway's sharp perceptions for noticing this plaque.

Chapter 20. Anti-ending

1. http://www.matsiman.com/matsiman.htm.

2. Lu-Min Vaario, Alexis Guerin-Laguette, Norihisha Matsushita, Kazuo Suzuki, and Frédéric Lapeyrie, "Saprobic potential of *Tricholoma matsutake*: Growth over pine bark treated with surfactants," *Mycorrhiza* 12 (2002): 1–5.

3. For related research, see Lu-Min Vaario, Taina Pennanen, Tytti Sarjala, Eira-Maija Savonen, and Jussi Heinonsalo, "Ectomycorrhization of *Tricholoma matsutake* and two major conifers in Finland—an assessment of in vitro mycorrhiza formation," *Mycorrhiza* 20, no. 7 (2010): 511–518.

4. Heikki Jussila and Jari Jarviluoma discuss tourism in depressed contemporary Lapland: "Extracting local resources: The tourism route to development in Kolari, Lapland, Finland," in *Local economic development*, ed. Cecily Neil and Markku Tykkläinen, 269–289 (Tokyo: United Nations University Press, 1998).

5. Another world, indeed, is forming. Through the recruiting activities of Thai women married into depressed rural Finland, a network of Thai pickers has entered the forest, picking berries, and, recently, mushrooms. Pickers come independently, using their own funds. Like pickers in Oregon, they sell what they pick and pay their own expenses. They crowd into abandoned schoolhouses in the shrinking villages of Finland's countryside; they maintain their own forms of living, sometimes bringing their own cooks—and even some of their own food. Unlike their recruiters, the pickers are not from Bangkok, but from impoverished Lao-speaking northeast Thailand. Perhaps they are distant cousins of Lao pickers in the United States. The resemblance makes one wonder: How will Finnish foresters and community builders speak with these new pickers? Will their experience and expertise come into dialogue?

Spore Trail. The Further Adventures of a Mushroom

1. Ursula Le Guin, "The carrier bag theory of fiction," in *Dancing at the edge of the world*, 165–170 (New York: Grove Press, 1989), on 167–168.

Index

Note: Page numbers in italics indicate photographs.

accounting, scalable, 42–43
affirmative action, 101–2
agriculture, 24
akamatsu pine. *See* Japanese red pine
Akemi Tachibana, 7
alienation, 5–6; defined, 121; as feature of
    capitalism, 122, 133, 301n3; in logging,
    41; matsutake trade and, 121, 128,
    271–72; In plantation labor, 39–40;
    value making and, 122–23
allelic differences, 304n19
Amanita muscaria, 235, 236
American dream, 103
animals: mushroom foraging by, 247;
    pines and, 170; reaction of, to mat-
    sutake, 45–46, 51. *See also* nonhumans
Anthropocene era, 19–20, 292n6
Armillaria root rot, 231
Arora, David, 51, 57
Asian Americans, Japanese vs. Southeast
    Asian, 99–106
Asian Canadians, 67
Asian Development Bank, 115
assemblages: concept of, 22–23, 43, 292n8;
    coordination in, 23; lifeways in, 23;

method of analyzing, 158; narratives
    of livability and, 157–58; political
    economy and, 23; politics and,
    134–35; polyphonic character of,
    22–23
assimilation: coercive, 99–100, 106; of
    Japanese Americans, 99–101, 103–4;
    of Native Americans, 197; Protestant
    secularism and, 103; of Southeast Asian
    Americans, 101
auctions, 69, 262, 268–69
automobile industry, 115
autumn aroma, 1, 2, 6, 7, 14

"babies," 128
bacteria, 138, 141–43, 238
bamboo, 183, 260
Basho, Matsuo, 45, 46
bears, 45, 247
Becket, Samuel, 257
Benjamin, Walter, 50
birch, 172
Black Ships, 110
blasted landscapes, 181, 195, 282
Bohr, Niels, 37, 38

Borneo, 24, 48, 131
bosses, matsutake, 269–74
Bracero program, 99
brain mushrooms (*Gynomitra esculenta*), 174
Braudel, Fernand, 38
Brazil, 38–39
broadleaf trees: as matsutake host, 231, 233–34; as nemesis of pines, 6, 7, 49, 151, 157, 169, 171, 185, 202, 258, 260
Brown, Beverly, 254
bubble worlds, 156, 304n5
Buddhism, 91, 93, 104
bulkers, 67–68, 80, 127
buyers, 77–78, 80–83, 91–92, 124, 271–72

Cage, John, 45; *4'33"*, 46; *Indeterminacy*, 46
Cambodians: attitudes of, toward the government, 253; matsutake foragers, 92, 245; war experiences of, 87–89. *See also* Khmer
candy cane (*Allotropa virgata*), 243, 247
capitalism: alienation as feature of, 122, 133, 301n3; analysis of, 61–62, 133; assemblages and, 23; buying/selling of mushrooms as, 82; collaborative survival hindered by, 19; ecologies exploited by, 62–63; employment situation resulting from, 3, 109–10; environmental impact of, 19; factories as exemplar of, 62; noncapitalist elements as part of, 66, 122–23, 133–34 (*see also* pericapitalist sites); patchiness of, 5, 61; progress as ideology of, 5; salvage accumulation in, 63–66, 134, 301n2; and scalable accounting, 42–43; supposed unity and homogeneity of, 65; and translation, 62, 133, 301n2; value making in, 122; wealth accumulation in, 61–62
Cascade Forest Reserve, 195
Castley, Robert, 114
cedar. *See* sugi
Cham, 57
Chao La, 32–33
Chapela, Ignatio, 231–33
charcoal, 7, 152, 180, 182–84, 186, 190, 259, 260, 279
Cheney, Dick, 87
Chin, Vincent, 115
China: Japanese importation of lumber from, 315n24; matsutake in, 162, 187–90, 231, 233–34, 236, 268–74,

286–87, 315n24, 321n6, 321n10; matsutake science in, 219, 223–24; photographs of, *10, 26, 146–47, 178, 226, 250, 266, 276*; privatization in, 267–74, 320n2; species research in, 229–30
Chinese Americans, 100
Christianity: conversion to, 104; revival movements in, 298n6. *See also* Protestantism
Chu, Nellie, 24
citizenship, 99, 101–2
Civilian Conservation Corps, 207
clear-cutting, 41, 173–74, 314n18
Cleveland, Grover, 195
codevelopment, 142
Colby, William, 32
collaborative survival: in assemblages, 23; capitalism as danger to, 19; components of, 20; matsutake as exemplar of, 2, 4; mushroom picking as exemplar of, 19; necessity of, 28
Collins, Jane, 66
commercial pickers, 105, 246
commodities: gifts compared to, 122–23; matsutake as, 37, 121, 123–28, 271; scholarship as, 285
commodity chains: defined, 296n1; matsutake, 66–69, 110, 118, 123–28; types of, 299n10. *See also* supply chains
commons, 78
conjunctures, local results of global, 205–13
Conrad, Joseph, *The Heart of Darkness*, 63
contaminated diversity, 30–34
contamination, 27, 29
Convention of Kanagawa (1854), 111
copper tops (*Tricholoma focale*), 13
coppicing, 180, 182, 183, 185, 260, 309n3, 309n7
Cronon, William, viii
curiosity, 2, 6, 21, 144, 281–82
Curran, Lisa, 138
currency, 111, 116–17
cypress. *See* hinoki

Darwin, Charles, 139, 302n1
Dawkins, Richard, 28
deer, 45, 247
Deleuze, Gilles, 293n8
disturbance: defined, 160; ecologies resulting from, 5, 160–61, 186–87; perspectival nature of, 161

diversity: contaminated, 30–34; economic, 65–66; fundamental role of, 29
DNA, 140–41, 143, 229–31, 236, 304n19
dollar, 111, 116–17
durian, 48

ecologies: assemblages in, 22–23; capitalist exploitation, 62–63; disturbance-based, 5, 160–61, 186–87; fungi-based, 137–39; movement of, 235; restoration of, 151–52
economic diversity, 65–66, 301n2
economics, neoclassical, 28
ecosystems engineering, 161–62
ectomycorrhizas, 138–39
Edo period, 6–7
elk, 45, 247
encounters: central role of, 20, 29; contamination through, 27; disregard for, 28, 38; evolution and, 141–43; identity formation through, 29; indeterminacy in, 29, 37, 38, 46–47; knowledge in relation to, 34, 37; matsutake growth resulting from, 40; speciation and, 235–36; transformation through, 20, 28–29, 46–47
enslaved Africans, 39
entanglement: alienation as disruption of, 5–6, 133, 255; assemblages characterized by, 83; biological, 137–44; histories of, 168; latent commons characterized by, 135, 255; living-space, 5–6; matsutake foraging and, 243, 247–48; privatization involved in, 267, 272–74
environment: capitalism's impact on, 19; human disturbance of, 3
erosion, 131, 317n1 (Ch. 18)
ethnography, 37, 159
evolution, 139–43
evolutionary developmental biology, 141–42
expansion: epistemological emphasis on, 22, 29; plantations and, 38–40; progress as, 28; scalability and, 38–40; science based on, 37–38
exporters, 127–28

factories: as exemplar of capitalism, 62; labor in, 24; scalability and expansion of, 40
Faier, Lieba, 237
feminist anthropology, 134

fever, for mushroom picking, 40, 75, 79, 132, 242
field agents, 67–69, 77, 80–81, 128
Finland: appearance of forests in, 167; forest management in, 167–69, 172–76; matsutake in, 174, 280, 322n5; photographs of, 166; post-glacial growth in, 172
Finnish Forest Research Institute, 279
fire: lodgepole pines and, 200; pines and, 169–70; ponderosa pines and, 196; swidden, 172
fire exclusion, 30, 196, 200–201, 207–8, 312n22, 313n5
firs, 30, 41–42, 51–52
first nature, viii
foragers. See matsutake foragers
forest management: Chinese approach to, 162, 187–90; Japanese approach to, 151, 161, 207–11; modern approach to, 168, 207–8; national affiliations of, 218; in Pacific Northwest, 193–202; time scales in, 172, 175; U.S. approach to, 162, 207–11
forestry, 29–30, 41–42
forests: Chinese classification of, 320n2; conservation of, 29–30; global factors shaping, 205–13; resurgence of, 179; treated as scalable, 41. See also logging and timber industry; peasant landscapes; trees
freedom: citizenship and, 101; commodity chains and, 118–19; exchange of, 126–27; in matsutake picking, 68, 75–77, 79–80, 82, 94; in mushroom buying, 126–27; Southeast Asian immigrants and, 102, 104, 106; trophies of, 62, 75, 80, 121, 126; in United States, 93–94; war experiences and, 85–90
Freidberg, Susanne, 65
Fremont, John Charles, 195
frontier romanticism, 86
Fujiwara, Mitsuo, 211
fungi: destruction of, by human intervention, 202; growth patterns of, 137; indeterminacy of, 47; and interspecies relations, 137–39; matsutake and, 171; nourishment of, 137–38; pines and, 170; propagation of, 232, 236–38; species of, 230; symbiotic attachments of, 143–44; trees and, 138–39, 174–75, 201; world-building activities of, 137–39

Garbelotto, Matteo, 233
Geddes, William, 32
genet, 316n9
genetics, 139–41. *See also* population
    genetics
ghosts, 73–74, 76, 79
Gibson-Graham, J. K., 65–66
gifts: matsutake as, 6, 67, 122–28, 244,
    245; other foods as, 301n6; as social
    exchange, 122
Gilbert, Scott, 142
Goto, Kokki, 260–61
Great Awakenings, 298n6
Grey-faced Buzzards (*Butastur indicus*),
    181–82
Guthrie, Woody, 64
Guyer, Jane, 302n4
Gynomitra esculenta, 174

Hamada, Minoru, 219–21
happenings, 23, 27
Haraway, Donna, 292n6, 293n10
Harding, Susan, 103
Hardt, Michael, 65–66
Hathaway, Michael, 188, 206, 228, 269, 271,
    282, 286–87
Healthy Forests Restoration Act (2003),
    311n3
Heidegger, Martin, 304n5
herbaria, 229
heritage pickers, 105
hikikomori, 263
Himalayas, 233–34
hinoki (Japanese cypress, *Chamaecyparis
    obtusa*), 183–84, 209–11, 260
Hiroshima, 3
history: as component of evolution, 142–43;
    embodied in survival, 33–34; indetermi-
    nacy in, 23; matsutake and, 171; mean-
    ings of, 168; mythology in relation to,
    306n1; nonhuman contribution to, 168;
    pines and, 168–72; trees and, 168,
    175–76. *See also* narratives/stories
Hmong: background on, 31–33; Christian
    conversion of, 104; matsutake foragers,
    33, 57, 73–74, 76, 92; war experiences
    of, 89–91
holobiont, 142
hologenome theory of evolution, 142
Homo economicus, 28
Hosford, David, 221

human disturbance: attitudes toward,
    218–19; of the earth's ecology, 3; forest
    restoration utilizing, 151–52; in geolog-
    ical perspective, 19; matsutake growth
    after, 6, 30, 49–50, 171–72, 218–19,
    257–64; matsutake speciation and,
    234–35; pines and, 170–71; red pine
    and, 6, 185
human nature, 21
hunting, 87, 89–91
hyphae, 137, 279

identities: formation of, 29; Hmong, 31–33;
    Mien, 30–33; names and, 293n4; role
    of, 23
immigration policy, 93
importers, 67, 69, 123–24, 128
indeterminacy: assemblages and, 23; in
    encounters, 29, 37, 38, 46–47; fear
    engendered by, 1, 20; in history, 23;
    matsutake and, 50; mushrooms and,
    46–47; smell and, 46. *See also* precarity
Indonesia, 113–14, 210, 315n24
industrial forests, 167–68, 171–76, 205–13
interchangeability, 39–40
internal transcribed spacer (ITS) region,
    229–31, 234, 236
interspecies relations. *See* multispecies
    environments
inventory, matsutake as, 127–28
inventory management, 64
iriai rights, 184, 262
ITS region. *See* internal transcribed spacer
    (ITS) region
Iwase, Koji, 228

Japan: climate in, 184; forest management
    in, 151, 161, 207–11, 259–60; Korea in
    relation to, 49; matsutake in, 6–8, 48–51,
    123–28, 211–12, 258–64; matsutake sci-
    ence in, 218–21, 223–24; peasant land-
    scapes in, 171, 180–87; photographs of,
    16, 36, 44, 108, 154, 204, 216, 240, 256;
    salvage accumulation in, 70; U.S. eco-
    nomic encounters with, 109–19
Japanese Americans: assimilation of, 99–101,
    103–4; early immigration of, 98; mat-
    sutake foragers, 97–98, 105; Southeast
    Asian Americans compared to, 99–106;
    World War II experiences of, 98–99
Japanese cedar. *See* sugi

Japanese cypress. *See* hinoki
Japanese red pine (akamatsu, *Pinus densi-flora*), 6, 49–50, 185–86, 261
jobs, 3, 19, 109–10, 280. *See also* labor
Jonsson, Hjorleifur, 31, 32

keiretsu (enterprise groups), 113
Khmer: attitudes of, toward the government, 253; matsutake foragers, 33, 57, 74. *See also* Cambodians
Klamath Tribes, 197–99, 209
knowledge: complex character of, 33–34; encounters and, 34, 37; individualistic perspective on, 28; scale and, 38; stories in relation to, 37; vernacular/peasant, 159, 161, 219, 220, 263
Knudsen, Henning, 228–29
Koi Nagata, 7
Korea, 49, 114–15. *See also* North Korea
kula exchange, 122, 126
Kuramoto, Noboru, 257

labor: factory, 24; interchangeable, 39; matsutake picking compared to, 77–78; noninterchangeable, 40; on sugarcane plantations, 39. *See also* jobs
landscapes: active nature of, 152; as assemblages, 158; concept of, 304n3; methodology for studying, 159–60; stories of, 158–63
Lao: buyers and entrepreneurs, 91–93; matsutake foragers, 33, 57, 74, 92–94
Lapland. *See* Finland
Large Blue butterfly (*Maculinea arion*), 141–42
latent commons: entanglement characteristic of, 135, 255, 258; features of, 255; matsutake lovers as, 279; privatization dependent on, 267, 271; uncultivated vegetation as, 282; value arising from, 274
Latinos, 94
Latour, Bruno, 305n12, 315n1
Law, John, 315n1
Lefevre, Charles, 317n19
Le Guin, Ursula K., 17, 287–88
life lines, of matsutake, 241–43, 247–48
livelihood: patches of, 132–33; Southeast Asian American strategies for, 101–3, 106
lodgepole pines (*Pinus contorta*), 30, 41–42, 194–95, 199–202, 312n22, 313n26

logging and timber industry: decline of, 41–42; diversification of, 314n18; in Finland, 173; forestry policies and practices and, 29–30, 41–42; in Oregon, 17–18, 193, 195–96, 198–200, 205–13, 314n18; scalability applied in, 41
logic, 28

Malinowski, Bronislaw, 122
Man-nyo Shu, 1
Marx, Karl, 61, 296n3
masting, 174–75
matsutake: alienation of, 271–72; in China, 162, 187, 187–90, 231, 233–34, 236, 268–74, 286–87, 315n24, 321n6, 321n10; and collaborative survival, 2, 4; as commodity, 37, 121, 123–28, 271; commodity chain based on, 66–69, 110, 118, 123–28; as delicacy, 4; description of, 3–4; duration of fruiting, 201; elite associations with, 6–7, 49; emotions and memories evoked by, 48–52; environmental conditions for, 3–4, 6, 30, 40, 49–50, 151–52, 171–72, 195, 200–202, 220–21, 269–71, 279–80, 306n21; fantasies of eating, 125; finding, 241–48, 277; in Finland, 174, 280, 322n5; fungi and, 171; gifts of, 6, 67, 122–28, 244, 245; as global commodity, 4; history making of, 171; and indeterminacy, 50; as inventory, 127–28; in Japan, 6–8, 48–51, 123–28, 211–12, 258–64; laboratory cultivation of, 220–21; life lines of, 241–43, 247–48; nematodes' effect on, 156–57; non-humans' reactions to, 45–46, 51; nonscalability of, 40; in Oregon, 42, 51–52, 57, 69, 75–83, 193, 212, 233, origin designations for, 301n5; origins of, 233–35; outings revolving around, 6–7, 185–86; pines and, 162, 171, 220–21; preparation of, as food, 44, 47, 51, 96; prices of, 4, 8, 58, 67, 69, 75, 262; quality of, 124–25; ranking of, 8, 126; relational quality of, 122–28, 220; reproduction of, 237–38; research on, 48–50; small, 128; smell of, 2, 6, 8, 14, 45–48, 51–52; sorting of, 81, 127, 301n9; speciation of, 228–29, 233–35; species/names of, 8, 51, 229–34, 291n11, 291n12; spores of, 237–38; supply chain based on, 118; supply of, 262. *See also* matsutake trade

Matsutake Crusaders, 258–59, 264
matsutake foragers: animals as, 247; atti-
    tudes of, toward the government, 78,
    253; attitudes of, toward their work,
    77–78; background experiences of,
    85–94; buyers' courting of, 81–82;
    camps of, 72, 73–74, 100–101 (see also
    Open Ticket, Oregon); and collabora-
    tive survival, 19; commercial, 105, 246;
    earnings of, 82; freedom of, 68, 75–77,
    79–80; heritage, 246; invisibility of, 18;
    methods of, 241–48; permits for, 78–79,
    297n1; political action involving,
    253–54, 319n1 (Part IV); status of, 4
matsutake science, 218–25, 287, 317n19
matsutake trade: and alienation, 121, 128;
    buying and selling practices in, 75,
    80–83, 126–27, 272, 321n9, 321n10;
    international, 8; middlemen in, 66–69;
    misconceptions about, 58; in Oregon,
    18; psychology of, 83; regularization of,
    69; risks in, 67; translation of commodi-
    ties and gifts in, 123–28
Matsutake Worlds Research Group, 223,
    286
Meiji Restoration, 7, 111–12
Melville, Herman, Moby-Dick, 63
Mendel, Gregor, 139
middlemen, 66–69
Mien: background on, 30–33, 246; Chris-
    tian conversion of, 104; cultural per-
    sistence among, 100–101; matsutake
    foragers, 14, 57, 74, 76, 92, 245–46
Mintz, Sidney, 40
modernity, 40, 140, 180, 315n2
modernization: deforestation from Japa-
    nese, 186; harms resulting from, 1–3;
    narrative of, 2, 20–21; process of, 40.
    See also progress
modern synthesis, 140–43
Moncalvo, Jean-Marc, 229–30, 234–36
money, 111, 116–17
moso bamboo (Phyllostachys edulis), 183,
    260
Moua, Mai Neng, 27
multiculturalism, 100
multispecies environments: growth and
    development in, 137–44, 309n3; living
    spaces of, 5–6; participation in, 264,
    281–82; time making in, 21; world mak-
    ing in, 22

Munger, Thornton, 312n22
Murata, Hitoshi, 237–38
mushroom foragers. See matsutake foragers
mushrooms: Cage and, 46; and indetermi-
    nacy, 46–47
music, 23–24, 46, 158
mutualism, 40, 139, 220, 303n16
mycorrhizas, 138–39, 170, 174–75
mythology, 306n1

Nakashimura, Leke, 285
narratives/stories: alternative, viii, 2, 5–6,
    18, 22–23; concepts vs., 159; details as
    essential to, 111; foraging metaphor
    for, 287; knowledge in relation to,
    37; of landscapes, 158–63; about the
    nonhuman, 155–58; of progress and
    modernization, viii, 2, 5–6, 18, 20–25;
    science's disregard for, 37, 157; units of,
    162. See also history
National Environmental Policy Act (1970),
    210
national forests, 41, 196
Native Americans: dispossession of, 197–99;
    forest stewardship of, 196; matsutake
    foragers, 57; sacred areas for, 74
natural history, 37, 159
natural selection, 139–40
nature: capitalist view of, 62; conceptions
    of, vii, 217, 218; first, second, and third,
    viii; humans in relation to, 3, 180, 183,
    186; interspecies relations characteristic
    of, 142; romantic view of, 5, 7; scalabil-
    ity imposed on, 38, 132, 135, 140
Negri, Antonio, 65–66
neighborliness, 279–80
nematodes, 156–58, 261
neoclassical economics, 28
neoliberalism, 42, 70, 100
networks, 292n8
Nike, 117–18
nonhumans: histories of, 168; narratives
    about, 155–58; reaction of, to mat-
    sutake, 45–46; world-making projects
    of, 22, 292n7. See also animals
nonscalability: disregard for, 38; emergence
    of, 42; of matsutake foragers, 40; of
    production, 64; scalability in relation
    to, 42–43
North Korea, 223–24
nostalgia, 48–51, 91, 186–87

noticing: in landscape analysis, 160; as method, 23–24, 143; modern perspective as hindrance to, 22, 37–38; pleasures of, 279; precarity as condition for, 3, 4

oaks, 162, 180–81, 184–85, 188–90
Ogawa, Makoto, 48–50, 220
Ohara, Hiroyuki, 221
Olwig, Kenneth, 304n3
Ong, Aihwa, 301n3
ontology, 292n7
open ticket, 75
Open Ticket, Oregon (pseudonym), 72, 75–83; attitudes toward work in, 77–78; buying and selling practices in, 75, 80–83, 126–27; character of, 76–77; "ghosts" in, 76; as livelihood patch, 132–33; regulations in, 78–79, 297n1, 297n2; Southeast Asian cultural persistence in, 97, 100–104
Oregon and Pacific Northwest: forest management in, 193–202; forests of, 29–30; frontier romanticism of, 86; industrial development in, 17–18, 21; logging and timber industry in, 193, 195–96, 198–200, 205–13; matsutake in, 42, 51–52, 57, 69, 73–83, 195, 212, 233; mushroom picking in, 13–14, 18–19, 30, 42; photographs of, xiv, 54, 60, 72, 84, 96, 120, 130, 136, 192, 284; whites' beliefs and lifestyles in, 86, 193–94
outsourcing, 143–44

Pacific Northwest. See Oregon and Pacific Northwest
panspermia hypothesis, 234
Pao, Vang, 32–33, 89, 102
Papua New Guinea, 315n24
patchiness: of capitalism, 5, 61; in contemporary life, 4–5; in science, 218, 225, 227
Pathet Lao, 32
Pearson, Thomas, 104
peasant knowledge. See vernacular knowledge
peasant landscapes: in China, 187–90; destruction of, 7; ecological development of, 180–87, 189–90; in Japan, 180–87, 189–90; matsutake in, 171, 185–86; privatization of, 267–74; restoration of, 8. See also satoyama

Pegues, Juliana Hu, 99
performance, in buying/selling of mushrooms, 81–83
pericapitalist sites, 63, 65, 278, 296n4, 301n2. See also capitalism: noncapitalist elements as part of
Perry, Matthew, 111
Peters, Pauline, 159
Philippines, 210
pines: animals and, 170; environmental conditions for, 169, 173–74; in Finland, 167–69, 172–76; and fire, 169–70; forest management and, 168; history making of, 168–72; human disturbance as condition for, 170–71; matsutake and, 162, 171, 220–21; nematodes and, 156–57, 261; oaks and, 180–81, 184–85, 190; in Pacific Northwest, 194; prolific nature of, 169; seed production of, 174; uses of, 188. See also Japanese red pine
pine wilt nematodes (Bursaphelenchus xylophilus), 156–58, 261
plantations, 38–40
plants, 138
Plaza Accord (1985), 117
political economy, 23, 24
politics: assemblages and, 134–35; forager–Forest Service meetings, 253–54; nature of, 254
polyphony, 23–24, 158
ponderosa pines (Pinus ponderosa), 30, 41–42, 195–200, 312n22
population genetics, 28, 303n16, 304n19
Portuguese, and colonial plantations, 38–39
postcolonial theory, 217, 315n2
precarity: adaptation as intrinsic to, 27; central role of, 20; common experiences of, 1–2, 20; in contemporary America, 98; defined, 20, 29; of the earth, 3; of mushroom foragers, 4; mushrooms' adaptation to, 2–3; of postwar development, 3. See also indeterminacy
Prigogine, Ilya, 305n13
privatization, 267–74, 285
progress: business linked to, 132; as capitalist ideology, 5; end of expectations of, 110; harms resulting from, 1, 5; human-centered nature of, 155–56; ideology of, viii, 5, 18, 20–25; process of, 40; and scale, 38. See also modernization
property, 78–79

Protestantism, 103, 104
Pyne, Stephen, 159

quorum sensing, 238

race to the bottom, 64–65
racial profiling, 253
raking, 222, 247–48, 260
raw materials, 62–63
Rayner, Alan, 46–47
red pine. *See* Japanese red pine
refugees, political vs. economic, 93
resurgence, 179
Richardson, David, *Ecology and Biogeography of Pinus*, 168
Robbins, William, 195, 210
ruins: creation of, 6; industrial forest, 205–13; vitality of, 6, 40–41

salvage: ambivalence of, 131; defined, 63; violence associated with, 63, 64; in Yunnan matsutake trade, 273–74
salvage accumulation: capitalist, 63–66, 134, 301n2; defined, 296n3; in matsutake trade, 128; in supply chains, 63–66, 110
salvage rhythms, 131–32, 134
Sarawak, 315n24
satoyama: defined, 151–52; revitalization of, 151–52, 160, 162–63, 180–81, 220, 258–64, 281; social and personal enrichment fostered by, 261, 263, 281. *See also* peasant landscapes
Satsuka, Shiho, 62, 112, 124, 217, 228, 258, 281, 287
scalability: in accounting, 42–43; emphasis on, 40; expansion and, 38–40; failures and ruins of, 38, 40–42; in inventory management, 64; meanings of, 38; nonscalability in relation to, 42–43; obstacles to, 142; plantations and, 38–40, 294n2; of science, 221; in species reproduction, 140–43, 304n19
scale, 37–38
scholarship, 285–86
science: machinic character of, 217; matsutake, 218–25, 287, 317n19; narrative ignored in, 37, 159; parochial character of, 218–19; patches in, 218, 225, 227; role of description in, 221; in satoyama revitalization, 263; scalability of, 221; spores

as model for, 227–28; as translation, 217–18, 287
seasonal enclosure, 270
second nature, viii
secularization, 103
self-containment, 28, 33–34, 140–41
self-interest, 28
selfish gene, 28, 140
shareholders' revolution, 116
Shaw, Rosalind, 161
shiros, 171, 219–20, 227, 237–38, 316n9
Showers, Kate, 159
single nucleotide polymorphisms, 236
Smalley, William, 32
smell: emotions and memories evoked by, 48–52; indeterminacy and, 46; of matsutake, 2, 6, 8, 14, 45–48, 51–52
Southeast Asian Americans: assimilation of, 101; attitudes of, toward the government, 78; cultural persistence among, 103; differences among, 102; discrimination against, 74, 78; Japanese Americans compared to, 99–106; livelihood strategies of, 101–3, 106; matsutake foragers, 18, 73–74, 105. *See also individual groups*
speciation, 228–29, 233–36
species: classification of, 229–32; of matsutake, 8, 51, 229–34, 291n11, 291n12; traditional evolutionary understanding of, 139–43
spores, 227–28, 234, 237–39
spotted owls, 18
squid, 141
Stengers, Isabelle, 305n13
stories. *See* narratives/stories
Strathern, Marilyn, 293n10
sugarcane, 39
sugi (Japanese cedar, *Cryptomeria japonica*), 183–84, 209–11, 260
sukiyaki, 97, 186, 258
supermarkets, 124
supply chains: characteristics of, 61–62; defined, 296n1; global, 109–10, 117–18; Japanese model of, 113–15; matsutake, 118; Nike model of, 118; roots of, 113; salvage accumulation through, 63–66, 110; supply chains as means of, 70; translation through, 70; U.S. use of, 116. *See also* commodity chains
survival: history embodied in, 33–34; individual vs. collective, 27–29; narrative

as means of, 34. *See also* collaborative survival
Suzuki, Kazuo, 220–21, 231, 279
swidden, 172
symbiopoiesis, 142

Takeuchi, Kazuhiko, 186
termites, 143–44
third nature, viii
ticks, 156
timber industry. *See* logging and timber industry
time, varieties of, 21
trade. *See* matsutake trade
trading, as translation, 112
trading companies, 113–15
traditionalism, 106
transformation: disregard for, 28; in encounters, 20, 28–29, 46–47
translation: capitalism and, 62, 133, 301n2; of commodities and gifts, 123–28; defined, 315n1; middlemen as means of, 66; mishaps in, 217; science as, 217–18, 287; trading as, 112
trash, 247
trees: fungi and, 138–39, 174–75, 201; history making of, 168, 175–76; matsutake and, 195. *See also* forests
Tricholoma caligatum, 291n11
Tricholoma magnivelare, 8, 51, 230–31, 233, 235, 291n12
Tricholoma matsutake, 8, 51, 230–31, 235
Tricholoma nauseosum, 51
trust, 272

Ueda, Koji, 48
Uexküll, Jakob von, 156, 158, 304n5
unintentional design, 152, 162
United States: forest management in, 162, 207–11, 259; freedom in, 93–94; Japanese economic encounters with, 109–19; matsutake science in, 218–19, 221–23, 317n19; precarity in, 98
universal product codes (UPCs), 64
Uriuda, Sanou, 97–99
U.S. Forest Service: environmental goals of, 201; financial status of, 41, 211; fire

policies of, 30, 200–201, 207–8; matsutake research and policies of, 13, 73–74, 105, 201–2, 221–22, 224, 278; policies of, 29–30, 41, 79, 92, 212, 247, 253–54, 311n3; whites' attitudes toward, 194
utilitarianism, 40

Vaario, Lu-Min, 279–80
Vancouver, 67
Vang, Chai Soua, 90
vernacular knowledge, 159, 161, 219, 220, 263
Verran, Helen, 50, 295n8
vertical keiretsu, 115
vulnerability, in precarity, 20, 29

Wal-Mart, 64, 78
war, matsutake foragers as survivors of, 85–94
wasps (*Asobara tabida*), 141
Weber, Max, 140
welfare, 101–2
whites: attitudes of, toward Southeast Asian Americans, 33, 73, 106; attitudes of, toward the government, 78, 193–94; frontier romanticism of, 86; matsutake foragers, 68, 74, 76, 278; war experiences of, 86–87
woodlands. *See* forests; peasant landscapes
world-making: concept of, 21–22; fungal, 138–39; ontologies compared to, 292n7; unintentional design in, 152. *See also* narratives/stories

Xu Jianping, 227, 234, 236

Yamaguchi Sodo, 9
Yamanaka, Katsuji, 233–34
Yanagisako, Sylvia, 302n3
Yang Huiling, 224–25
yen, 111, 116–17
Yin Shaoting, 310n17
Yolngu, 50, 295n8
Yoshimura, Fumihiko, 186
Yunnan, China. *See* China

zaibatsu (conglomerates), 112–13
Zeigle, Tim, 90